American Gardens

Ferns for American Gardens

JOHN T. MICKEL

TIMBER PRESS

Portland • Cambridge

Front cover, clockwise from upper left, *Athyrium otophorum, Osmunda cinnamomea, Phyllitis scolopendrium, P. scolopendrium* 'Crispa'; spine, *Matteuccia struthiopteris*; back cover, above, *Blechnum spicant,* below, *Adiantum venustum* (photographs by John T. Mickel).

Published in 2003 by
Timber Press, Inc.
The Haseltine Building
133 S.W. Second Avenue, Suite 450
Portland, Oregon 97204-3527, U.S.A.

Timber Press
2 Station Road
Swavesey
Cambridge CB4 5QJ, U.K.

Printed in China

Library of Congress Cataloging-in-Publication Data

Mickel, John.
    Ferns for American gardens / John T. Mickel.
      p. cm.
    Originally published: New York : Macmillan, ©1994
    Includes bibliographical references and index.
    ISBN 0-88192-598-5 (pbk.)
    1. Ferns, Ornamental—North America. 2. Ferns, Ornamental. I. Title
SB429.M515 2003
635.9'373—dc21

2003048405

I acknowledge with thanks permission from the W. C. Brown Publishing Co., Dubuque, Iowa, to reproduce the drawings on pages 12–15, 19, 23, 64, 65, 66, 68 by Edgar Paulton, first published in J. T. Mickel, *How to Know the Ferns and Fern Allies*, 1979.

To my wife, Carol

Contents

Acknowledgments

This book is the product of my personal experience with ferns, both in gardens and in the wild in various parts of the world. I have been helped and inspired by many gardening friends. Ethelyn Williams has been especially instructive over the past twenty years as both a friend and also the primary spore grower at the New York Botanical Garden. Other members of the New York Chapter of the American Fern Society who have been of assistance are Charles Anderson, Gordon Foster, Carol Johnston, Dorothy Linde, Virginia Otto, and Mayneal Wayland.

Many people around the country have been very generous in sharing their plants and experience and in allowing me to take photographs in their gardens. Notable among them have been Thomas Morgan, of Carmel, New York; Henrette Suhr, of Chappaqua, New York; Virginia Otto, of Westborough, Massachusetts; Bunkie Hopkins, of Northeast Harbor, Maine; James Montgomery, of Berwick, Pennsylvania; Nancy and Leon Swell, of Richmond, Virginia; the late Kathryn Boydston, of Niles, Michigan; Mary and Robert Burks, Edythe Crumpton, Ginny and Edwin Lusk, and Ruth Schatz, of Birmingham, Alabama; Virginia Ault, Marilyn Johnson, Bruce McAlpin, and Milton Piedra, of Miami, Florida; Ruth Radcliff, of Lake Placid, Florida; Dorothy and Edward Linde, of Austin, Texas; Naud Burnett, of Dallas, Texas; Barbara Hoshizaki, of Los Angeles, California; Don Armstrong of Vancouver, British Columbia; and several people in the Seattle area, including Torben Barfod, Sylvia Duryea, Neill Hall, Jocelyn Horder, Guy Huntley, Judith Jones, Mareen Kruckeberg, Jeannette Kunnen, Marshall and the late Edna Majors, Sue Olsen, the late Mrs. Corydon Wagner, and others connected with the Hardy Fern Foundation.

Several keen fern gardeners in England have been most hospitable: Peter Boyd, the late Bert Bruty, Ray and Rita Coughlin, Jimmy Dyce, Clive and Alma Jermy, the late Reginald Kaye, Hazel Key, Martin and Hazel Rickard, Trevor and Molly Walker, and John Woodhams. Malcolm Hutcheson, head gardener at Sizergh Castle (Cumbria), and John Bond, Keeper of Savill Garden (Windsor) were also quite helpful.

I appreciate the help of the botanical authorities who have read parts of the manuscript and identified plants relating to their specialties: Ed Alverson, Christopher Fraser-Jenkins, Richard Hauke, Barbara Hoshizaki, Kunio Iwatsuki, David Johnson, Masahiro Kato, Irving Knobloch, James Montgomery, Iván Valdespino, and Terry Webster.

I could not have written this book without the support of the staff and facilities of the New York Botanical Garden. The Fern Committee has been very supportive for many years. I have learned a great deal from Mobee Weinstein and the late Joseph Beitel, members of the horticulture staff. The library staff of the New York Botanical Garden, especially Dora Galitzki and Marie Long, has always been most kind in helping me locate reference works and answering horticultural questions. The outstanding library, herbarium, and living collections have been extremely valuable.

I give special thanks to Ruth Clausen, Judy Garrison, Judith Jones, Ruth Nastuk, Ruth Russell, Ethelyn Williams, and my wife, Carol, for their careful reading of the manuscript and for offering many valuable suggestions.

The drawings were made by Dick Rauh and the late Edgar Paulton. The closeup photographs of sori were taken by Charles Neidorf. Although most of the color photographs are my own, other photographs were taken by the late Joseph Beitel, F. Gordon Foster, Barbara Hallowell, Pamela Harper, Judith Jones, Sue Olsen, and Alan Smith.

I greatly appreciate the meticulous work of my editor, Pam Hoenig, her assistant, Justin Schwartz, and the rest of the staff at Macmillan.

Ferns for American Gardens

Introduction

Several years ago I had the pleasure of taking part in a New York Botanical Garden–sponsored perennials symposium together with Ruth Clausen and others. At that time Ruth and Nicolas Ekstrom were finishing their outstanding book on perennials, *Perennials for American Gardens* (Random House, 1989), and I asked Ruth how many ferns they were including. She replied that there were none; they were leaving the ferns for me.

Ferns are undoubtedly the most overlooked and underutilized class of perennial garden plants. There is probably no other group with so little published modern information on its outdoor culture. Ruth and Nicky's book is certainly no exception in giving ferns short shrift. Virtually all books on perennials, shade plants, and other gardening themes offer but a token page or paragraph on ferns, often with out-of-date names and sometimes even misinformation.

Over one hundred years ago, Charles Druery, in his introduction to *Choice British Ferns* (1888), lamented, ". . . it is a matter of surprise, and even bewilderment, that popularly they [ferns] should be so little known and so rarely cultivated."

Several interdependent factors have resulted in this horticultural vacuum. Because there is little information on outdoor fern cultivation in America, there is a general unawareness or even fear of ferns. This ignorance of ferns leads to little demand for them at the nurseries, and as a result the growers do not supply them. Or perhaps conversely, without availability there is little interest. Even when a list of ferns for the garden is available, common queries are: What do they look like? How do I know I want them in my garden?

Are they difficult to grow? Will they do well in this climate? Several misconceptions have arisen regarding ferns. The first myth is encapsulated wonderfully in a cartoon I saw many years ago in which a lady in a plant nursery says to a friend, "The trouble with ferns is that they come up and that's it." That is *not* "it"! Ferns have many valuable qualities, and that's what this book is all about.

Although ferns lack the bright colors of flowers, they are tremendously diverse in frond size, shape, division, texture, and even color, and are especially useful in the shady garden and landscape. Ferns can fill niches in swampy situations and even in full sun. To quote from Abraham Stansfield's fern nursery catalog published in 1858 in England, "The bright colours of flowers are admired by [even] the least intellectual, but the beauty of form and textures of ferns requires a higher degree of mental perception and more intellect for its proper appreciation."

Some gardeners are afraid that ferns are difficult to grow. Perhaps they are wary of plants that don't have flowers or seeds, or think ferns are too delicate, recalling the finicky behavior of their leaflet-dropping Boston ferns inside the house. For the most part, hardy ferns are easy to grow and a procrastinator's delight. Personally, I am one of the great procrastinators of our day. This is not something to be ashamed of. There are so many things to do in this world, and although I want to work in the garden, I rarely find the time. Happily, ferns fit into this schedule very nicely. When I get a fern for my garden—from a friend, or one I've purchased—I dig a hole, plant the fern, water it once or twice, and it's on its own. Even with this benign neglect I have more than 130 kinds of ferns in my garden. The point is that you don't need to be a slave to the garden in order to raise ferns. They look good, they fill a need in our shady gardens, and they require very little care. What more can you ask of a plant?

Most ferns are easily cultivated and multiply, though others are more challenging. They can be used among flowering plants or shrubs, or, as in my own case, some flowering plants can be used among the ferns. Ferns are a small enough group that you can quickly become familiar with them and learn the common genera and species.

I am happy to report that the public perception of ferns is changing. More articles are being written. Ferns are appearing with greater frequency in flower shows, and fern display gardens are developing around the country. And perhaps most important, more species are becoming available in nurseries. Fern interest in North America is now at its highest level and is still on the rise.

HISTORY OF HARDY FERN GARDENING

Gardening with hardy ferns in a serious way began in Britain in the mid-nineteenth century. Its beginning was marked by the publication of Neuman's *British Ferns* in 1845, in which he described the British fern flora, listed the many variations of the native fern species, and gave localities in which the plants had been found. This work was soon followed by a wave of volumes on the subject. Thomas Moore published several books on the British ferns. Especially noteworthy were his "nature-printed" volumes, in which the actual fronds were pressed into lead to make the book's plates. Lowe, Schneider, and Druery followed with extensive listings of every variant reported. Nearly every species native to the British Isles had a few varieties described—some markedly different, some only marginally distinct. A few species—*Athyrium filix-femina*, *Dryopteris filix-mas*, *Phyllitis scolopendrium*, and *Polystichum setiferum*—had more than three hundred varieties each.

The British were attracted to growing ferns. With the development of Wardian cases (terrariums), many people grew ferns indoors, and they brought many native species and varieties into their gardens (see page 26). It became a social activity to visit a woodland on a Sunday afternoon to search for fern variants and dig them for one's garden. Several nurseries specializing in ferns offered a broad selection of largely British species and varieties.

This obsession with fern culture was described and analyzed perceptively in David Allen's book, *The Victorian Fern Craze* (1968). In addition to being grown, ferns were a common motif on pottery, picture frames, silverware, and even chamber pots. If you are ever in southwest England, be sure to visit the Museum of North Devon in Barnstaple, where there is a delightful display developed by Peter Boyd devoted to the Fern Craze, including an array of attractive and diverse Victorian fernabilia.

In 1891 the British Pteridological Society was organized (pteridology being the study of ferns and fern allies, which include clubmosses, spikemosses, horsetails, quillworts, and psilotum). This venerable society recently celebrated its centenary in London with an outstanding symposium on fern cultivation and a tour of several magnificent fern gardens.

British interest in fern cultivation has continued to this day. The most authoritative book of recent years on temperate fern cultivation, *Hardy Ferns*, was written in 1968 by Reginald Kaye, who lived in northwestern England. Unfortunately, this excellent book concentrates on British species and is out of print. Other valuable British booklets on hardy fern gardening include

The common Victorian activity of digging native ferns is illustrated in this 1871 figure, "Gathering Ferns," from the *London News* (displayed at the Museum of North Devon, Barnstaple, England)

Richard Rush's "A Guide to Hardy Ferns" (1984) and James Dyce's "The Variation and Propagation of British Ferns" (1991).

In Australia, David Jones's *Encyclopaedia of Ferns* (1987) contains much useful information, but it is written from an Australian perspective and does not cover the North American ferns and their hardiness in depth.

Fern cultivation has not enjoyed the same popularity in America that it has in Britain. Toward the end of the nineteenth century a few ferns crept into horticulture in American conservatories and homes. The Boston fern (*Nephrolepis exaltata* 'Bostoniensis'), discovered in 1897, gained instant popularity as an indoor fern and is still the most widely grown fern in America, but an overall acceptance of ferns in cultivation has been slow in coming.

In 1893, just two years after the British Pteridological Society was organized, the American Fern Society was founded, but whereas the British were intent on growing all the wild-found forms in their gardens, Americans were more interested in preparing dried specimens and studying the wider selection of species on this continent. Relatively few Americans grew ferns in their gardens.

In the United States most of our cultivation has involved tropical species,

Fern motifs were frequently included on Victorian pottery, furniture, and other objects. (Museum of North Devon, Barnstaple, England)

both in the conservatories of botanical gardens and as houseplants. Consequently, fern gardening has flourished most conspicuously in southern Florida and California, where the climate permits the growing of a wide range of ferns out of doors.

Several people have laid the groundwork for the development of hardy fern cultivation in America. Ralph Benedict of the Brooklyn Botanic Garden was one of just a few professional botanists in the early twentieth century who had an interest in both science and horticulture. He was involved in scientific fern studies, the cultivation of ferns, and their interpretation to the public. He edited the *American Fern Journal* and was active in promoting the establishment of fern display gardens.

Edgar Wherry of the University of Pennsylvania, author of *The Fern Guide* (1961) for northeastern species and *The Southern Fern Guide* (1964), was a keen student of ferns and their habitats, and was especially knowledgeable about their garden possibilities. His early work as a mineralogist led to an interest in the association of plants and soils, and he was instrumental in developing the first soil-testing kits. His books include comments on the cultivability of many of our native ferns and fern allies.

Another promoter of ferns in gardens was Kathryn Boydston, who is best known for developing her home, Fernwood, near Niles, Michigan, as a nature center. Here she grew hundreds of kinds of ferns from spores, partly for planting outside and partly for studies in hybridization by botanical scientists. She also began the American Fern Society's spore exchange in 1954, thus making many more species available to those interested in growing a wide variety of ferns. No longer were we limited to the few species offered in nurseries, which, unfortunately, for the most part collected their plants in the wild.

In his retirement years, Neill Hall, a dedicated amateur, took over the Fern Society's spore exchange in 1962 and managed it for twenty-six years. In his first year he sent out two hundred packets of spores. He then built up the exchange's bank so at one point he had over a thousand kinds of ferns on the list and sent out more than five thousand packets of spores in one year. He not only received and processed donated spores, but actively sought them out both through extensive correspondence and travel, personally collecting spores in the wild and in botanical gardens around the world. The American Fern Society's spore bank now boasts more than seven hundred kinds, of which more than two hundred are hardy.

Twenty years ago North America had very few organizations devoted to fern study and cultivation. The American Fern Society and Los Angeles International Fern Society have been around for one hundred years and thirty-five years respectively, but more recently over a dozen regional fern societies and study groups have come into being across the country, from Connecticut to Florida and Texas to Washington. The bulletin of the American Fern Society, *Fiddlehead Forum*, has become a source of fern information for the layman. Testing of new species is being carried out at the New York Botanical Garden and the Hardy Fern Foundation near Seattle (see appendix, page 333).

Perhaps the greatest herald of hardy fern cultivation in America has been F. Gordon Foster, an amateur fern gardener. His interest in photography and microscopy led to spore study and growing ferns from spores, finally resulting in his book, *A Gardener's Book of Ferns* (1964; now called *Ferns to Know and Grow* in its fourth edition, 1993). In it he describes cultivation and propagation procedures, and a small sampling of hardy species suitable for the garden. He spoke before innumerable garden clubs, promoting fern study and cultivation, and recently donated his living ferns to the New York Botanical Garden; these became the nucleus of its extensive hardy fern collection.

Another highlight in the development of American fern cultivation was the publication of Barbara Hoshizaki's excellent *Fern Grower's Manual* (1975). This book has marvelous introductory chapters on cultivation practices and a listing of species in cultivation, concentrating on tender species.

There are many books on fern identification—for states, regions of the country, and even the continent of North America—but these have only sparse information on fern cultivation.

Until 1970 the selection of available fern species was limited almost entirely to a smattering of native American species, a few English crested ferns, and two species from Japan, *Athyrium niponicum* 'Pictum' and *Dryopteris erythrosora*. Siskiyou Rare Plant Nursery of Medford, Oregon, had an especially rich offering of native western species in the 1960s. A major impetus for public interest in fern cultivation was the establishment of two nurseries in the Seattle area that concentrated on hardy ferns in the early 1970s: Sue Olsen with her mail-order nursery, Foliage Gardens, and Judith Jones with a similar nursery, Fancy Fronds. These two nurseries have greatly enriched the hardy fern market and accelerated American awareness of ferns in cultivation. The major difference between these two nurseries and previous businesses is that plants are spore-grown and not collected in the wild. Unfortunately, there are still a number of nurseries that supply plants directly from the wild, one even boasting it collects only from virgin areas. Natural populations are diminishing, and every effort must be made to preserve them for future generations. Wholesale companies, both in Holland and the United States, are propagating more species of ferns, and today, nearly two hundred kinds of ferns are available in nurseries and mail-order businesses.

The purpose of this book is to provide information on growing the wide range of ferns suitable for culture in temperate gardens, especially in North America. It is not the last word on hardy fern cultivation, but only a beginning. We still need information on many aspects of fern cultivation, especially the degree of hardiness, ease of cultivation, and details of propagation of most species.

THE NAMING OF FERNS

I will use both the Latin names and common names in this book when referring to specific ferns. Good arguments can be made for the use of common names—they are in English, they probably are the names we learned first, and they may seem to be more stable than the botanical (Latin) names, which are sometimes changed by botanists. In addition, some ferns have such universal common names that their use causes no confusion. A good example is the ostrich fern, which is known in many countries and several languages by that name; its scientific name, on the other hand, has changed from *Struthiopteris pensylvanica* to *Pteretis nodulosa* to *Matteuccia struthiopteris*, the latter being its correct name today. Often, on the other hand, there is great confusion regarding common names. The same name can be used for different plants (for example, "shield fern" is used for both *Dryopteris* and *Polystichum*) and in other cases, multiple names are applied to the same plant (*Lycopodium clavatum*, for example, has twenty-four common names). Latin names are very specific and universally understood and in the long run are more stable, though it may not always seem so. Changes in scientific names are mostly the result of increased knowledge (botanists learning more about the distinctness of groups) or differences in opinion. Closely related genera that are considered distinct by some botanists (the so-called botanical splitters) are combined by others (the so-called botanical lumpers). For example, the hart's-tongue is closely allied to the spleenworts, so some botanists consider them in the same genus, *Asplenium*, while others (including myself), through tradition, or believing them distinct enough, put the hart's-tongue in a separate genus, *Phyllitis*.

The scientific, or Latin, name of a species is made up of two parts. The first part, which is capitalized, is the genus name, and each genus encompasses one to many species. The second part, which is not capitalized, is a specific epithet, often descriptive. Thus, *Asplenium montanum* is the mountain spleenwort. The epithet can describe some feature of the plant, such as *hirsuta* (hairy), or indicate the place or region where it was first found or is largely found, such as *virginiana* (of Virginia), or honor a person, such as *andersonii* (of Mr. Anderson; Ms. Anderson would be *andersoniae*)—perhaps the person who discovered it. The species name is given a Latin ending which agrees in gender with the genus.

Some species are variable enough to have resulted in botanists or horticulturists recognizing categories within the species. These are called subspecies, varieties, forms, or cultivars.

The term "variety" can be loosely used to mean any distinct variant within a species, but in a botanical sense "variety" and "subspecies" apply to a deviation from the "typical" plant in a definite geographic area, and where the two overlap, they interbreed to form fertile intermediates. ("Variety" and "subspecies" are used nearly interchangeably in ferns although some botanists recognize a fine distinction between these categories.) A "form," on the other hand, is a plant with an unusual feature that occurs here and there without a discrete range. *Osmunda cinnamomea* occasionally has glandular hairs (those plants are called *O. cinnamomea* f. *glandulosa*) in scattered populations in New Jersey, Maryland, Alabama, Mississippi, and Arkansas. "Cultivar" is applied to a variety or form that occurs entirely or primarily in cultivation and is designated by cv. (e.g., *Dryopteris affinis* cv. Cristata) or more commonly within single quotation marks (e.g., *Dryopteris affinis* 'Cristata'). The vast majority of fern varieties in cultivation are really in a botanical sense "forms," as well as cultivars. However, in this book I will treat them all as cultivars, designated by single quotation marks, unless a plant is known definitely to be botanically a variety (var.) or subspecies (ssp.). Occasionally, I also use the word "variety" in the loose manner mentioned above.

Hybrids are designated by a formula involving the parent species names, and some hybrids are also given binomial names. Sterile hybrids are shown with an × before the specific epithet. Thus, *Dryopteris celsa* × *ludoviciana* is also known as *D.* × *australis*. Occasionally hybrids are fertile and act as distinct species. These have no × in the binomial. For example, the fertile hybrid between *Dryopteris cristata* and *D. goldiana* is known as *D. clintoniana*.

I do not use family names here. Fern families have been construed in such diverse ways by different botanists that it is confusing to the nonprofessional botanist, and even for many botanists. For an overview of the relationships of the ferns treated in this book, see page 331 in the appendices.

Fern Structure

"Nature made ferns for pure leaves to show what she could in that line."
—HENRY DAVID THOREAU

Ferns have been with us for more than 300 million years and in that time the diversification of their form has been phenomenal. There are amazing fossil impressions of fern or fernlike foliage, especially from the Coal Age (Carboniferous Period), which is also referred to as the Age of Ferns as they were a dominant part of the vegetation at that time. During this era some fern groups actually evolved seeds—the seed ferns—making up perhaps half of the fernlike foliage in Carboniferous times. Most of the ferns of the Coal Age became extinct but a few remnants later evolved into our modern ferns. Today there are about twelve thousand species of ferns in the world, the vast majority inhabiting wet tropical forests.

This is not the place for a detailed discussion of the morphology and anatomy of the ferns, but it is important to understand some of the basic structure and life history in order to appreciate them and grow them well.

Stem

The mature fern plant is constructed in the same manner as other kinds of plants we are familiar with, possessing roots, stems, and leaves, but in ferns these organs take on a different proportion and appearance from those of most other plants. The most conspicuous part of the fern—nearly all of the visible part of the plant—is the leaf, commonly called the frond. This highly visible part is attached to the stem, which is relatively inconspicuous. The stem is responsible for the production of leaves and roots, and the storage

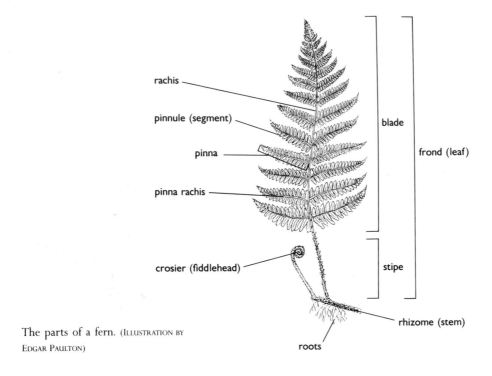

rachis

pinnule (segment)

pinna

pinna rachis

blade

frond (leaf)

crosier (fiddlehead)

stipe

rhizome (stem)

roots

The parts of a fern. (Illustration by Edgar Paulton)

of food. Most ferns have stems (rhizomes) that creep horizontally, right on or just beneath the soil surface, often branching. Whether long-creeping or compact, horizontal or erect, the stem is the growth center of the plant, for it not only grows in length, but its growing tip initiates all the leaves of the plant. This growing tip is the essence of the plant and its vegetative growth, and great care must be taken not to damage it.

Inside the rhizome the conducting tissue (the vascular bundles) carries water, minerals, and food throughout the plant. The vascular bundles can be seen when the rhizome is cut across with a knife; they may appear as a continuous ring but more often they are in the form of a discontinuous ring.

Fern roots are usually very slender and wiry, and arise along the length of the stem. They help anchor the plant to the soil (or rocks or tree trunks), and absorb water and minerals for the plant.

It is important to know the habit of a particular fern before selecting one for your garden. You don't want to find out too late that the fern you purchased spreads rapidly when you need a plant that will stay in one place. If the rhizome is short-creeping, the fronds will appear as a compact clump. If it is a species with a more widely creeping rhizome, the fronds will arise an

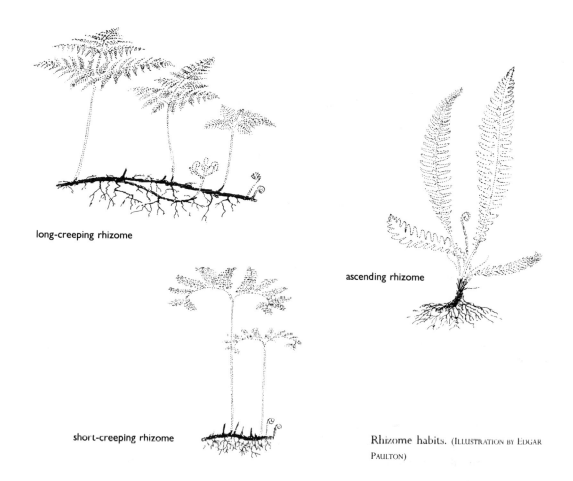

long-creeping rhizome

ascending rhizome

short-creeping rhizome

Rhizome habits. (ILLUSTRATION BY EDGAR PAULTON)

inch or more apart, sometimes forming extensive colonies (for example, *Thelypteris phegopteris* and *Gymnocarpium dryopteris*) and in extreme forms becoming decidedly aggressive (like *Dennstaedtia* and *Pteridium*). These colonies can occupy an entire hillside or meadow, often crowding out all other forms of plants. Bracken is the most notorious example. It has been suggested in jest that bracken is so widely creeping under the ground that all the bracken in the world is really a single plant!

On the other hand, some ferns have their rhizomes ascending (horizontal but turned upright at the end) or even fully erect, forming all the fronds around this erect crown. These do not creep at all and usually do not make many branches. The stem grows very slowly, usually remaining close to the soil with several leaves arising from the crown—the stem tip—to form a vase-shaped plant. This is especially noticeable in the holly ferns (*Polystichum*), the wood ferns (*Dryopteris*), and the ostrich fern (*Matteuccia*).

But there are some ferns with erect rhizomes that produce many offshoots, the ostrich fern being a prime example. In addition to the short, trunklike, erect stem, it sends out two or three slender runners, or stolons, beneath the ground that produce new plants several inches to a couple feet away from the original plant. The result is an abundance of young plants in the vicinity, which gives you a constant supply of ferns to give away or move to another part of the garden. It is good to know this about your plant ahead of time!

Perhaps the most striking of all fern stems are those of the tree ferns, with their graceful, slender trunks crowned at the top with long, gently arching dissected fronds. Some tree ferns are marginally hardy in southern Florida and coastal California.

Fronds

The fern frond is divided into two main parts, the stipe (leaf stalk or petiole) and the blade (the leafy, expanded portion of the frond). A cut through the stipe shows the vascular bundles and provides a useful tool for distinguishing some major fern groups. For example, *Dennstaedtia* and *Osmunda* have a single U-shaped bundle, whereas *Thelypteris* and *Athyrium* have two strap-shaped bundles, and *Dryopteris* and *Polystichum* have several round bundles, still reflecting the basic U-shape.

The blade may be undivided (simple) to finely cut, each degree of division having a specific term. *Pinnate* blades are divided into leaflets (pinnae), with each leaflet narrowly attached to the central axis, or rachis. Blades more divided are designated as *bipinnate* or *tripinnate*, with some divided four or five times, the ultimate divisions being called pinnules or segments. To determine how many times divided a leaf is, imagine a beetle climbing up the leaf stalk and count the number of turns it must make to reach an ultimate segment. For intermediate degrees of dissection the word *pinnatifid* is used;

Stipe bundles. (ILLUSTRATION BY EDGAR PAULTON)

Dennstaedtia

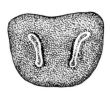

Athyrium

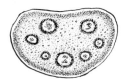

Dryopteris

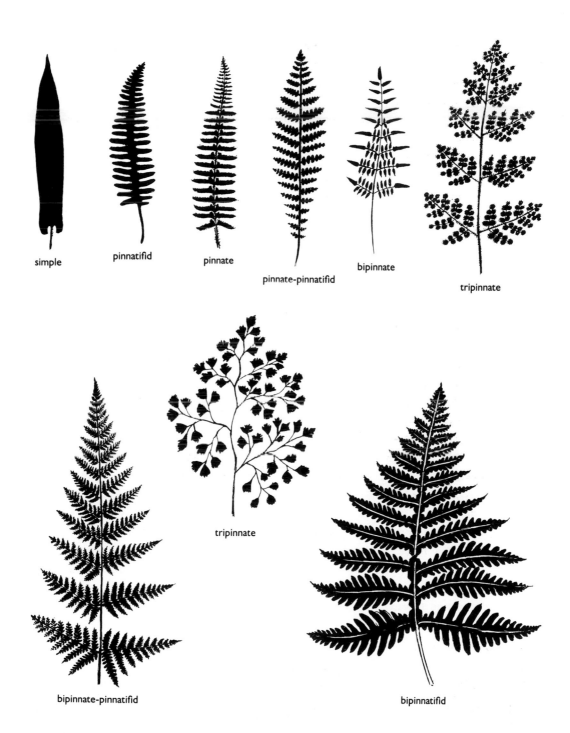

simple

pinnatifid

pinnate

pinnate-pinnatifid

bipinnate

tripinnate

tripinnate

bipinnate-pinnatifid

bipinnatifid

Frond dissections. (ILLUSTRATION BY EDGAR PAULTON)

thus, a *pinnatifid* blade is one cut nearly to the midvein, *pinnate-pinnatifid* is not quite divided enough to be called bipinnate, or a bipinnate frond with deeply cut segments is *bipinnate-pinnatifid*.

Generally each primary leaflet (pinna) is further divided, with the segments on the side pointing toward the frond tip (the acroscopic side) being about the same size as their counterparts on the side pointing toward the frond base (the basiscopic side), but in some genera, such as *Dryopteris* and *Arachniodes*, the basal pinnae and sometimes other pinnae will have the basiscopic segments much larger than those on the acroscopic side of the same pinna (see the entries for *Dryopteris dilatata*, *D. campyloptera*, *D. carthusiana*, *D. formosana*, and most of the species of *Arachniodes*). Often an undivided pinna or pinnule will have a single lobe near its base on the acroscopic side. This lobe is called an *auricle* (ear) and is characteristic for some species.

Ferns vary greatly in frond size. In temperate regions the extremes that are found in the tropics are lacking: tree ferns with ten- to twelve-foot fronds on trunks sixty to eighty feet tall are in marked contrast to some of the filmy ferns with ever-so-delicate and elusive fronds the size of a little fingernail. Temperate regions still do produce a surprising variation in size. Although most have leaves two to three feet tall, the ostrich fern is commonly six feet (and uncommonly eight or nine feet) tall. In contrast, the maidenhair spleen-wort is usually only four to six inches long and the mosquito fern (*Azolla*) has leaves only one sixteenth to one thirty-second of an inch long. Even within some species, there are many forms (cultivars) showing unbelievable variation. Most notable is the lady fern, *Athyrium filix-femina*, usually with fronds two to four feet tall, but with miniature forms that are only three inches high.

The habit of the fronds is also quite variable. Some ferns, such as *Dryopteris filix-mas* 'Barnesii' and *Polystichum tripteron*, hold their fronds stiffly erect. Many others have fronds gently arching, as in *Athyrium filix-femina*, while others (e.g., *Adiantum venustum*) have fronds that are broadly arching so the frond tips are pointing toward the ground. *Camptosorus rhizophyllus* spreads its fronds horizontally on moist, mossy rocks.

In the tropics there are some ferns with twining fronds, like the stems of morning glories. In the case of the climbing fern (*Lygodium*), it is not the stem that twines but rather the main axis (the rachis) of the fern frond. This twists about adjacent foliage or slender woody trunks while the fern stem continues its growth horizontally under the ground surface. *Lygodium* is a genus of about forty species found in tropical regions of both the New and Old Worlds, but there is one native to the eastern United States (*L. palmatum*) and one to Japan

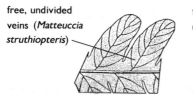
free, undivided
veins (*Matteuccia
struthiopteris*)

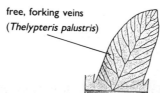
free, forking veins
(*Thelypteris palustris*)

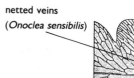
netted veins
(*Onoclea sensibilis*)

Venation patterns. (Taken from H. A. Gleason, *The New Britton and Brown Illustrated Flora of the Northeastern United States and Canada*, Vol. 1. New York Botanical Garden, New York, 1963, with permission from the New York Botanical Garden)

(*L. japonicum*) that are hardy north to New York and Massachusetts. Both make intriguing garden plants but the former is more difficult to cultivate.

There is broad diversity in the details of the fronds as well.

Venation.   In most North American ferns the veins of the leaf are free, i.e., they run from the midvein to the margin without forming a network. They may branch but they do not unite with other veins. However, when ferns do form a vein network, it is often very distinctive and thus very helpful in identification, as in *Onoclea*, *Woodwardia*, and several species of *Thelypteris* and *Polypodium*.

Texture.   Delicacy is the name of the game among ferns and there are many species with beautiful, membrane-thin fronds, such as species of *Dennstaedtia*, *Athyrium*, *Adiantum*, and *Thelypteris*. These delicate ferns easily dry out, giving all ferns the reputation of being difficult to grow as houseplants. Many, indeed, require high humidity, but not all species are so thin-textured. Fronds of *Dryopteris* and *Polystichum* are leathery and often evergreen.

Color.   Although we think of ferns as being plain and simple green, there is a surprising range of colors and shades in the ferns. The most popular fern with colorful fronds is the Japanese painted fern (*Athyrium niponicum* 'Pictum'), which has a combination of green, gray, and burgundy red in the fronds. Another Japanese *Athyrium*, *A. otophorum*, has very pale green blades with dark red rachises and pinna axes. Red stipes and rachises are common in species of *Athyrium*, and some species have both red and green forms.

Another colorfully impressive plant is the autumn fern, *Dryopteris erythrosora*, whose expanding fronds are a bronze color, gradually turning to a dark green as the fronds mature. In addition, the young fruiting dots (sori) on the back of the frond are a brilliant red, hence the specific name *erythrosora*, meaning

Japanese painted fern (*Athyrium niponicum* 'Pictum').

red sori. Shorter-lived but still striking are the juvenile leaves of the maidenhair ferns (*Adiantum*) and the blechnoid ferns (*Blechnum*, *Doodia*, and *Woodwardia* genera). Their uncurling fronds (called crosiers, or fiddleheads) and freshly expanded leaves are varying shades of pink until they finally mature and become the more traditional green.

Even the green fronds come in varying shades. Although many ferns have a fairly true green color, a large number of species are really more yellow-green. This is especially typical of those having a thin texture, such as *Thelypteris noveboracensis* and *Dennstaedtia punctilobula*. Some species of *Dryopteris* and *Polystichum* are a dark green hue, or even have a distinct bluish cast, as in *Dryopteris marginalis*. At the dark end of the scale is *Athyrium japonicum*, which has a sedate blackish green color.

Several ferns in arid regions of the southwestern United States are a gray-green or bluish green color, as in *Pellaea* and *Cheilanthes*. Some species have beautifully variegated forms which are commonly cultivated. *Pteris cretica* var. *albolineata*, *P. ensiformis* var. *victoriae*, and *Arachniodes simplicior* var. *variegata* have a broad white to yellowish band in the center of each pinna or segment.

In addition to the spring beauty of the unrolling crosiers and pink juvenile fronds, ferns can also provide some very impressive fall color. Species of *Osmunda* (*O. regalis*, *O. cinnamomea*, and *O. claytoniana*) have fronds as bright a

Fall color of *Osmunda cinnamomea.*

gold as the autumn leaves of sugar maples. Others, such as *Dennstaedtia* and *Onoclea*, turn from green to a muted yellow while species of *Athyrium* turn almost directly to brown with the first hard frost.

Scales and hairs.   Adding to the beauty of the ferns, the rhizome, stipe, and crosiers of most ferns are covered with hairs or scales. *Dryopteris atrata* and *D. uniformis* have glossy black scales, *D. remota* and *D. affinis* are shaggy

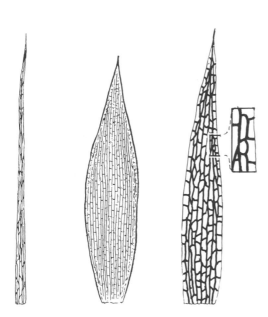

Fern scales. (ILLUSTRATION BY EDGAR PAULTON)

with golden scales, and the *Osmunda* fiddleheads are densely clothed with white to tan hairs. Although the blades may appear naked, closer examination with a hand lens reveals hairs and scales there as well.

Hairs are linear structures one or more cells long and only one cell wide. The hairs on the fronds of *Thelypteris* are characteristically sharp-pointed and often one-celled. Some long hairs have a glandular tip that secretes a volatile substance that may give the plant a distinctive smell, as in the hay-scented fern (*Dennstaedtia*). In some ferns, short, gland-tipped hairs produce a conspicuous white or yellow wax, as in the silverback and goldback ferns (*Pentagramma* and some *Cheilanthes*). Scales are somewhat like hairs but broader—several cells wide—although generally only one cell thick. They are often linear or lance-shaped. Usually they are uniform in color (concolorous) but in some species there is a dark brown or black streak down the center of each scale, in which case we call the scales bicolorous.

The leaf surfaces often have scales and/or hairs in varying degrees of abundance. The leaves in some species are completely covered, especially the undersurface, whereas others are virtually naked.

Evergreenness

None of the ferns are truly evergreen but we use the term, knowing it is not applied in quite the same way as in conifers and flowering plants. In the higher plants the leaves remain on the plant two or three years, whereas in the ferns, the leaves stay green through most of the winter months, finally turning brown just before the new fronds arise in the spring. Some people prefer the term "wintergreen" instead of evergreen, but there is no need for two terms; besides, wintergreen can be applied to a few ferns, such as some *Botrychium* and *Polypodium* species, that are green in the winter but die down from spring to late summer.

My fern garden is dotted with green through the winter, including specimens of *Dryopteris intermedia*, *D. marginalis*, *Polystichum acrostichoides*, and *P. braunii*. Although the fronds remain green, the stipes become mushy a couple inches up from the base, and with the fronds' support gone, they pass the winter flat on the ground but green. *Dryopteris erythrosora* and *D. championii*, though, remain standing and bright green through the whole winter.

Evergreen ferns are also good all winter as cut fronds in arrangements, even those lying down, at least in the earlier parts of the winter; many become somewhat discolored by winter's end.

In the great majority of ferns, the fronds die in the autumn (or if evergreen, the next spring) but remain attached to the rhizome, turning brown and gradually decaying. This brownish skirt around the base of the plant actually helps as a mulch and is best not removed (although some gardeners do so for cosmetic reasons). These ferns are called "deciduous," although again it is not the same sort of "deciduous" as in trees, where the leaves fall cleanly from the plant in the autumn. Very few ferns lose their leaves completely—the polypodiums do, along with a few other largely tropical genera.

As a perennial, fern rhizomes remain alive, even with leaves down, and the following spring the growing tips send up new sets of fronds. Several of our common deciduous ferns (e.g., *Athyrium*, *Dryopteris*, and *Polystichum*) store food in the old leaf bases, keeping these as food reserves. If a rhizome is cut lengthwise, the greenish living tissues can be seen extending well up into the old stipe bases.

Fiddleheads

Don't wait until the fronds are up and fully expanded in the spring to appreciate your ferns. As the first wildflowers and bulbs begin to bloom, pull back some of the dry leaves around the fern crowns and watch for the awakening of the new fronds. Fern leaves do not expand in all directions at once as do the leaves of higher plants, but rather are tightly coiled and mature first at the base, with maturation gradually progressing to the tips as the fronds unroll. These coiled, developing leaves are called fiddleheads (alluding to their similarity to the scroll of a violin), or crosiers (because of their resemblance to a bishop's coiled staff by that name).

Fiddleheads are amazingly diverse in size, color, and clothing, allowing one to distinguish many ferns on the basis of the crosiers alone. The *Cystopteris* and *Woodsia* crosiers are the first to unroll. They are so small and green and early (starting with the crocuses) that it is easy to miss them. The early silvery haired osmundas (*Osmunda cinnamomea* and *O. claytoniana*) are the first con-

Crosiers of *Polystichum braunii*.

Crosiers of *Cyrtomium fortunei*.

Crosiers of *Adiantum pedatum*.

spicuous fiddleheads on the scene. These gorgeous clusters of young crosiers arising in swamps and wet ditches in late April with their heads all huddled toward the center look like groups of conspirators discussing their spring strategy. They are clothed in dense white hairs that turn cinnamon-colored as the fronds mature. *Dryopteris* and *Polystichum* fiddleheads are also stout and clothed with scales of white, gold, brown, or even lustrous black. The crosiers of the delicate maidenhairs are pink and nearly invisible against a background of dry leaves. The pink to reddish expanding young fronds gradually turn to green and the stipes to black as they develop.

Dimorphism

In most ferns, all of the leaves perform two functions—the manufacture of food through photosynthesis and the production of spores for reproduction. Sometimes the fertile leaves, those that produce spores, will appear slightly narrower or taller than the strictly vegetative leaves, but look basically the same. In more extreme cases, however, there is a dramatic contrast between fertile and sterile leaves. The fertile leaves or fertile parts of leaves may be

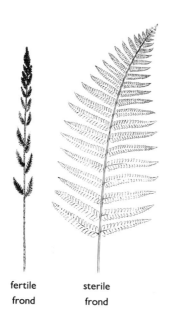

fertile
frond

sterile
frond

Three expressions of dimorphism in *Osmunda*: left to right, *O. cinnamomea*, *O. claytoniana*, *O. regalis*. (Illustration by Edgar Paulton)

completely devoid of leafy tissue, being composed of hardly more than the veins and spore cases (sporangia). At maturity these fertile leaves will appear brown or golden and contrast markedly from the green vegetative leaves. Such frond dimorphism generally runs in a family or genus, so often all members of a genus will show this phenomenon. In *Osmunda*, different species exhibit dimorphism in different ways. *Osmunda cinnamomea* has leaves that are entirely fertile or entirely sterile, the fertile ones being the first ones up in the spring, dropping their spores in early summer, and withering away. On the other hand, *O. claytoniana* has the sporangia borne on only a few pairs of pinnae in the middle of each frond, hence its common name of "interrupted fern," whereas *O. regalis* is fertile in the terminal third of the frond, thus giving rise to the colloquial name "flowering fern." The adder's-tongue (*Ophioglossum*) and rattlesnake ferns (*Botrychium*) have their sporangia borne on a fertile spike or branch arising from the leaf stalk and held erect. The ostrich fern (*Matteuccia struthiopteris*) and its close relative the sensitive fern (*Onoclea sensibilis*) have distinct fertile fronds that are brown, but, unlike most dimorphic-fronded species, they are not tender and do not wither right away. Instead, they are tough and woody, their segments inrolled, resembling bunches of grapes. After the vegetative leaves have died down for the winter, these fertile sentinels stand at attention throughout the winter. Their segments open in late winter to release their spores, dramatic when it happens on top of the snow.

WATER FERNS

The water ferns look so different from most ferns that it is difficult to imagine them as ferns. Among the water ferns the water clovers (*Marsilea*) with seventy species are found mostly in warm regions. Their leaves look like those of four-leaved clovers arising from creeping rhizomes rooted in the mud. The leaves rise through the water and float on the surface or the plants can be found growing on muddy shores, holding their shamrocks upright. The spores of the water ferns are not found on the leafy part of the frond at all, but in oval, nutlike structures, called sporocarps, at the base of the leaf stalk.

Two genera closely related to *Marsilea* show an interesting series of fewer leaflets. *Regnellidium diphyllum* of Brazil (not hardy) has only two leaflets, and *Pilularia* (which has three temperate species) has no leaflets at all. The leaves of the latter consist of nothing more than naked leaf stalks, looking much like a grass, but on careful examination one can see the unrolling fiddleheads (the leaf stalks unrolling) and the sporocarps nestled among the leaf bases.

Another group of water ferns is the floating ferns. The water spangles, *Salvinia*, float on the water and have oblong or round leaves (one half to one and a half inches long). Peculiar four-pronged hairs on the leaf surface keep the water droplets off the leaves. The leaves occur in pairs on the floating rhizome, and hanging down from each pair is what looks like a branched root. Actually, this is a third leaf that has become dissected. The plant grows rapidly over the water, sometimes compeletely covering the surface. It grows well in aquaria or in an urn or pool outdoors in the summer. In more tropical regions it can cover large areas of lakes and ditches.

Another floating fern, the mosquito fern, *Azolla*, has leaves only about one thirty-secondth of an inch across. The leaves occur in pairs, crowded on a stem floating on the water or occasionally rooted on the muddy shore. It looks more like duckweed or a moss than a fern.

FERN ALLIES

The term "fern allies" is given to several plant groups—clubmosses, spike-mosses, quillworts, and horsetails—that are at roughly the same evolutionary level in the plant kingdom as the ferns; that is, they have conducting (vascular) tissue and reproduce by spores. They are really not related to the ferns. Fern allies have small leaves with simple, unbranched veins and large sporangia, each often containing several hundred spores. The sporangia of most of the allies are produced in cones at the tip of the stem or the branches. In contrast, the ferns have a more complex branched vein system and generally small sporangia with only sixty-four spores each. The several groups of fern allies are distinctive and are more likely to be mistaken for mosses or some kinds of flowering plants than for ferns. They arose even before the ferns, some of them more than 400 million years ago, and, like the ferns, reached their greatest development during the Carboniferous Period, some of them becoming hundred-foot trees with trunks three feet in diameter. These eventually became much of the world's coal deposits.

Together, the ferns and fern allies are called pteridophytes, or lower vascular plants. Botanists studying ferns usually work on the fern allies as well.

The fern allies fall into two major groups: One, the clubmosses (*Lycopodium*), spikemosses (*Selaginella*), and quillworts (*Isoetes*), all have leaves spirally arranged on the stem with the sporangia borne at the leaf bases. The leaves bearing sporangia are usually smaller than the purely vegetative leaves and are set closer together forming cones, although in a few clubmosses and all the quillworts the fertile leaves are not distinctly different. The other, the horsetails (*Equisetum*), have minute, whorled, white or black leaves fused to form sheaths on hollow, jointed, ribbed stems, and the sporangia are borne on special umbrellalike structures in a cone.

The fern allies have not been used much in cultivation. Certainly many of them would be interesting curiosities as they introduce textures and forms not seen in the ferns. Several of the native horsetails and Asian spikemosses are readily cultivated although most of the clubmosses are challenging to grow. Quillworts grow mostly underwater, and although they can be grown, they are too inconspicuous to be considered further in this book. The fern allies are not grown from spores, partly because they are readily propagated vegetatively and partly because the spores are mostly difficult to germinate (some requiring long periods in the dark and special nutrients).

BRITISH VARIETIES

Occasionally in the wild or in spore cultures one can find an unusual fern specimen having forking tips or some other peculiar feature. Some of these abnormalities are the result of environmental quirks such as a sudden drop in temperature that causes developing leaves to be peculiar at maturity. These phenomena are only ephemeral, future leaves being normal, and are of no particular horticultural interest. Some variants, however, are caused by mutation, which would result in all or most of the leaves having a particular feature. Such characteristics can be passed on genetically via the spores, enabling similar plants to be produced. Some such variants breed true 100 percent of the time, whereas others produce a mixture of offspring with wide variation, perhaps only 5 to 10 percent having the desired form.

One of the great mysteries of ferndom is the remarkable abundance of fern variations in the British Isles. This phenomenon was integral to the Victorian fern craze of the nineteenth century, and even with the vast quantities of such plants removed from the wild over the past 140 years, there is still a frequent occurrence of these abnormal plants. Pteridophiles in Britain and Ireland can still go out in the wild and expect to find examples of these unusual forms. There seems to be no other place in the world with such a concentration of species aberration. Over the past thirty years on field trips in the United States, Mexico, the West Indies, and other parts of the world, I have never encountered variations of this sort in the wild other than as ephemeral oddballs. I don't mean to say that the British Isles are the only region in the world where this occurs, since we do indeed have several interesting variations in North America, such as the crested and dissected forms of the Christmas fern, but these are quite rare compared with the numbers of such mutants in Britain and Ireland.

These peculiarities can arise in one form or another in perhaps many genera but are found most frequently in a limited number of species. The species most heavily endowed in this way are *Athyrium filix-femina*, *Phyllitis scolopendrium*, and *Polystichum setiferum*. Each of these species has literally hundreds of named varieties.

The following are the most frequent kinds of variation found in the ferns.

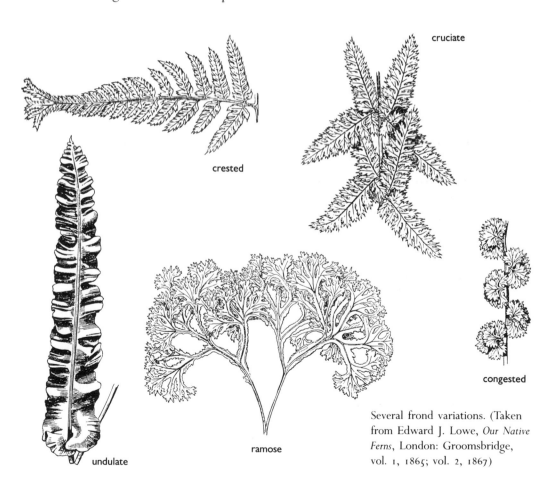

cruciate

crested

undulate

ramose

congested

Several frond variations. (Taken from Edward J. Lowe, *Our Native Ferns*, London: Groomsbridge, vol. 1, 1865; vol. 2, 1867)

Forking or cresting.   The most common type of variation is forking or cresting, in which the tip of the frond and often the tips of all the pinnae fork, once or twice or more repeatedly, maybe in a single plane or, less commonly, more tightly twisted in multiple planes to form tassels. These forms are often given names like *bifida* (for once-forked), *cristata* (frond tip and often pinnae crested), *capitata* (tip crested, but not the pinnae), and *percristata* (crested throughout—on frond tips, pinnae, and pinnules). *Polydactyla* ("many-fingered," repeated forkings), *corymbifera* (tasseled), *multifida* (many forkings), and *grandiceps* (compact multiple forkings to form a "large head") all apply to this phenomenon in different degrees, but unfortunately the names are not all applied uniformly.

"*Ramosa*" (branching) involves a forking farther down the main axis, on the rachis or even from the stipe, giving a branched appearance to the frond as a whole.

Frond division. Another dimension of change is to have fronds more divided (dissected) than usual. Finely cut fronds are often called "plumose" (*plumosa*). In the case of the undivided fronds of *Phyllitis*, the margins are incised (shallowly cut) or lacerate (deeply cut). More often than not, highly dissected fern varieties are barren, with no sori found. (The term "sterile" is often applied in descriptions of highly dissected varieties, but "barren" is a better term since "sterile" can also mean that sporangia are formed but the spores abort, as in most hybrids between species.)

Dwarfing and congestion.   In some cases the mutant plants are merely smaller plants, even down to four to six inches tall, but aside from their size appearing much as the typical species. *Athyrium filix-femina* 'Minutissimum', for example, is a dwarf form of the European lady fern. Often the reduction in size also involves the overlapping of segments, as in *Adiantum aleuticum* 'Subpumilum' and *Athyrium filix-femina* 'Congestum Cristatum'. Many of these diminutive plants are ideal for rock gardens and other small spaces, such as terraria. The reduction and congestion may not apply to the entire frond but only the pinnae. A fine example of this is *Athyrium filix-femina* 'Frizelliae', in which the pinnae are reduced to congested buttons along the length of the rachis.

Sometimes the pinnae or some of the pinnules will be lacking, usually irregularly (depauperate). *Dryopteris filix-mas* 'Linearis Polydactyla' is especially attractive with its segments small to nearly absent and the pinna tips multifingered. Other species with pinna parts missing, irregular, or imperfect may appear insect-eaten and are not worth growing.

In some of the less divided species, especially *Polypodium*, the tip of the frond may be elongated, like a tail (caudate), for example, *Polypodium glycyrrhiza* 'Longicaudatum'.

Cruciate. A very dramatic pinna modification is the cruciate condition. In this case, found most commonly in *Athyrium*, the pinnae fork at their base to form two equal pinnae at right angles to each other, one directed downward at a 45-degree angle from the horizontal, the other ascending at a similar angle with each pinna half crossing an adjacent pinna half. The epitome of this form is *Athyrium filix-femina* 'Victoriae', in which the entire frond is a series of crisscrosses.

Margin. The margin of the frond or its segments can be undulating rather than in the usual single plane. This can vary from a slight waviness of the margin (*crispa*), as in some *Dryopteris*, to a strong roller coaster, giving the appearance of lasagna or ribbon candy, as in *Phyllitis scolopendrium* 'Undulata'.

In some forms the margin of the segments is rolled downward (*revoluta*, *revolvens*).

Surface. The upper surface of the hart's-tongue fern (*Phyllitis*) is sometimes very rough or wrinkled, a condition called "muricate" (*muricata*).

Buds. One of the most curious variations is the production of buds on the frond, usually along the rachis in the axils of pinnae in varieties of *Polystichum setiferum*. Plantlets usually do not develop very far unless the frond is pegged down onto moist soil or sand. Plantlets are produced on the upper surface of the blade in *Dryopteris erythrosora* 'Prolifica' and the rare *Phyllitis scolopendrium* 'Vivipara'.

The occurrence of the same sort of mutations in different species may cause some to end up looking superficially alike. They are not really the same, of course, as evidenced by other features such as scales, anatomy, and sori, but their general form can be amazingly similar, as in congested forms of *Athyrium filix-femina*, *Polystichum setiferum*, and *Dryopteris filix-mas*.

A more elaborate discussion of these variations can be seen in Dyce, "Classification of Fern Variation in Britain" (*Pteridologist* 1(1987): 154–155) and Kaye, *Hardy Ferns* (1968; pp 100–101).

Chapter Two

Growing and Gardening with Ferns

I t is not complicated to develop a fern garden, but there are three main requirements that must be met: 1) shade, 2) loose, rich soil, and 3) moisture.

Shade

Nearly all ferns do best in shade—not the full shade of maples or hemlocks, but rather a mixed, dappled shade, with sunlight for part of the day and patches of light moving across the garden, or a high shade that allows light to come in from the side. A common mistake is to think that ferns enjoy deep shade. Sometimes articles claim that if you have a corner of your property that is so dark that nothing else will grow, ferns are the perfect solution. Wrong! Ferns require protection from the burning rays of afternoon sun and from drying winds, but they also need light to grow well. The kind of light they need might be found at the edge of a wooded area, or in woods with patches of sunlight. If you observe where ferns are found in forests, you will see that most of those ferns are located in rather light woods or at the edges of clearings. Deeply shaded forests have few ferns or none at all.

Shade need not be present in the form of trees. It can also be found on the north side of buildings, in city courtyards among tall buildings, in window wells, or behind a wall or fence. No matter the location, there should be plenty of "skyshine." A lath structure is often used in warmer areas and can be useful for situations lacking shade.

Soil

Basically, most ferns require a rich, humusy soil with good drainage, such as that found in woodlands. When I moved into my house, the garden had nearly pure sand fill and lots of shade. Grass had been planted over most of the area, but, being on a slope, parts of the lawn would wash downhill after every major rain and I had to bring it back with a wheelbarrow, filling in the canyons and replacing the sod. I turned to ferns. With each fern I planted I put a shovel or two of compost or peat in the hole before putting in the fern. A mulch of wood chips and leaves has gradually changed the soil of the entire area so that it is dark and well drained. And the soil erosion is no more!

Heavy clay soil can be more of a problem as the heaviness does not allow enough oxygen for optimal fern root growth. It must be made lighter and richer by working in organic matter, especially compost for nutrients, and coarse sand and perhaps small stones to loosen it up and let in more oxygen. Builder's sand is too fine to help. An ongoing compost pile is most helpful, but if you don't have your own, limited amounts can be purchased at garden centers, and some villages have community leaf piles available for the taking.

Most ferns grow well in a soil with good drainage, rich in organic matter, and slightly on the acid side. There are a few ferns that prefer some lime in the soil or grow on limestone rocks. These include a number of the spleenworts (*Asplenium*), some maidenhairs (*Adiantum*), the cliff brakes (*Pellaea*), and the walking fern (*Camptosorus rhizophyllus*). Marble chips can be sprinkled around such lime-loving plants or if you have limestone rocks available for a limestone rock garden, so much the better. Some ferns, such as the bulblet bladder fern (*Cystopteris bulbifera*), normally occur on limestone but can take slightly acid soil as well. Others, such as *Pellaea atropurpurea* and *Gymnocarpium robertianum*, are strictly lime-loving (these plants are known as calciphiles). Strictly acid-loving species (calciphobes) include *Blechnum spicant*, *Gymnocarpium dryopteris*, and *Lygodium palmatum*.

A very important aspect of your fern site is the matter of judging the effect of tree roots. Your fern planting area must be cultivated. Ferns are not strong competitors, and the roots of trees and shrubs rob the area of moisture as well as physically vie for space. Your planting area should be far away from such root invasion or you should actively cultivate the area, periodically cutting around the bed but not close to the ferns as they do not appreciate disturbance. Extra watering in such an area may be needed.

Moisture

Choosing the best location for a fern garden also involves assessing the available moisture of an area. Drainage should be moderate but the soil must never get bone-dry. If the soil is so porous that it is dry all the time, you can remedy it in several ways. Organic matter can be added to the soil to enhance its water-holding capacity. You can divert downspouts to a "dry well" (a pit filled with coarse stones) in the vicinity of the garden, which will allow the water to slowly percolate through the soil. My own ferns reside mostly over a septic field, and for the areas not moistened that way, dry wells from three downspouts and the washing machine help. Of course, you can also resort to using a hose or installing a watering system. A few ferns will tolerate dry situations, including *Dennstaedtia*, *Pteridium*, and some of the desert ferns (e.g., *Cheilanthes* and *Pellaea*), and even *Dryopteris affinis* and *D. filix-mas*, but all will do better with moisture.

When first transplanted, the ferns should be watered well several times and kept moist for the first couple weeks until they are established. In times of severe drought I try to give my ferns a deep watering. In midsummer, if there is a lack of regular rain showers, some of the ferns will show signs of stress in the form of wilting and browning, and added water helps alleviate the situation. *Adiantum pedatum*, especially, develops brown fronds or tips, as do *Matteuccia* and *Onoclea*, and sometimes *Athyrium* if they are allowed to be dry too long. Judge your own moisture situation as some growers recommend a minimum of two seasons of regular watering to fully establish the root system.

In the wild, ferns are found in a wide range of habitats. *Dennstaedtia punctilobula* and *Dryopteris intermedia* are often seen in dry rock crevices whereas *Woodwardia areolata* and *Onoclea sensibilis* are usually in swamps, but overall in the garden nearly all ferns will do well with moderate moisture. The swamp-lovers such as *Matteuccia*, *Dryopteris cristata*, and *Thelypteris palustris* may reach a greater size in wetter situations but will still do quite well in a general garden. My ostrich ferns, for example, are regularly four to six feet tall.

PLANTING YOUR FERNS

Once you have the site selected and the soil prepared, you are nearly ready to plant your ferns. If this is a large project, such as planting an entire bed, plan where you want the ferns placed, and perhaps even set the plants in position to see what they will look like, always making sure the roots do not dry out. When we planted the New York Botanical Garden's F. Gordon Foster Hardy Fern Garden, we first visited Mr. Foster's garden in Sparta, New Jersey, estimating the number of plants and listing the kinds to be moved. Before we even dug a single plant, we went back to the NYBG site and placed a marker in the soil for each plant.

Let's digress a moment to consider where you might acquire ferns for planting. You may be dividing existing plants or even growing them from spores (see Chapter 3). If you are just beginning, it is more likely that you are purchasing plants from a nursery. Local nurseries will have a selection of some native ferns or even a few native to Japan or Europe that have been in turn obtained from wholesalers, who are stocking an increasing number of species and varieties. Carefully consider the sources of these purchased plants. Wholesalers, for the most part, to get an adequate number of plants, grow them from spores or through tissue culture, but some local nurseries or mail-order establishments still collect plants in the wild. Especially with the growing interest in ferns, this has put increasing pressure on the wild populations and this is to be discouraged. Plants collected in the wild, when grown in a pot for a few months, can be sold as "nursery-grown" plants. All known plants of walking fern (*Camptosorus rhizophyllus*), grape ferns (*Botrychium* species), and clubmosses (*Lycopodium*) in the trade come from wild sources. Inquire specifically for their origin. For the individual gardener, wild material is a practical source of plants when the area is being developed for housing or highway construction or if the plant populations are large. Of course, permission must be obtained from the landowner, and no plants should be removed from public lands, no matter how large the populations. In the appendix on fern sources, I have listed some nurseries known to be reputable and responsible in this regard, and references for additional source lists.

Once you have the plant, dig a hole somewhat larger than the rootball of the fern. Add peat or compost and a little bonemeal, and water the hole to make sure the roots will have sufficient moisture. One common mistake is to let the roots dry out before getting the plants into the ground. If you dig the fern yourself, try to get enough soil with it to cover the roots. If the plant comes to you nearly bare-rooted, soak it and keep it covered with moist newspapers or burlap, or in a plastic bag and in the shade until you are ready to plant it. Great disturbance shocks the plant and kills some of the rootlets, reducing its ability to take in water from the soil until it can produce new rootlets for absorption. As you plant the fern, cut off any broken fronds and about one third of the total fronds to reduce water loss from the leaf surfaces.

Cutting off good leaves is not necessary if you have kept a good size root ball and provide sufficient water as the fern gets established. Ferns bought in containers should be ready to plant without frond removal (other than broken ones). Keep the old fronds off to the side and use them as a mulch skirt around the plant to help keep the soil moist and reduce soil erosion.

Note the habit of the rhizome (or check the species entry in this book)—whether it was ascending or creeping horizontally—and orient the rhizome accordingly. Plant the fern at the same level as it was growing, with the growing tip—the center of the crown—slightly above the ground. This is most important for it may rot if left underground. Firm the plant in place; add compost as a topdressing and mulch. Some ferns have rather slender, long-creeping rhizomes and cannot be held on the surface of the soil easily. These you can lay in a shallow trench and then lightly sprinkle soil on top to hold them in place. These should not be planted more than an inch deep, but be sure to cover loose roots and the dead ends of the rhizome; birds sometimes try to pull them up for nesting material. Once the ferns are planted, water everything again to make sure they get a good start.

The addition of wood chips or other mulch around the plants preserves the moisture and keeps down the weeds. Alternative mulches include buckwheat hulls and cocoa shells.

Once the ferns are in the ground, there is little care needed to maintain the fern garden. Watering should be necessary only when the plants are freshly planted and in times of drought. The addition of compost once a year is as much nutrient as the ferns need. Fertilizer makes the plants grow faster, in which case they may become weaker and less resistent to insects or freezing in the fall. Neglect has its limits, though. Encroachment and competition from other plants can become a problem. Ferns do not take competition well and can be readily overtaken by weeds or other garden plants. Mulching and adding wood chips help keep weeding to a minimum.

Occasional thinning of the more aggressive species may be necessary. The ostrich fern (*Matteuccia struthiopteris*) with its stolons and young plants popping up around it, the widely creeping rhizomes of the sensitive fern (*Onoclea sensibilis*), the New York fern (*Thelypteris noveboracensis*), and the beech ferns (*Thelypteris decursive-pinnata*, *T. hexagonoptera*, and *T. phegopteris*) are all candidates for thinning. Some species are not especially assertive but do produce offshoots that you may wish to remove for planting elsewhere. It does not harm the parent plant to leave them, but in the case of the crown-formers, the smaller offsets detract from the symmetry of the large crown and even displace it with time. These make fine giveaways, or they can be used in other parts of the garden. In addition to making your friends happy, you have a chance of getting divisions back if your own plant dies later. An old adage among gardeners is, "the best way to keep a plant is to give it away."

In the spring, the fern garden should be cleaned before the crosiers start to unfurl. At this stage, ferns are very fragile and break off easily once the fronds begin to elongate; the work is best done when the crosiers are still tightly curled in the crown. Removal of weeds, branches, and leaves should be done by hand. Hoes or rakes should not be used as these may cause damage to the shallow root systems or break off the fiddleheads.

In the autumn, fallen tree leaves may be left on the fern garden for additional winter mulch. When the leaves have fallen, carefully rake off the greater accumulation but let a layer remain. They insulate the ferns during the cold months and then break down, adding nutrition and texture to the soil. In late fall protect those ferns that are marginally hardy for your area by burying them in leaves or salt hay and covering them with branches to keep them from heaving out of the ground in late winter and early spring. Sometimes open-topped boxes with coarse screens are used over tender plants for added protection before heaping on the leaves and branches. Old fronds may be carefully cut away if preferred, or left on as added natural mulch.

Ferns grown from spores can be placed outside after their second winter indoors but must be protected. For the first and perhaps even the second winter outside the young ferns should be given special care, as outlined above for marginally hardy ferns.

The transplanting of ferns can take place any time during the growing season, or just before it. Some gardeners prefer to do it in the spring so the plants will become well-established before winter. Others like to plant in late summer, as soon as the nights become cool, to avoid the heat and drought of the summer, which can easily kill freshly planted ferns. Transplanting is possible even in the midst of summer, as long as the plants are kept moist and not exposed to too much strong sun before they have settled in. Late in the fall is risky, though, since the plants may not have time to put down their root systems before the onset of winter weather.

One cannot judge on the basis of a single try whether a plant will be hardy or do well in one's garden. Sometimes it takes several attempts at transplanting, perhaps planting at different times of the year or in a different place, realizing that every garden has many microhabitats. Individual care makes a great difference too, of course, as do the amount of soil on the roots, the age of the plant, the time between digging and replanting, etc. Common ferns native to your area should be a good bet. However, selection need not be limited to your own area or to identical ecological conditions. Plants have broader tolerance than their natural ranges might suggest. You cannot always determine in advance whether a particular fern will be hardy in your area based on the actual range of the species. *Dryopteris ludoviciana* and *D.* × *australis*, for example, are limited to the southeastern United States but are hardy much farther north. *Dryopteris erythrosora* occurs in warm temperate regions of Japan but is fully hardy in most of the United States. We don't know the full effective range or full hardiness of most fern species, and extensive testing is needed. The only rule is to go ahead and try.

PESTS IN THE FERN GARDEN

Ferns are generally free of major pest damage. In a few areas of North America slugs and snails are a problem. They chew off entire young crosiers or creep out on the fronds and eat holes in the leaf tissue. Although they seem to enjoy most kinds of ferns, there are some species that are very difficult to grow because of the passion slugs have for them. The walking fern (*Camptosorus rhizophyllus*) and some of the spleenworts (*Asplenium*), for example, are especially difficult to cultivate in the garden for this reason. Slug bait sprinkled about the plants will usually take care of this problem. Some people use diatomaceous earth or sand on the ground immediately around the plants. Deadline administered in a ring around the plants is especially effective and does not wash away easily.

Leaf-rolling insects occasionally will disfigure a few fronds, but not much can be done other than to remove and destroy the damaged frond tips.

Birds will often peck at the small ferns, especially those growing among rocks, and will pull them from the soil to use as nesting material. Cover small rhizomes and loose roots so as not to tempt the birds. Young plants just getting established might be enclosed with a wire mesh to protect them until their roots are well-attached to the soil.

Fortunately, deer do not seem to be attracted to ferns in a serious way. A major deer run passes directly through our fern glen at the New York Botanical Garden's Cary Arboretum in Millbrook, New York, and only rarely is a fern nibbled. More often the damage is from deer lying on the ferns.

A greater threat to the ferns is playing children and pets. Ferns are generally fragile plants; the fronds of many species are brittle and break easily.

LANDSCAPING WITH FERNS

Much of landscape design is a matter of individual taste, but I think suggestions of possible ways ferns can be used in the garden could be helpful. There are many situations where ferns can fit beautifully, either in small groupings or larger plantings. Perhaps the most useful and natural-looking plan is the mixed shade garden filled with a diversity of ferns chosen to include a variety of size, texture, and evergreenness and flowering plants.

One of the first questions to arise is how many of each species of ferns should be planted, which is, in part, a matter of practicality. If you are given a single plant, you don't have much choice, but if the options are open and you have the space, try to use three or five of a kind to form a small group.

This mixed fern bed includes fifteen species of ferns along with English and Japanese primroses and dwarf iris.

Ferns on a rocky pool bank in Tacoma, Washington (left to right): *Athyrium cyclosorum*, *Adiantum aleuticum*, *Polystichum munitum*, and *Phyllitis scolopendrium*.

Athyrium filix-femina gives a feathery texture among other waterside plants.

Large rocks make an impressive background for *Blechnum spicant*.

Some of the smaller ones, especially, such as *Athyrium filix-femina* 'Frizelliae' or 'Minutissimum', look rather lonesome by themselves. Even the larger ferns, like *Dryopteris goldiana*, make a fine clump in the right situation. On the other hand, single specimen plants draw more attention to a peculiar form. I like to use *Athyrium filix-femina* 'Victoriae' by itself. It is striking as an individual plant, showing off its remarkable crisscross architecture. I have seen it as a clump of a dozen or more plants and its unique patterns seem to fade into a general ferniness. The extreme is to plant large beds of single species. The

Savill Garden at Windsor, England, is a wonderful example of this type of planting with thirty to forty plants well spread out in large beds. But then, that garden has 4,500 acres.

The choice of which ferns to use and how many depends, too, on the effect you wish to achieve. The Christmas fern (*Polystichum acrostichoides*), with its lustrous, spreading, dark green fronds, makes a low mass. Some of the larger vase-shaped species, such as the ostrich fern (*Matteuccia struthiopteris*), look better contrasting with a smaller species of a different texture, such as the northern maidenhair (*Adiantum pedatum*). Large dark green dryopterises go well with the small, pale green oak fern (*Gymnocarpium dryopteris*) or the colorful Japanese painted fern (*Athyrium niponicum* 'Pictum'). In planting several species together, naturally, place the larger ones toward the back, whether they be upright or arching, with the smaller ones nearer the front. Consider habit and size of the mature plant and don't crowd your plants. Most important, give them irregular spacing (not in rows) for a more natural effect. They don't always have to be spread far apart; they can be overlapping.

Ferns mix very well with many shade-loving flowering plants. Ferns provide

An array of native ferns makes a charming entry to this country home in Mount Desert, Maine (*Athyrium angustum, Dennstaedtia punctilobula, Osmunda claytoniana, Polystichum acrostichoides, Thelypteris noveboracensis*).

Thelypteris phegopteris (with *Athyrium angustum* to the left) frames these stone steps.

a symphony of green throughout the growing season, and careful selection of flowering plants can provide continuous bits of color. Such native plants as wild geranium (*Geranium maculatum*) and species of campanula, columbine (*Aquilegia*), hepatica, bloodroot (*Sanguinaria*), and violets (*Viola*) all look beautiful together in the mixed shaded garden, giving a touch of color in the spring and variation in texture the rest of the season. The jack-in-the-pulpit (*Arisaema triphyllum*) is especially dramatic as it rises above the smaller ferns with its handsome trifid leaves and hooded inflorescences in the spring. The leaves are beautiful all summer, and it adds bright late summer color with its orange-red fruits. Solomon's seal (*Polygonatum biflorum*), foamflower (*Tiarella*), and bishop's cap (*Mitella diphylla*) add a delicate touch of white to the garden.

Nonnative flowers and shrubs can also be used. Azaleas make a bright backdrop to unrolling fiddleheads, and the spring-flowering bulbs—daffodils, tulips, and crocuses—act as harbingers of the more subtle show to come later. By the time they are finished flowering, the ferns are up and discreetly hide the fading leaves of the bulbs. Astilbes with their plumes of white or pink mix well with the ferns, as do the foliage plants, such as the many forms and textures of hosta. A border of English and Japanese primulas helps show off the ferns during the spring and summer respectively, and the hardy begonia (*Begonia grandis*) complements ferns beautifully with its pink flowers and red-bottomed leaves through the late summer and fall. Thus, ferns are the continuo as the orchestra of flowering plants play their brief solos through the growing season. Other excellent fern companions are listed on pages 42–44.

The curious leaves and flowers of *Arisaema dracontium* give interesting variety among the ferns.

The creeping habit and erect, bright blue flowers make *Phlox stolonifera* an outstanding companion to ferns in a shady garden.

The pendent pink flowers of *Begonia grandis* add color to the garden in the late summer and early fall.

BOTANICAL NAME	COMMON NAME	PERIOD OF BLOOM
Actaea pachypoda	doll's-eyes	late spring— early summer

Inconspicuous flowers but white, porcelainlike fruits in summer and fall. Fruits are poisonous to children.

Actaea rubra	red baneberry	late spring— early summer

Divided leaves and bright red berries in summer.

Anemonella thalictroides	rue anemone	spring

Small plants with delicate divided leaves and white flowers.

Arisaema dracontium	green dragon	early summer

The long yellow dragon's tongue of the inflorescence and the arc of the dissected leaf add attractive touches.

Asarum canadense	Canada wild ginger	early summer

The gingers are grown for their rounded, heart-shaped leaves. The flowers are inconspicuous, three-parted, purplish brown, and borne close to the ground. The leaves are deciduous.

Asarum caudatum	British Columbia wild ginger	early summer

Flowers with long, taillike petal tips. The leaves are deciduous.

Asarum europaeum	European wild ginger	early summer

Striking for its lustrous, dark, evergreen leaves.

Caulophyllum thalictroides	blue cohosh	spring

Inconspicuous flowers but nice foliage and round blue fruits.

Convallaria majalis	lily-of-the-valley	late spring

White wands of fragrant flowers but invasive and needs control each year.

Dicentra cucullaria	Dutchman's-breeches	spring

Mound of dissected leaves and white to yellowish flowers. The leaves disappear soon after flowering.

Dicentra eximia and cultivars	fringed bleeding heart	spring and summer

The pink, red, or white flowers are attractive, as are the dissected leaves, which stand up well all summer.

BOTANICAL NAME	COMMON NAME	PERIOD OF BLOOM

Dicentra spectabilis *bleeding heart* *spring*
Impressive with its arching racemes of large heart-shaped pink-and-white or white flowers. The leaves tend to become somewhat shabby late in the season.

Epimedium species and cultivars *barrenwort* *spring*
Sprays of delicate white, yellowish, pink, lavender, or red flowers; leaves rimmed with reddish or bronze when young, some species semievergreen.

Erythronium americanum *dogtooth violet* *spring*
The smooth, mottled leaves and erect stalks of yellow flowers contrast well with the young fern fronds.

Erythronium tuolumnense *giant dogtooth violet* *spring*
Similar to *E. americanum* but with unmottled leaves and much larger in all dimensions.

Galium odoratum *sweet woodruff* *late spring*
Small, delicate flowers to give just a touch of white, but the foliage is more important, with a mound of small, whorled leaves and erect stems; spreads but not obtrusive.

Helleborus niger *Christmas rose* *late winter*
Gives flowers before anything else is up.

Helleborus orientalis *Lenten rose* *early spring*
Flowers as early bulbs and first fiddleheads (*Cystopteris* and *Woodsia*) are coming up.

Heuchera species and cultivars *coralbells* *spring–summer*
Long stalks of small pink, red, or white flowers; foliage sometimes colored as well.

Hosta species and cultivars *plantain lily* *summer*
Plants of many sizes and colors, 3 feet to only 2 inches tall. The leaves come in many shades (green and blue, to variegated with yellow or white borders) and textures (smooth, grooved, puckered).

Iris cristata *dwarf crested iris* *spring*
Blue flowers on plants only a few inches tall. Slugs are fond of it.

Mertensia virginica *Virginia bluebells* *spring*
Flowers pink in bud, turning to blue on opening; deer like it.

BOTANICAL NAME	COMMON NAME	PERIOD OF BLOOM
Phlox divaricata	*wild blue phlox*	*spring*

Erect plants with pale blue flowers.

Phlox stolonifera	*creeping phlox*	*late spring*

Low foliage with erect (6- to 8-inch) flower stalks, blue flowers with yellow eye; invasive but worth it; lots to give away.

Podophyllum peltatum	*mayapple*	*spring*

Interesting umbrellalike leaves and drooping, waxy white flowers, but spreads quickly. Leaves occur 1 foot or so apart on a long rhizome.

Polemonium caeruleum	*Jacob's ladder*	*late spring*

Ladderlike compound leaves and abundant blue flowers; deer wipe mine out occasionally.

Sanguinaria canadensis *'Multiplex'*	*double-flowered bloodroot*	*spring*

Produces flowers that look like miniature water lilies.

Smilacina racemosa	*false Solomon's seal*	*spring*

Terminal raceme of white flowers; produces red fruits in summer and fall.

Trillium grandiflorum	*white trillium*	*spring*

The 3-parted leaves are attractive after the white flowers are gone; other species have yellow or maroon flowers, some with mottled leaves.

Uvularia grandiflora	*bellwort*	*spring*

Erect, forked, leafy stems and weeping yellow lilylike flowers.

For a touch of humor you can add the dissected fernlike foliage of nonferns, such as yarrow (*Achillea*), tansey (*Tanacetum*), and even parsley in sunnier locations. Visitors to the New York Botanical Garden's rock garden are commonly fooled by the dissected foliage of *Corydalis lutea* and even look for the sori until they see the sprays of yellow flowers.

Be careful in the use of widely creeping species with ferns, such as *Pachysandra*, *Vinca* (myrtle), *Ajuga*, and *Hedera helix* (English ivy). Most ferns do not compete well with aggressive plants. I take care to pick species or varieties of ground cover that do not overrun the ferns. For example, common bugleweed (*Ajuga reptans*) is a rampant grower, but the cultivars 'Metallica' and 'Burgundy Glow' grow much more slowly and work well with ferns. Ferns

*Onoclea sensibilis
in pachysandra.*

used with ground covers need to be tall, strong growers. *Matteuccia, Onoclea,*
and *Osmunda* are able to hold their own when used with such bold ground
covers as pachysandra and myrtle, although you will miss seeing the bases of
the fern plants. The large fronds emerge well from the dark green ground
cover.

In addition to the fleeting color of flowers in the garden, a more lasting
touch of pale streaking can be achieved by using a few plants with variegated
foliage. Below are a few of the ones I have found especially attractive.

BOTANICAL NAME	COMMON NAME	PERIOD OF BLOOM
Aegopodium podagraria 'Variegatum'	*bishop's weed*	*summer*

Makes good ground cover in shade but spreads widely.

Arum italicum 'Pictum'	*Italian arum*	*spring*

Dark green arrowhead leaves with pale veins arise in the fall; the plants
flower in the spring and die down.

Liriope muscari	*lilyturf*	*fall*

Evergreen grasslike leaves with white and green streaks, or entirely green.
Spikes of purple flowers like those of grape hyacinth (*Muscari*).

Polygonatum odoratum 'Variegatum'	*variegated Solomon's seal*	*late spring*

The arching stems, variegated leaves, and creamy, pendent flowers make
this one of the most beautiful plants for a shade garden.

Pulmonaria officinalis	*lungwort*	*spring*

White spots on oblong leaves. Pink buds open to sky blue flowers.

Arum italicum 'Variegatum' has
showy leaves from late summer
through the winter and spring.

The arching stems and white-
margined leaves make *Polygonatum
odoratum* 'Variegatum' an interesting
addition to the garden.

Foundation Plantings

Large ferns work well in front of building foundations and similar locations,
such as along the bases of walls and fences, and to cover bare bases of shrubs
and large hedges. They can also be used to mark boundary lines of a neighbor's
property or the edge of a garden. In addition to hiding foundations or large
objects, ferns look lovely planted more sparsely in front of a fallen log or
beside a large rock. Ferns used in these ways should be erect or only slightly
arching and be planted in a solid row or in clumps. *Matteuccia* is the traditional
and most widely used choice. It is the tallest of our ferns and among the
most dependable. It is an outstanding plant, especially if you have a space to
fill, because it will send out stolons and quickly add more plants each year.
We have it hiding the bare trunks of a hemlock hedge that marks our boundary
line. It comes up strongly each year and even invades the pachysandra.
Occasionally, a stolon goes in the other direction, under the fence and into
my neighbor's garden. Perhaps he enjoys the gift.

Any of the larger dryopterises (*affinis*, *filix-mas*, *marginalis*, *australis*, *goldiana*),

Osmunda claytoniana and other tall ferns can be used along a fence or foundation.

athyriums (*filix-femina, angustum, thelypteroides*), and osmundas are good as tall background or foundation plantings. *Thelypteris kunthii* and *T. ovata* are popular in the South (zones 8 to 9), and *T. torresiana* should be used more widely. In the West the larger polystichums (*munitum, andersonii*) and *Woodwardia fimbriata* are outstanding strong growers where there are not great temperature extremes.

Edges

The species named above can also be used when you are seeking a tall border plant, such as for use along driveways or paths. The all-purpose ostrich fern is also an excellent choice. Our son took a load of my ostrich ferns to line his driveway. He made a fine mass planting, two plants deep, staggered, along the length of the drive. They hid the bases of the neighbor's overgrown shrubs beautifully, and also provided our son and his neighbor with fiddleheads to eat each spring!

Some species are used effectively as borders along walkways—the northern maidenhair and Japanese painted fern do especially well since they are arching and graceful. They only look delicate; they are extremely hardy and spread well. The colors of both are spectacular.

Thelypteris phegopteris is a top choice in the ten-inch and under category. It has beautiful triangular leaves and stays small with firmly arching fronds. *Cystopteris protrusa* and *Athyrium niponicum* (both 'Pictum' and the green form) are outstanding and extremely sturdy. These, besides making fine edges, can be divided every few years since they have a creeping, much-branched rhizome. The Japanese painted fern (*A. niponicum* 'Pictum') does best in the shade, as the intense reddish color gets washed out and pale in too much sunlight.

Athyrium niponicum 'Pictum' makes a colorful edging to a bed.

The adiantums are another favorite for edges and come in several sizes. *Adiantum venustum* is a special favorite of mine—so delicate and always an eye-catcher. *Adiantum pedatum*, a little taller, is also extremely effective along a path. The delicate and feathery fronds make it one of our most popular ferns. *Adiantum capillus-veneris* is another excellent selection for low edges, though it seems to be happiest south of zone 7.

The smaller edging ferns do well with stones. A margin of stones not only defines the bed but provides crevices for the roots of the smaller ferns (e.g., *Cystopteris*), keeping them cool and moist.

A stiff boundary must be used for assertive species; metal or plastic strips sunk in the ground limit the subterranean rhizome's advances.

Rock Gardens

The group of people who have made the best use of ferns are the rock gardeners, who seem to agree with Reginald Kaye that no rock garden is complete without them—". . . to my mind, the rock garden planting scheme is not complete without some foil of foliage, some cool verdure on which to rest the eyes." In the rock garden there are innumerable opportunities to use a multitude of diverse ferns. Usually it is the smaller species that have found happy homes among the rocks. The major question to answer before making your choices is whether the rocks are acidic or calcareous. There are fewer lime-loving ferns, but those few present interesting possibilities. Some of the calciphiles can even be used among acid rocks if limestone chips or oyster shells are added to the soil around the plants. These are marked with an asterisk on the list on page 326.

Whole books have been written about the construction of rock gardens and one of my favorite discussions on the topic is a chapter in Reginald Kaye's *Hardy Ferns,* where he states, "When building a rock garden I usually leave a few vertical gaps an inch or so wide between the rocks, filling up the bottom few inches with well-fitting stones and [soil] mixture, pressed firm. Then a layer of mixture in which the fern roots are spread, covered, and then a few more tight-fitting stones, then perhaps another fern, and so on up to the top of the crevice." The most important thing to remember is to incorporate the vertical gaps and to use tight-fitting stones after planting the rock fern in soil and compost to wedge in the plant so it does not wash out. You might even wrap the roots of the fern with moss for added moisture-holding capability. If possible, incorporate moisture-holding materials in the rock garden construction so it will not dry out—e.g., keep it in the shade, add organic material, keep the rockwork from being too tall, have it built into the side of a slope, or even install a dry well nearby.

Many small ferns do well among the rocks. The woodsias occur naturally on rock ledges. The delicate fragile fern (*Cystopteris fragilis*) is excellent, and its relative the bulblet bladder fern (*C. bulbifera*) is especially interesting. It has very slender, long-triangular, gracefully arching fronds, but it needs especially good moisture, growing naturally near waterfalls and streams. It has

Woodsia polystichoides is one of the best ferns for a partially sunny rock garden.

the added attraction of producing tiny bulbils, like buds, on the underside of the frond. These readily fall off, root themselves in the moist soil, and spread quite rapidly in this way. The aspleniums are mostly rock ferns, and several grow rather well in cultivation. Ebony spleenwort (*Asplenium platyneuron*) is one of the taller ones, reaching twelve to eighteen inches in height, whereas the maidenhair spleenwort (*A. trichomanes*) has four- to six-inch fronds that spread in nearly a rosette. There are incised forms of both species. Some of the polypodies are outstanding rock ferns; the hart's-tongue fern (*Phyllitis scolopendrium*) can be planted with great success on calcareous rocks. Its long, glossy, leathery green straps add an interesting texture and form to the garden. In drier areas, species of the lip ferns (*Cheilanthes*), cliff brakes (*Pellaea*), and other dryland ferns can be used.

Some of the very small ferns show off beautifully in the rock garden. The parsley fern (*Cryptogramma acrostichoides*), little hard fern (*Blechnum penna-marina*), walking ferns (*Camptosorus*), wall rue (*Asplenium ruta-muraria*), and *Ceterach* are all excellent choices. There are also lovely minature varieties of some larger species, including *Adiantum aleuticum* 'Subpumilum', *Polystichum setiferum* 'Congestum', and *Athyrium filix-femina* 'Minutissimum', all of which are particularly beautiful when used in an old wall or the rock garden.

Large Spaces

For broad spaces, there are several fern species that will fill in nicely. *Matteuccia*, growing to five or more feet high and vase-shaped, is a perennial favorite. It is a sturdy, rapid grower and always impressive. For a delicate, feathery appearance, *Dennstaedtia* at two to three feet in height is a good choice. I have seen it used en masse with huge rocks and it is spectacular and carefree. In the shade *Thelypteris noveboracensis* is outstanding in large groupings. It is a bit smaller than *Dennstaedtia* but a similar pale green.

In the Sun

Believe it or not, there are some ferns that can be used effectively in the sun if there is adequate and consistent soil moisture. Naturally occurring in the sun are *Matteuccia*, *Onoclea*, *Thelypteris palustris*, and the osmundas, all of which grow with moist feet in the wild. *Dryopteris affinis*, *D. filix-mas*, *Athyrium filix-femina*, and *Dennstaedtia punctilobula* are others that commonly thrive in open areas. *Cheilanthes* and its relatives, however, can take the driest conditions of all, once they are well-established. Soil moisture is the key, though, in predicting which species will survive.

Recently I was involved with the "fernishing" of a restored rock garden at Lyndhurst, a national trust estate along the Hudson River in Tarrytown, New York. I was apprehensive about the site for ferns as several diseased trees had been removed, exposing most of the garden to midday and afternoon sun. The first recommendation I made was to add some shade trees. A grove of river birch (*Betula nigra* 'Heritage') was planted as fast growers to provide shade as well as to display their decorative peeling, yellowish gray bark, but it would be some time before they would provide significant protection from the sun. Amazingly, most of the ferns survived the harsh exposure. *Adiantum pedatum*, *Thelypteris phegopteris*, *T. decursive-pinnata*, and *Cystopteris protrusa* always appear quite delicate, but they were among those which survived. Only *Polystichum acrostichoides* did not live through the crisis. In addition to the natural gentle slope providing soil moisture to the garden, the Taconic Garden Club, organized under Gray Williams, watered this outstanding collection twice a week for two months of summer heat to ensure the remarkable survival rate. After two years the birches are now casting enough shade to protect many of the ferns during the summer heat.

Wet Places

Though some might find a stream, a marshy spot, or even a ditch difficult to landscape, ferns find them a prime locale. Ponds, streams, and pools are ideal for *Athyrium*, *Osmunda*, *Adiantum*, and *Phyllitis*. *Matteuccia* normally grows near streams and thrives in wet soil, and *Osmunda cinnamomea* and *O. regalis* are both swamp-lovers. *Onoclea sensibilis*, *Thelypteris palustris*, *Dryopteris carthusiana*, and *D. cristata* occur on hummocks in swamps, and in nature *D. goldiana* grows near water but not in it, so they are all good choices for wet places. *Woodwardia areolata* and *W. virginica* also can take very wet conditions. But keep in mind that although these ferns normally grow in wet places, they also do very well in drier situations.

If an area is really wet and boggy, you might try some more esoteric species, such as *Marsilea*, along the edge of the water, and *Salvinia* and *Azolla* floating on the water's surface. A boggy site is the place to try some of the fern allies as well. *Equisetum fluviatile* grows with its rhizome in the mud underwater, and *E. hyemale* and *E. variegatum* can be set close to the edge.

Selaginella species do well here too, especially the creeping ones (*S. apoda, S. kraussiana, S. uncinata*), which seem to survive better near water.

A number of moisture-loving perennial flowering plants, such as Japanese primrose, Japanese iris, and yellow flag iris, make fine companions to the ferns.

Naturalizing

Another interesting way to use ferns is to naturalize them in or at the edge of an existing woodland. In such a setting paths can be created using wood chips, which can often be obtained free from the local highway department. Log steps and split-log benches offer convenient places for meditation and add to the natural setting. If there are no ferns there already, there is probably a good reason for it, such as poor soil, deep shade, lack of moisture, or too many tree roots. Maybe you can alter the conditions, but beware; not all woodlands are ideal for ferns.

The low competitive level of ferns suggests that they would have a difficult time becoming established or persisting for long in the wild. I have been asked on several occasions whether introduced ferns in the garden are likely to escape and become an established part of the local flora. In most of North America it seems highly unlikely that ferns could accomplish this. Of the more than one hundred kinds of ferns in my garden, only a very few ferns reproduce themselves by spores, and the few that do, do it in well-cultivated sites. *Cyrtomium falcatum* and *Woodwardia radicans* have escaped in California, and *Athyrium japonicum* in Florida. *Pteris multifida* has become established from North Carolina to Texas. *Lygodium japonicum* and *L. microphyllum* are serious pests in southern Florida. In warmer parts of the country a few fern species have become naturalized. The chances of exotic ferns becoming naturalized seem to be minimal in the colder parts of the country.

Ferns in Pots

Ferns don't always have to be in the garden or woodland to be enjoyed. It is possible to grow many ferns outside in pots. This is especially practical for people with condominiums or apartments or those who confine their gardening efforts to the porch or patio. Nina d'Ambra and Martin Goldberg reported in the *Fiddlehead Forum* that they grew more than one hundred pots of ferns from twenty genera in their small backyard in Brooklyn, New York. They had good shade from the surrounding buildings but the soil was too dry and alkaline (from mortar and concrete) and tree roots were too invasive. So they used ferns in pots as foundation plantings and as decorations on the porch and in the yard, with the advantage of their being mobile. They moved them around and kept a beautiful show going all summer long.

Ferns grown on the patio or porch do best in plastic pots. Plastic helps cut down on water loss and keeps the pot lighter in weight. Use a soil mixture of two parts organic matter, one part topsoil, and one part perlite. For ferns that prefer drier conditions, use a mixture of equal volumes of organic matter, topsoil, and perlite (perlite rather than sand which is much heavier). For calciphiles, add dolomitic lime to adjust the pH to about 7.0 to 7.5. Full-sized pots work best even though ferns usually have shallow roots. (D'Ambra and Goldberg reported they found roots all the way to the bottom of full-sized pots.)

Ferns grown in pots need watering on a daily basis in hot summer weather. Mulching the tops of the pots with pine bark or small stones reduces moisture loss and looks attractive.

The only serious insect problem faced by potted ferns is ants, which seem to find them a perfect place to build a nest. In doing so, they destroy the root system. This problem can be solved easily by immersing the pot in water for six to eight hours.

Potted plants need more winter protection than in-ground ferns. The severe low temperatures and temperature shifts in the northern United States take their toll on fern roots. There are two ways this can be solved. One is to dig a trench and bury the pots up to their rims, then mulch with straw or another dry, fluffy material such as Styrofoam (not peat or soil) about the time regular freezing weather begins. For more tender species or as an alternative to sinking the pots, the plants can be plunged into a pit. In choosing a location, find one where the pit will be in complete shade for the entire winter so it does not heat up on sunny days. Dig a hole about two feet deep (the length and width depend on the number and size of the plants), place the plants in the pit, and cover with a layer of Styrofoam pellets. You can add another layer of pots and more Styrofoam, and still another layer if you have the depth. Top off with Styrofoam and put a plywood lid over the top. Every few weeks, or more often during warm spells, water the top layer of pellets enough for the water to trickle down and irrigate to the bottom. (This method will probably not work so well with dryland ferns as the high humidity in the frame may cause crown rot.)

WHERE TO START?

How does the beginner get started? The most direct way to acquire a few ferns is to visit your local nurseries, where you will probably find some of our native ferns and perhaps a few from Europe and Japan. Another good source of ferns is the specialty mail-order nurseries, a few of which you will find listed in the appendix. More than two hundred kinds are available. Avoid taking ferns from the wild, although rescuing plants from areas being destroyed is recommended.

Joining forces with others is the best way to develop a fern collection and learn more about these fascinating plants. You can share plants and grow them from spores. If there is a local fern society in your area, get together for sharing plants, spores, and expertise. Volunteering at a preserve or botanical garden where there is a fern collection often allows you to get spores or even plants.

The next question: which ferns should you choose? There are many reliable favorites which are good for beginners and seasoned gardeners alike. In the appendix I have listed my favorite ferns. For my own garden, I look for three things in a fern to consider it a great candidate: It has to look good, be easy to grow, and should reproduce vegetatively so I can have some to give away. Nearly all of the ferns on my beginner's list are hardy to zone 5, which covers most of the United States. There are even more possibilities if you live in the milder climates of the South or Northwest. Several genera are especially rich in dependable species for the temperate garden. *Dryopteris* tops the list for the most species, nearly all of of which are easy and tough, and many are evergreen. *Athyrium* is one of the most diverse in form. Its species are deciduous but highly dependable. Most *Polystichum* species have lustrous, evergreen fronds. Also very satisfying are *Adiantum*, *Cystopteris*, *Matteuccia*, and *Onoclea*.

Chapter Three

Propagating Ferns

Propagation means multiplication and there are two basic ways of accomplishing this in plants: vegetatively and sexually. To propagate vegetatively is to take part of the plant or take a young plant that has grown by a bud directly from the original plant and plant it. To propagate sexually, in ferns, involves the sowing of spores and raising the resulting offspring.

Vegetative propagation is by far the easiest and most direct; new plants reach maturity quickly. However, one is limited to the divisible stock available, either through a friend or one's own plants, which usually results in relatively few new plants. In many cases the desired plant is not available, or the plant does not make offspring vegetatively. Propagation by spores gives access to a much broader array of ferns from around the world and the end result is greater numbers of new plants. But spore growing requires time, patience, and care. I would suggest your acquisition program take a balanced attack: start some plants vegetatively, graduating to growing from spores as your confidence and hunger increase.

VEGETATIVE PROPAGATION

Compared with the number of spores produced, very few new plants actually result from spores in nature. Most of the spores land in inhospitable surroundings or the young plants die before they become established. In contrast,

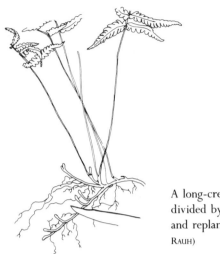

A long-creeping rhizome can be divided by cutting a rooted branch and replanting it. (Illustration by Dick Rauh)

many plants are produced in the wild by vegetative reproduction. The rhizome may branch or some part of the plant may develop buds to form new plants. Mature plants are obtained instantly or in a few months by vegetative reproduction, which is much faster (and more gratifying in the short run) than propagation by spores. Most ferns participate in some form of vegetative reproduction, some slowly and others quickly, and they have several ways of doing this.

The simplest form of vegetative reproduction is the branching of the rhizome. Creeping rhizomes, in addition to producing new leaves and roots, develop branch buds that grow out laterally. Widely creeping species, such as the hay-scented fern (*Dennstaedtia*) and bracken (*Pteridium*), may develop extensive colonies that completely cover a hillside or forest clearing. The branches continue to grow, and as the rhizome dies off at the older end, the branches separate from one another. We can speed the process by merely cutting off a rooted branch and replanting it. The Japanese painted fern (*Athyrium niponicum* 'Pictum'), for example, has a rather compact rhizome but it branches profusely. It usually doubles its rhizome system each year. After three or four years the painted fern can be dug up and, with a sharp knife, be cut into four to eight plants (I divided one that made fifteen!), keeping at least one or two growing tips with each division.

Even crown-forming rhizomes may branch to form small plants around the base of the plant. These can be separated by carefully breaking them apart and replanting both parts. Carefully remove the soil from the side with the child-fern. With a sharp knife cut slightly into the side of the parent

Crosiers mark the location of the growing tips in this short creeping rhizome. (ILLUSTRATION BY DICK RAUH)

A plant of ostrich fern arising from the stolon (left) of the parent plant and three new stolons arising from the base of the new plant.
(ILLUSTRATION BY DICK RAUH)

crown with the baby so you get the entire offspring together with some parent tissue and some roots, the latter being very important. Without roots, the offspring will need to be covered with a plastic bag after planting to reduce water loss until roots form. It is also possible, with some nerve, to divide your single crown by cutting the rhizome in half lengthwise, and planting both halves. It is frightening to inflict such damage on your prized plant, but a healthy plant has strong recuperative power and can survive.

Some plants have an upright rhizome (like a short trunk), with side branches that are much longer and more slender than the main stem. These branches, called runners or stolons, result in young plants appearing some distance away from the rhizome of the parent plant. The ostrich fern (*Matteuccia*) is the most notable example among temperate ferns. (*Nephrolepis*—the Boston fern and its relatives—is a good tropical example.) The ostrich fern has a series of young plants appearing one to three feet from the base of the parent plant. The young develop their own roots and can be removed by carefully cutting their stolon connections (their version of an umbilical cord) to the parent plant. *Thelypteris decursive-pinnata* has short stolons forming a cluster of young within an inch or two of the plant base.

Rachis buds of *Polystichum setiferum* 'Rotundatum'. (ILLUSTRATION BY DICK RAUH)

Large rachis bud of *Woodwardia radicans*. (ILLUSTRATION BY DICK RAUH)

In some species, buds may be found on the rachis (the central stalk) of the leaf, usually at the base of the pinnae. These generally remain on the plant, developing into young plants when the leaf becomes old and touches the ground. Some forms of *Polystichum setiferum* form copious babies along the rachis in this way. The European chain fern (*Woodwardia radicans*) has one large bud near the tip of the rachis that weighs the frond tip down and then develops rapidly when it touches the soil. *Polystichum lentum* and *P. proliferum* also bear a single bud near the tip of the rachis. The ebony spleenwort (*Asplenium platyneuron*) will occasionally produce an inconspicuous bud in the axil of a basal pinna (about one out of seven fronds), which develops into a small plant at the base of the parent plant.

Sometimes round vegetative buds, like little bulblets or beads, on the main rachis and major lateral veins easily fall off. The bulblet bladder fern (*Cystopteris bulbifera*) has copious bulblets on the lower side of the rachis and pinna midveins. Each one looks like a round pea with two fleshy lobes and the growing tip in the middle. They are easily jarred loose, and hundreds of young can be found beneath plants of this species in the garden and in the wild.

One of the most conspicuous means of vegetative reproduction is the development of plantlets on the surface of the leaf. Ferns that do this are called "mother ferns." *Asplenium bulbiferum* of New Zealand and *A. daucifolium*

Bulblet on rachis of *Cystopteris bulbifera*. (ILLUSTRATION BY DICK RAUH)

of Madagascar have such abundant babies that the leaves droop to the ground, but this is very unusual among temperate ferns. *Dryopteris erythrosora* 'Prolifica' has a few such babies, mostly along the rachis and pinna axes on the upper surface. To speed the rooting process the frond can be pinned to the soil; the youngsters will quickly take root and become independent. In *Woodwardia orientalis*, the abundant surface babies, each consisting of a growing tip and a single, small, winglike leaf, drop off readily or can be picked off and easily rooted in peat or moist soil. Plantlets, occasionally, will appear on the surface of the hart's-tongue (*Phyllitis scolopendrium*), too.

A very striking means of bud reproduction is the rooting of an extended rachis. Many examples of this may be seen in *Asplenium* and its close relatives, especially among tropical species, but it is by no means limited to this group. The rachis of the leaf extends well beyond the last pinnae, and produces a baby plant on contact with the soil. It in turn develops leaves with extended tips that root down; thus, it appears to walk across rocks or the forest floor. In North America, the walking fern (*Camptosorus rhizophyllus*) is a familiar example. Another beautiful "walking fern" is the much larger *Polystichum lepidocaulon* from eastern Asia, not yet common in the trade.

In some groups of ferns the roots form buds that can grow into new plants. A new stem and leaves are formed and then the new plant produces additional roots of its own. One that commonly develops root buds is the adder's-tongue fern (*Ophioglossum*). The cultivated species, *O. petiolatum*, quickly fills a pot with its root proliferations.

Plants on the frond surface of *Woodwardia orientalis* and a single enlarged plantlet. (Illustration by Dick Rauh)

Plants arising from the root buds of *Ophioglossum*. (Illustration by Dick Rauh)

Extended rachis of *Polystichum lepidocaulon*. (Illustration by Dick Rauh)

In recent years a tissue culture technique has been developed to greatly speed up the vegetative reproduction of ferns in cultivation. By carefully culturing a small piece of plant tissue, it is possible to cause it to develop several growing points which in turn can be separated and cultured to form many plants. This method has the advantage of having a single plant as the source of many more offspring than is possible by natural vegetative means, and mature plants can be obtained more rapidly than by sowing spores. However, most tissue culturing is done commercially and is not for the amateur.

It is still interesting to follow the process, though. A growing part of the plant, such as a stem tip or stolon, is cut from the plant, sterilized in a bleach solution, and placed on a special nutrient agar (a jellylike substance with nutrients and vitamins dissolved in it). After about five weeks, roots are formed, and then the tip is transferred to another agar containing hormones to promote multiplication. After another five weeks the tip has multiplied to produce many small plants. These can be separated, hardened with stronger light, and then planted in soil or recultured to produce more growing tips.

Similar techniques can be applied to the gametophyte generation (the prothalli). Spores are sterilized in a bleach solution and sown on nutrient agar. Developing prothalli are macerated in a blender with nutrients and hormones, and poured onto sterile soil, with each prothallial fragment developing into a mature prothallus. Resulting plants develop rapidly. This technique is especially useful when available spore material is limited. Tissue culture requires extremely sterile conditions and specialized equipment and, as I said previously, is best left to the commercial growers.

LIFE HISTORY OF A FERN

To grow ferns from spores requires an understanding of their life history.

Ferns have no flowers or seeds, but rather reproduce sexually by spores. The mature fern produces spores in spore cases (called sporangia) that are usually located on the underside of the leaf. Each sporangium produces sixty-four spores, except in the more primitive ferns, where each sporangium produces 128, 256, 512, or more spores in each case. The spore cases are generally found in small clusters, called sori (singular, sorus), comprised of several to one hundred sporangia. The sori take many different forms but the form is generally consistent for each genus or group of genera. Most often

Sorus patterns, clockwise from the upper right: *Adiantum pedatum*, *Dryopteris remota*, *Dryopteris erythrosora*, *Athyrium japonicum*.

SORUS PATTERNS

Polystichum braunii. (Photo by Charles Neidorf)

Polypodium virginianum. (Photo by Charles Neidorf)

Woodwardia virginica. (PHOTO BY CHARLES NEIDORF)

Pellaea atropurpurea. (PHOTO BY CHARLES NEIDORF)

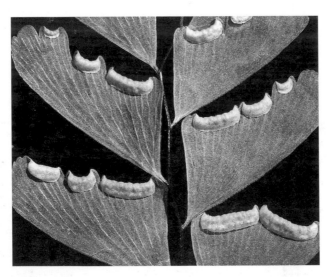

Adiantum pedatum. (PHOTO BY CHARLES NEIDORF)

the sori appear as round dots on the lower surface of the frond (as they do for *Dryopteris* and *Polystichum*), but they may be elongated along a vein (*Asplenium*, *Athyrium*), or along the midvein (*Blechnum*, *Woodwardia*). Frequently, however, sori are produced along the margin of the leaflet, either as a continuous line

(*Pellaea*, *Pteris*) or as several small lines (*Adiantum*), or in small cuplike structures (*Dennstaedtia*). More frequently than not, the sori are protected by a special flap, called the indusium. The indusium covers the sorus when it is young, but as the sporangia mature and are ready to release the spores, the indusium bends back or withers. In most ferns, the indusium is a discrete structure, but in those with marginal sori, it is the specialized margin of the leaf that folds over to protect the sorus. Since this protective margin is not a separate structure, it is called a false indusium.

Some of the more ancient fern groups do not have the sporangia organized into discrete sori, but rather the sporangia are found individually in *Lygodium* or in large masses in *Osmunda*.

As the spores mature and develop their final wall markings, the sporangium opens to release them. The opening of the sporangium is not a random splitting. Rather, there is a band of special, thick-walled cells around the sporangium, the annulus, that contracts to effect the opening. The sporangium opens slowly, and then the spores are suddenly catapulted out into the surrounding air. The spores either fall to the ground or are carried by air drafts for several feet or even miles before they fall to the earth.

With sixty-four spores per sporangium, perhaps fifty sporangia per sorus, hundreds of sori per leaf, and several fertile leaves per plant, it is common for a single plant to produce millions of spores in one season. Thus, it would seem that the world should be covered with ferns, but this is obviously not

Two different shapes and surface patterns of fern spores.

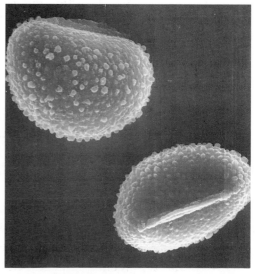

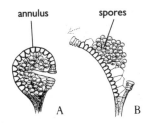

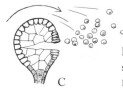

annulus

spores

Release of spores from a sporangium. (ILLUSTRATION BY EDGAR PAULTON)

A   B   C

Stages in spore germination.
(ILLUSTRATION BY EDGAR PAULTON)

germinating spore

— rhizoid

the case. Nearly all of the spores are destined to die before they are able to produce a new plant. Most fall in places that are not suitable for germination. Others germinate but die from lack of water. To be successful, germination must take place in a shaded, moist place where there are not a lot of other plants that could crowd out the incipient ferns. Often this is a muddy, shaded bank that has a constant supply of moisture.

Germination consists of the spore absorbing water and splitting open, the one cell inside enlarging and elongating. The cell turns green, thus making it able to manufacture its own food by photosynthesis. Its chief need is for water, and it sends out a hairlike structure, a rhizoid, that acts like a root, absorbing water and minerals from the soil. The green cell continues to elongate, and divides to form two cells. A filament is soon formed with more rhizoids sent down into the soil. Soon some of the cells near the tip divide laterally to broaden the filament, and this plantlet, called a prothallus or gametophyte, continues to grow, longitudinally and laterally, to form a heart-shaped pad of green tissue about the size of a fingernail, clothed at its base with many rhizoids. Prothallial development takes one to three months, or, in extreme cases of some tropical genera, a year or more.

The prothallus is only one cell thick on its "wings" and a few cells thick in its midrib, and the entire plant is usually only one quarter of an inch across, making this part of the fern's life history difficult to see in nature.

Fern prothalli, or gametophytes, are generally heart-shaped, and for a long period it was considered that the gametophytes of all ferns were nearly alike. Studies in the last forty years, however, have shown that there is great diversity among the ferns in this regard. Some gametophytes remain as filaments, making them difficult to distinguish from those of mosses or algae; others are ribbon-

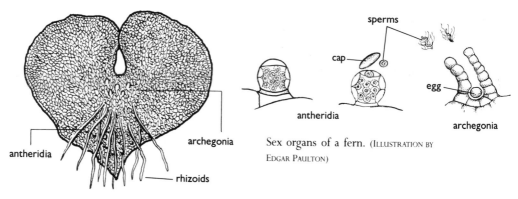

Sex organs of a fern. (ILLUSTRATION BY EDGAR PAULTON)

Fern prothallus. (ILLUSTRATION BY EDGAR PAULTON)

shaped, and a few are only half heart-shaped, developing only one side of the prothallus.

It is on the lower surface of these prothalli that the sexual part of the plant's life history takes place. On the wings and toward the base among the rhizoids are tiny beadlike structures, the antheridia, which produce sperms. When a surface film of water is present, the antheridial lid comes off and several sperms emerge, which then begin swimming rapidly. Each sperm is spiral-shaped and propelled by numerous hairlike structures.

Along the thickened midrib of the prothallus there are several tiny, chimney-shaped projections, the archegonia. Each archegonium has a single egg cell located in its base, which is embedded in the prothallus. When the egg is mature, the tip of the chimney opens, releasing the fluid contents of the neck. This effluent attracts the swimming sperms, the sperms swim down the neck canal, and one sperm fertilizes the egg. As soon as fertilization takes place, the other archegonia on the prothallus become nonfunctional; only one fertilization takes place per prothallus.

The sex cells, both sperm and egg, are called gametes, and thus the prothallus is often referred to as the "gametophyte" generation; the plant we see—the fern plant that produces the spores—is the "sporophyte."

The fertilized egg, embedded in the prothallus, grows and divides to form a multicellular structure. Part of it differentiates into a root that absorbs water and minerals from the soil, part becomes the first leaf that manufactures the food for the young fern through photosynthesis, and another part protrudes as the young stem that will grow out, producing new roots and leaves. Once the organs of the new sporophyte are established, the function of the prothallus is finished, and it withers away. Each new leaf produced is a little larger and often more dissected than the previous one until the mature leaf

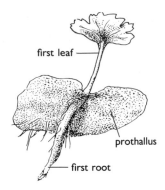

first leaf

prothallus

first root

Prothallus and sporeling.
(ILLUSTRATION BY EDGAR PAULTON)

form appears. After several months or up to a few years of growth, the plant is mature enough to produce leaves with sporangia on them, thus continuing the cycle of life.

The time it takes for a fern to grow from a spore to a plant that can produce spores varies considerably in different groups of ferns. Most often it will take three to four years or more to become mature enough to produce spores. On the other hand, some species of *Thelypteris* take only six months, and a tropical water fern, *Ceratopteris*, may complete its life history in only three months. This variation in life cycle reveals a lot about the plant's ability to compete in the world, its aggressiveness in taking over bare soil, and its ability to fill available spaces for germination. The percentage of germination also varies and the relative vigor of the prothalli helps determine which species are the weeds of the fern world and which are the rarities.

It is a real challenge to find prothalli in the wild, or even in the greenhouse. They are so small and inconspicuous that it is not surprising most people cannot find them. Look for them near mature ferns. Often they are found on mud in swamps or on mossy banks in woodlands. The easiest place to find them is in a humid greenhouse on the sides of moist pots or on undisturbed surfaces of soil or sphagnum moss. Generally, if there are ferns in the green-house, there will be prothalli and young ferns can be found, unless there is scrupulous housekeeping.

Apogamy

Although most ferns pass through the above stages in their life history, there are occasional irregularities in the plant's makeup that direct it to follow a slightly different route. One situation bypasses sex entirely. Spores germinate to form the prothalli, and the sex organs (antheridia and archegonia) may form, but the archegonia do not function. Rather, the prothallus develops a bud, which appears first as a slight swelling, usually on the underside of the prothallial notch, with hairs around it. As it continues to enlarge, the bud first produces a leaf (as opposed to the root being first, as is the case in normal fertilization). Several leaves may form before the first root appears. Once the plant is established, the prothallus withers and disappears. Since there is no fusion of gametes (sperm and egg), the process is called apogamy (without gametes).

Apogamy is found in many groups of ferns and is more common than is normally thought. It is found in some of the more commonly cultivated plants, such as the Japanese holly fern (*Cyrtomium falcatum*) and the Cretan brake (*Pteris cretica*). In normal sexual prothalli, fertilization is often slowed by a lack of water in which the sperms can swim. Since fertilization is not needed in apogamous plants, production of young ferns is more rapid and success more certain than in sexually reproducing ferns. Ferns native to dry regions, especially species of *Cheilanthes* and *Pellaea*, have a higher frequency of apogamy than do those from wetter areas. Hybrid ferns that would normally be sterile, with abortive spores, are able to reproduce by spores if one of the parents is apogamous. Although fertilization does not take place in apogamous species (the archegonia not functioning), the antheridia produce functioning sperms and can (and do) fertilize eggs of gametophytes of other species to form hybrids. *Dryopteris remota*, the hybrid of *D. affinis* and *D. expansa*, volunteers in my garden; none of my other species of *Dryopteris* do this.

HYBRIDIZATION

Hybridization is a frequent phenomenon among ferns in nature. It occurs when the sperm of one prothallus fertilizes the egg on the prothallus of another species. Hybrid fertilization is successful only if the two species are of the same genus or closely related genera. Hybrid ferns are mostly sterile; that is, they cannot reproduce by spores, unless one of the parents is apogamous. The nuclei of the cells of the resulting hybrid sporophyte plant contain one set of chromosomes from each parent. In the nuclear division that forms spores, the chromosomes of the two parents pair up if it is a normal species, but if the sets are of different species, they cannot; therefore, the spores abort, appearing as crumpled blobs of spore wall material. The hybrid plant continues living and may reproduce vegetatively.

Occasionally there is a doubling of chromosomes. The chromosomes then have mates to pair up with and viable spores can be produced. This fertile hybrid is thus a newly formed species since it is different from all other species and can reproduce itself by spores. Scientific examination of the chromosome numbers in ferns reveals which of our ferns are sterile hybrids and which are fertile but of hybrid origin.

Hybrids are generally intermediate in appearance between the two parents. Sometimes the parents are markedly different and the hybrid is distinctly intermediate. The fronds of the ebony spleenwort (*Asplenium platyneuron*) are once divided, those of the mountain spleenwort (*A. montanum*) are three times divided, and their hybrid, Bradley's spleenwort (*A. bradleyi*), is twice divided. On the other hand, some species of *Dryopteris* are so closely allied that their

Asplenosorus ebenoides (center), the hybrid between *Camptosorus rhizophyllus* (left) and *Asplenium platyneuron* (right). (ILLUSTRATION BY EDGAR PAULTON)

hybrids are difficult to distinguish without microscopic examination of their spores and chromosomes.

The members of some genera are extremely promiscuous, forming great hybrid complexes. *Dryopteris*, *Asplenium*, and *Diplazium* are especially noteworthy. One of the most interesting complexes occurs in the Appalachian spleenworts. What were thought forty years ago to be fourteen species today are known to be only four basic species and ten hybrids. Some of the hybrids are fertile and are able to hybridize in turn with their parents or with other species to form additional intermediates. In spite of the large number of known hybrid combinations, in actual numbers of plants, hybrids are generally infrequent or rare and are a challenge to find.

There are many possibilities for interesting hybrid combinations, and although spectacular results are not guaranteed, they are exciting to pursue. Sometimes hybrids are made intentionally by horticulturists and research botanists. The simplest method is merely to sow the spores of two distinct species together and watch the offspring, hoping for a cross to occur. Some people place a gametophyte of one species in a drop of water to allow the discharge of sperm, and then place a gametophyte of the other species in that drop for an hour before replanting it. To eliminate the possibility of self-fertilization, the part of a gametophyte with the archegonia (around the notch) is carefully cut off and placed by the basal, antheridial portion of the gametophyte of another species, but this requires care and surgical mastery.

In contrast to flowering plants, induced hybridization is not a practical method of producing new horticultural fern varieties. For the commercial grower it is tedious and unreliable work, and the number of plants obtained is very small. Instead, new varieties are formed from random, natural mutations—oddballs that are found in the wild or among the masses of sporelings.

Occasionally hybridization in cultivation may occur accidentally. *Asplenosorus crucibuli* is an impossible cross in nature, involving two species from different continents—*Asplenium platyneuron* of North America and *Camptosorus sibiricus* of eastern Asia—that occurred by accident in a greenhouse. The most dramatic hybrid arising in cultivation involved species in three different genera: *Asplenium platyneuron* and *Camptosorus rhizophyllus* cross to form Scott's spleenwort, *Asplenosorus ebenoides*. This hybrid occurs naturally in many parts of the eastern United States, and a fertile form is grown commercially. When it grows in quantity near the hart's-tongue fern, *Phyllitis scolopendrium*, in greenhouses, a trigeneric cross can occur, forming a bizarre plant that is strap-shaped toward the tip and lobed toward the base. Its cells contain three sets of chromosomes, one from each of the species, and the spores are abortive.

SEXUAL PROPAGATION—GROWING FERNS FROM SPORES

Growing ferns from spores is a moderate challenge, taking a good deal of patience and care, but the rewards are great. Often it is the only method of obtaining unusual species. Propagation of ferns from spores, especially the rare species, is a much preferred alternative to collecting plants from the wild. The fern allies are not grown from spores except in the research laboratory. *Equisetum* spores live only a few days, *Lycopodium* spores take months or years to germinate and usually require special techniques, and *Selaginella* requires two kinds of spores and special care. Thus, the fern allies are best propagated by vegetative means. *Ophioglossum* and *Botrychium*, two primitive ferns, also take special handling (they germinate underground); they have never been grown from spores "in captivity" outside research laboratories.

Collecting the spores. The easiest way of obtaining spores is from fern plants directly. It takes some practice to recognize when the spores are ripe. Most ferns develop the sporangia soon after the fronds arise in the spring, which is late May and June in most of the colder parts of North America, a bit earlier in the South and Northwest. Some continue producing sori all summer and into the early fall, but several species wait until late summer before maturing their sori. These include *Athyrium pycnocarpon*, *Woodwardia areolata*, *Arachniodes standishii*, and *Dryopteris bissetiana*. Similarly, *Onoclea* and *Matteuccia* bear their sori on special woody fronds that appear in mid- to late summer but do not release the spores until winter.

Most spores are dark brown or black at maturity, and the ripe sori that hold the spores are that color, too. The sporangia will appear dark and glistening like caviar. The sporangia mature first at the bottom of the frond. Thus, the sporangia may be empty at the bottom of the frond, ripe in the middle, and too young at the tip. Even within a single sorus, not all the sporangia mature at once; there is a mixture of mature and juvenile sporangia, so it is best to collect a fertile frond when the majority of the sori or sporangia are mature. Some genera, like *Polypodium*, have golden spores, and therefore golden sori, so it may be difficult to distinguish mature golden sori from old tan sori without a hand lens. A few genera (e.g., *Osmunda*, *Matteuccia*, *Onoclea*) have green spores. A 10-power hand lens is adequate to distinguish the different stages of sorus development.

Break off a leaflet or whole frond bearing ripe spores and place it spore-

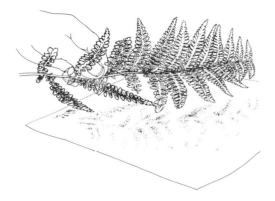

Spores are collected by laying a fresh fertile frond on a piece of white paper overnight. (ILLUSTRATION BY DICK RAUH)

side down on a sheet of white paper or in an envelope. The spores will be released in a few hours. The next day tap the frond again, then throw it away. What shows up on the paper looking like fine dust will be spores and perhaps some empty spore cases. Store the spores in glacine envelopes, paper envelopes, or glass vials, but never plastic bags as the spores adhere to the plastic. Keep the packets cool and dry.

To obtain spores of rare (or new to you) species, membership in one of the fern societies in the country which have spore exchanges is recommended. They have spores of species from all over the United States and many from abroad. The American Fern Society, for example, has more than seven hundred species in its spore bank. Most fern spores will remain alive for several years (some for more than fifty years), so they can be collected and stored for later sowing. Green spores are viable a few days to a month, or up to a year if refrigerated.

There are as many methods of growing ferns from spores as there are growers. Described below is a method I have found satisfactory.

The containers for sowing can be of almost any description. The goal is to have a container that can be sealed to reduce the loss of moisture and yet will still let light in. Clear glass or plastic dishes or cups with a tight-fitting cover do well. Clear plastic wrap can also be used over the top. Rows of glass dishes are a common sight in a fern fancier's home. Or one can use clear plastic shoeboxes (12 × 6 ½ × 3 ½ inches) which hold eighteen two-and-one-quarter-inch square plastic flower pots. This way many different species can be stored in a small space; a small amount of water in the bottom will keep the whole batch humid. Moisture is needed for the germination, growth, and fertilization of the prothalli and the young developing ferns after fertilization.

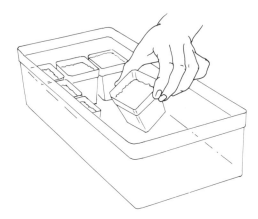

Eighteen 2 1/4-inch pots for spore culture will fit in a clear plastic shoebox. (Illustration by Dick Rauh)

For soil I prefer a mixture of one part soil, one part sand, and two parts peat or leaf mold, but many other soil types will work just as well; most ferns will germinate on any medium. Basically you need a loose mixture that gives good drainage yet holds moisture well. Milled or long-fiber sphagnum or a mixture of sphagnum and sand, or peat pellets, or a commercial African violet soil mix (presterilized) will also work.

A major problem in growing ferns from spores is contamination. Spores of mosses, fungi, and algae are everywhere—in the air, on all surfaces, in tap water, and in unsterilized soil. This must be kept in mind throughout the planting procedure until the new plants are on their own. To reduce the damage caused by these invading hordes, the following steps are recommended.

1. Use as clean a sample of spores as possible. See the section on procedure below.
2. Use presterilized soil or potting soil baked in the oven for two hours at 300 degrees Fahrenheit, or pour distilled water over peat pellets or sphagnum. Sphagnum is rather strongly acid and less likely to support contaminants. Some people do not sterilize it, but it is better to sterilize the sphagnum rather than throw out a contaminated mess later on. If you sterilize soil in the oven, be sure you keep it moist in a closed container or it will dry out and burn. Some people use a poultry roasting bag to keep the moisture (and smell) inside.
3. Pour boiling water over the containers you plan to use for spore growing or rinse with a 5-percent chlorine bleach solution.
4. Use boiled (five minutes at a rolling boil) or distilled water, not tap water for all watering of the plants.

When the paper is tapped gently, the spores will remain on it as the chaff falls off. (ILLUSTRATION BY DICK RAUH)

Moisten the soil with distilled water and fill each pot nearly to the top. There will be clearance in the box for the young plantlets. If you are using a covered dish, use perhaps one inch of soil or fill to half the depth of the container. Keep the container covered until you are ready to sow.

Next, make sure what you sow is primarily spores and not fern chaff. Remove the contaminating chaff by tapping the dustlike spores to the edge of the paper or a three-by-five-inch card. The spore cases are lighter and fall off first, leaving mostly spores which stick more strongly to the paper.

Open the container. Sprinkle the spores from the envelope or paper by gently tapping it. Try for even distribution. One of the most common mistakes in sowing is to tap too many spores onto the soil; too many spores make it too crowded for the prothalli to develop. Even distribution can be achieved by turning the paper or card bearing the spores upside down over the pot and tapping once to release the spores. To help guard against contaminating fungi, lightly mist the sown surfaces with a fungicide, such as Physan (⅛ teaspoon per 2 cups of distilled water). Add small plastic labels (sterilized)

Turn the paper upside down and tap firmly to sow the spores.
(ILLUSTRATION BY DICK RAUH)

and cover the container immediately. Make sure there is a tight fit to reduce water loss. Some people use Vaseline along the top edge to make it airtight.

Place the container on a north- or east-facing windowsill where there is light but no direct sun. Direct sunlight on your little greenhouse will "cook" the developing fern spores. Artificial light is even better because you can control the amount of light and the day length. Use cool white fluorescent tubes or commercial plant lights with the containers about six to ten inches below the tubes. High light at the beginning may inhibit germination in some species, so shade cloth can be used to reduce the light until germination has begun. Give them twelve to fourteen hours of light each day. Then wait.

Green will show on the soil surface in two to eight weeks or more, although you might see the germinating spores earlier with a 10-power hand lens. This signals that the spores have germinated and young prothalli are developing. If you don't see anything right away, don't throw the cultures out for several months since some kinds are very slow to germinate. Water will probably not be needed at this stage if the lid is not opened, but take care that the soil does not dry out. If water is needed, use sterile water and replace the lid right away. Pour the water into the box between the pots so they are watered from below to avoid disturbing the soil surface and the germinating spores. The prothalli will develop to maturity in another month or two.

When the prothalli seem to be as big as they are going to get, watch for young fern plantlets arising from the notches of the prothalli. If there is no sign of them, sprinkle or mist with sterile water because surface water is needed for fertilization.

When the plantlets are one half to one inch tall, thin them. Use tweezers to pinch out small patches and replant a few patches into another sterilized container, with sterilized soil, giving the ferns room to grow. Cover again to assure high humidity; the young leaves are very thin and dry out quickly. If you need to rewater later, always use distilled or boiled water. When the babies are two inches tall, transplant one per two-inch, sterilized pot. Keep the humidity high for a while longer as they produce new leaves. Gradually, lift the lid more each day to harden them off. This is perhaps the most critical time in the whole procedure and you can lose the whole batch if you get too anxious to expose them. Go slowly! If you're successful, you will have more ferns than you will know what to do with.

Throughout the process of growing ferns from spores, no fancy tools are needed. Tweezers are handy for separating young plants. Another good instrument to use is a vegetable peeler; you can dig with the gently curving

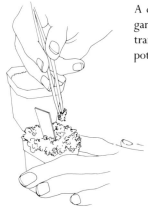

A crowded growth of gametophytes can be thinned by transplanting small clumps to other pots. (Illustration by Dick Rauh)

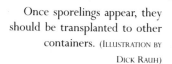

Once sporelings appear, they should be transplanted to other containers. (Illustration by Dick Rauh)

tip and tamp down with its back. Some people use a lobster pick, which has a two-tined end for cutting or dividing, and a small scoop for lifting the young ferns. Another useful tool is a long aluminum gutter nail, the point of which can be used for poking holes for planting, and the head end for tamping the soil. It is wise to dip the instruments in alcohol or a 10-percent bleach solution to sterilize them between use so as not to introduce mold or algae to other pots.

An easy variation of sowing procedure was described by Ethelyn Williams, the New York Botanical Garden's primary spore grower for the past twenty years, in the *Fiddlehead Forum* ("Spore Planting on Compressed Peat Plugs," 14: 23, 1987):

I have been planting spores on compressed peat plugs, instead of pasteurized medium in 2¼″ pots, and have found that the advantages outweigh any disadvantages.

After dipping a clear plastic shoebox and its lid in a boiling 5% bleach solution and rinsing them in distilled water, 18 compressed plugs are set on the bottom of the box, indented side up. Boiling distilled water is poured over them until they swell up to full size. Excess water may be removed with a roast baster before the lid is put in place, and the box is set aside until cool or until sowing time.

At planting time a table may be covered with paper towels, and a plug removed to plant. The plug's netting should be pushed back to the edge with a clean finger or tool to give maximum planting surface. Spores may be poured onto a clean 3 × 5-inch card, the chaff tapped off and the spores then tapped onto the plug, trying not to overplant.

When the planting is complete, labels may be stuck onto the plugs and card file entries made.

Any time the crowding of the gametophytes warrants it, gametophytes can be transplanted in about 1/4″ sections to 2¼″ plastic pots of pasteurized medium to give growing room. If the netting gets in the way, it can be cut, or little pieces of netting with gametophytes attached can be transferred to pots. Sometimes sporophytes develop on the plugs before the gametophytes are transferred; they should be transplanted before the roots become badly entangled.

Before the covers are put on the new boxes, a misting of Physan is an added safeguard against the development of algae, fungi, and bacterial infections. The boxes may be placed under fluorescent lights or in a window where there is good light, but no direct sun, and where a temperature of about 68–80 degrees Fahrenheit can be maintained.

Problems and pests.   Mold can be introduced to your humid container on the fern sporangia and from the air. It can be controlled by misting with a dilute solution of Physan. Algae in the form of a greenish black slime, and mosses, whose young stages are branching green threads, are not so easily controlled. They, too, can be introduced in water or soil that is not totally sterile. Mosses have to be removed with tweezers. If the algae have not gotten a stranglehold, a solution of Algex can be used to control them, but algal growth can quickly become so dense the pot has to be thrown out. Sometimes the gametophytes, growing with algae, will survive long enough to get the sporophytes growing. Transplanting the gametophytes or young sporophytes into sterile soil is often a good solution.

The fauna in soil that is not carefully sterilized can be controlled by the application of dilute water-soluble Sevin or malathion.

Above all it is essential that you use sterile soil, containers, and water to avoid problems.

Hardy Ferns for American Gardens

There are more than one thousand species of ferns found growing in temperate regions of the world but because of lack of availability and information, relatively few have been used in the garden. There are many excellent candidates in Asia, New Zealand, and high-elevation tropical America, and we expect that many of those species will be tested and brought into cultivation in the next few years.

In this book I consider about 530 kinds of ferns and fern allies in fifty genera. I stress the native North American species, of course, and even include some rarities, which can be grown from spores. A selection of British species and varieties is included, as well as recent imports from Japan and other regions. I emphasize ferns that are easy, strong growers for a wide range of climates in North America, and also include some that are challenging or perhaps hardy only in milder zones or with special conditions.

The genera discussed here are arranged alphabetically by genus. I include first comments regarding the genus as a whole—its significant characteristics, geographical and ecological distribution, and horticultural merit—and do not repeat these in the species descriptions. Under each genus, the species are listed, along with frequently used botanical synonyms and the most widely accepted common names. The species name is followed by items of special reference: description of the fronds, rhizome habit, availability, hardiness zones, and ease of cultivation. For some of the botanical and geological terms you may wish to refer to the glossary in the appendices.

Fronds.　　The frond length given is usually that to be expected in the garden. This may be different from the frond length of a plant found in the wild.

Also indicated here are *frond habit*, whether the fronds are held generally *erect* versus *arching* to nearly flat on the ground, and *evergreenness*, whether the fern is evergreen, semievergreen, or deciduous. This varies with the severity of winter; species that are usually deciduous in New York may be evergreen in Georgia or even in New York during an exceptionally mild winter. In this book evergreenness is judged by zone 5 winters or the most northern zone in which the fern is hardy. Semihardy means the fronds remain green into the cold weather before they turn brown, whereas the fronds of deciduous species die down shortly after the first hard freeze of the winter.

Rhizome habit. Most rhizomes are short-creeping and compact, with the fronds close to one another, but some are ascending, or make an upright crown, while others are more widely creeping with fronds distinctly apart.

Availability. This refers to the degree of availability of the species in American catalogs or nurseries. A rare species is not generally found for sale and is obtained only from individuals or botanical gardens, or must be grown from spores.

Hardiness zones. The hardiness zones are cited according to the USDA zone hardiness map (see page 323), but these should be taken only as rough approximations. Zones listed with each species are based in part on the natural ranges of some of our native ferns and in part on known successes. However, they can be misleading since there is much more to successful growth than the minimum temperature, which is the basis of the map. Zone 8 in the southern United States, for example, certainly does not have the same climate as zone 8 in Seattle. Humidity, summer temperatures, and distribution of rainfall through the year are other important factors. For some species, especially those not previously grown in North America, the cited zones are only an estimate, and more information from gardeners is needed.

For this book I have concentrated on species which grow well in hardiness zones 5 to 8. The temperate-area ferns described usually grow in areas with hard freezes, where most of my gardening experience has taken place. Milder regions of the South can grow a number of subtropical species which gives those areas many more possibilities, although some northern species may not do well there. We need more information on fern hardiness in zones 2 to 4 and in the West and Southwest. As a matter of fact, detailed information is needed for all parts of the continent since so many of the good species have not been thoroughly tested over a broad range of the country's climates over a span of time. More information is also needed on heat hardiness and aridity hardiness.

Ease of cultivation. *Easy* requires planting the fern in moist, shaded, rich, well-drained soil, and sitting back and watching it grow. Of course, there is the occasional weeding, trimming, and watering during drought. Most of the ferns I have chosen fall into this category. *Moderate* suggests that some special care or skill is required, such as the addition of lime or special drainage, or that the plants are not as strong, dependable growers. *Difficult* indicates a species for the experienced grower and indicates that your chances of success may be slim. Even so, because of differences in climate, soils, moisture, etc., what may be easy for us in New York may be difficult for someone in Texas. Take this as a general guide. I would be glad to hear your varying experiences.

After the reference entries, a brief description of the plant follows, including its outstanding features, country or region of origin, and, where applicable, comments on its cultivation or other information of interest, which has not been given under the genus. Significant varieties and cultivars are also listed. My selection of species and varieties is chosen with an eye to providing a wide range of diversity, including some less common ferns from other parts of the world that might be worth pursuing for their ornamental interest. More species, varieties, and even genera are becoming available every year.

More information on the plants' descriptions, ecology, and range can be found in the cited floras of the United States, Canada, British Isles, and Japan in the bibliography, since these are the source areas for most of the ferns in cultivation.

ADIANTUM, Maidenhair fern

Among our most beautiful and popular ferns, maidenhair ferns thrive in moist situations. The creeping, scaly rhizomes branch to form compact to diffuse colonies. They send up fronds which range in size from ten to thirty inches, with gorgeous shining, brittle, black (sometimes chestnut) stipes which are smooth or clothed with narrow scales or hairs. The blade is mostly three- to five-times divided, and the segments are oblong or fan-shaped, naked or with scattered stiff hairs. The sori are short to oblong, one to several per segment. An outstanding feature of these delicate ferns is the pink color of the crosiers and juvenile foliage. The fronds are deciduous to semievergreen.

Adiantum is a large genus, with about three hundred species, largely native to wet tropical regions. They grow in moist, rich forests or among rocks in exposed sites. Maidenhairs are easy to grow in rich, well-drained soil and can survive in the sun if the soil moisture is adequate. Hot weather may cause the fronds to brown by the end of the summer.

A. aleuticum (syn. *A. pedatum* var. *aleuticum*, *A. pedatum* subsp. calderi)

Serpentine maidenhair, Western maidenhair

FRONDS: 12 to 30 inches long, erect-arching, deciduous

RHIZOME HABIT: short-creeping

AVAILABILITY: common

HARDINESS ZONES: 2 to 8

EASE OF CULTIVATION: easy

This species was formerly included within *A. pedatum* but has recently been shown to be a distinct, though closely related species. It resembles *A. pedatum* in its purplish black stipe and rachis, the stipe forking to form a crescent-shaped axis from which radiate five to nine fingerlike pinnae, each bearing numerous delicate segments. The fronds are arching to stiffly erect with overlapping, oblong to narrowly triangular segments. The long triangular segments with deeper sinuses in the margin separate it from *A. pedatum*, which has segments more rounded at the tips.

Native mostly to western North America and eastern Asia, and some disjunct locations in serpentine habitats in eastern North America, *A. aleuticum* can be found in a variety of sites—ravines, stream banks, and sunny locations on talus slopes, serpentine barrens, and coastal cliffs.

Adiantum aleuticum.

A form of *Adiantum aleuticum* with overlapping segments.

Adiantum aleuticum hybridizes with *A. jordanii* in California to form *A.* × *tracyi*, a sterile hybrid, which is also hardy in the Seattle area and perhaps in the southern United States. The hybrid has the fan-shaped segments of *A. jordanii* and the forking frond architecture of *A. aleuticum*, and is extremely rare.

Adiantum aleuticum crosses with *A. pedatum* to form the rare hybrid *A. viridimontanum*, named for the Green Mountains of Vermont, where the hybrid grows on serpentine rocks.

A. a. 'Subpumilum' (syn *A. pedatum* subsp. *subpumilum*, *A. pedatum* var. *subpumilum*), dwarf maidenhair. The dwarf maidenhair is now considered to be a dwarf form of *A. aleuticum* rather than a subspecies or variety of *A. pedatum*, and at the same time it can be considered as a cultivar of *A. aleuticum*.

This form appears much like *A. pedatum* or *A. aleuticum* but is much smaller and more compact, three to four inches tall with overlapping segments. Native to and very rare in western Washington and on Vancouver Island, British Columbia, it is widely cultivated. It is not as strong a grower as *A. pedatum* or *A. aleuticum*, at least in the Northeast, and its hardiness zones are 5 to 8.

There is an intermediate size form available (*A. aleuticum* 'Imbricatum'), which is easier to grow, also in zones 5 to 8.

A. a. 'Tasselatum'. This lovely cultivar has crested pinna tips, causing them to droop and be more ruffled than the typical *aleuticum*. It can be grown in zones 5 to 8 but is not widely available. This form is very unstable in that it does not come true from spore, and plants may crest one year and not another.

A. a. var. *japonicum* (syn. *A. pedatum* var. *japonicum*), Japanese maidenhair.

Adiantum aleuticum 'Subpumilum'.

Adiantum aleuticum 'Imbricatum'.

This variety is hardly distinguishable from *A. pedatum* or *A. aleuticum*. The young foliage is a deeper red, and the red color lasts for a longer time on the expanding blade than in the American species. We do not have information on the hardiness zones of this variety in North America; it is native to eastern Asia and is only infrequently available for sale here.

A. capillus-junonis

FRONDS: 5 to 12 inches long, arching, deciduous
RHIZOME HABIT: short-creeping
AVAILABILITY: rare
HARDINESS ZONES: 6 to 8
EASE OF CULTIVATION: moderate

This beautiful East Asian maidenhair has once-pinnate fronds with six to eight pairs of fanlike pinnae. The tip of the frond is extended and roots to form a new plant. The fronds of this plant droop from walls and limestone cliffs in eastern China. I saw it in the mortar of walls in Beijing, where it made a fine, flowing display.

As far as I know, this species has not been tried yet in American gardens, but it should be hardy in North America.

A. capillus-veneris

Southern maidenhair, Venus maidenhair
FRONDS: 10 to 22 inches long, arching, deciduous
RHIZOME HABIT: short-creeping
AVAILABILITY: common
HARDINESS ZONES: 7 to 10
EASE OF CULTIVATION: easy

The delicate fronds of this maidenhair are bipinnate to tripinnate, arching or pendent. There are three to six pairs of pinnae; the segments are fan-shaped and small, only one quarter to three quarters of an inch long, and the sori oblong. The veins end in the teeth rather than in the sinuses between the teeth as they do in most adiantums. One sorus develops per segment lobe. In the wild this species can be found on limestone rocks and walls and circumneutral soil in southern and western North America and north to South Dakota and British Columbia. It is widespread in tropical and warm-temperate regions of the world. Whether the western North American plants (to zone 4) are a distinct part of a hardy race or not is not known but they should

Adiantum capillus-veneris. (PHOTO BY PAMELA HARPER)

Adiantum capillus-veneris sori. (PHOTO BY F. GORDON FOSTER)

be tried in northern gardens. Greenhouse specimens of *A. capillus-veneris* do not survive in zone 5.

A plant that passes under the name of *A. capillus-veneris* that is hardy in New York is really *A.* × *mairisii* (page 84).

A. hispidulum
Rough maidenhair, Rosy maidenhair
FRONDS: 8 to 14 inches long, erect, deciduous
RHIZOME HABIT: short-creeping
AVAILABILITY: common
HARDINESS ZONES: 8 to 10
EASE OF CULTIVATION: easy

This graceful maidenhair has an erect rhizome with bipinnate to tripinnate fronds; the pinnae segments are about three eighths inch long and hairy underneath. The pinnae taper toward the tip and the sori are round. The stipes and rachises are also hairy, with stiff, straight, erect, brown hairs. Rough

Adiantum hispidulum.

maidenhair is naturalized on clay banks and old walls in Louisiana (though rarely) to southern Georgia and northern Florida; it is a native of Asia, Australia, and New Zealand.

North of zone 8 *A. hispidulum* is usually treated as a tender species, and kept indoors.

A. jordanii
California maidenhair
FRONDS: 8 to 18 inches long, arching, deciduous in summer
RHIZOME HABIT: short-creeping
AVAILABILITY: infrequent
HARDINESS ZONES: 8 to 10
EASE OF CULTIVATION: moderate

This far-western beauty has bipinnate to tripinnate fronds with quite variable segments (three-eighths to one-and-one-quarter inches wide), which are broadly fan-shaped. The sterile segments are toothed, and the veins end in the sinuses between teeth. The sori are elongate, one to four per segment. This species is a native of the rocky slopes of California and Oregon, south to northern Baja California.

A. × mairisii
FRONDS: 12 to 16 inches long, arching, deciduous
RHIZOME HABIT: short-creeping
AVAILABILITY: rare
HARDINESS ZONES: 6 to 10
EASE OF CULTIVATION: easy

Adiantum × *mairisii.*

Richard Rush (*British Pteridological Society Bulletin*, 1983, vol. 2, p. 261–262) reported that *A.* × *mairisii* is a sterile hybrid between *A. capillus-veneris* and perhaps *A. aethiopicum*. It resembles *A. capillus-veneris* in its loosely arranged segments, arching fronds, and veins ending in the teeth. It is hardy farther north than that species (barely to New York) and is best grown near a damp, shady wall in a sheltered location if you want to stretch the hardiness zone.

A. monochlamys
FRONDS: 2 to 6 inches long in cultivation (12 to 16 inches in the wild), arching, deciduous
RHIZOME HABIT: short-creeping
AVAILABILITY: rare
HARDINESS ZONES: 8 to 10
EASE OF CULTIVATION: difficult

The rhizome is short-creeping and ascending in this delicate species from eastern Asia. The fronds are tripinnate, the segments narrowly wedge-shaped, smooth, and with a single sorus per segment. *Adiantum monochlamys* is similar to *A. venustum* but more compact; the rhizome does not form mats, and the species is not nearly as hardy.

A. pedatum
Northern maidenhair fern, Five-finger fern
FRONDS: 12 to 30 inches long, erect-arching, deciduous
RHIZOME HABIT: short-creeping
AVAILABILITY: common
HARDINESS ZONES: 2 to 8
EASE OF CULTIVATION: easy

This maidenhair's rhizome is short-creeping, horizontal, and colony-forming; the stalk of the frond forks nearly in half with the two parts curving

Adiantum pedatum.

back, each having three to five fingerlike divisions, each in turn bearing twelve to twenty pairs of delicate segments, the segments oblong, naked, and about one half inch long. The sori are oblong and develop on small segment lobes. *Adiantum pedatum* likes moist, rich, well-drained woods and is found in much of eastern North America. It forms large clumps in light to medium shade and can be divided by cutting with a spade or sharp knife. The rhizome is heavily branched so that any way you cut the rhizome system you are likely to include more than one growing tip. Plant the rhizome at or just under the soil surface, pressing the soil firmly about it.

Cathy Paris of the University of Vermont has recently studied this species group and found that it consists of several distinct species or hybrids. First there is *A. pedatum* itself. *Adiantum aleuticum* occurs on serpentine rocks and mostly in the West (and only in scattered sites in the Northeast) and is distinguished by its more upright pinnae and often somewhat overlapping, narrowly triangular, whitish segments (see page 80). These two species hybridize to form a fertile hybrid, *A. viridimontanum*, which is found only in the Green Mountains of Vermont. The oriental variety, which has generally been identified as *A. pedatum*, is now considered to be a variety of *A. aleuticum*. *A. p.* 'Miss Sharples'. This form of the northern maidenhair is available only infrequently. It has broader pinna segments than the western species, and it is yellow-green in color, unlike *A. aleuticum*.

A. poiretii
Mexican maidenhair
FRONDS: 10 to 20 inches long, erect, deciduous
RHIZOME HABIT: short- to long-creeping
AVAILABILITY: rare
HARDINESS ZONES: 8 to 9
EASE OF CULTIVATION: moderate

The Mexican maidenhair's stipe is chestnut to black and smooth; the blade is triangular to oval, three- to four-times pinnate with two to eight pairs of pinnae. The segments are wedge- to fan-shaped, one quarter to three eighths inch wide, mostly symmetrical, with a few teeth, a smooth surface, and a whitish undersurface. The stalk color runs into the segments and the sori are oblong. It is native to the cool forests of much of tropical America, usually at higher elevations. This charming species has rarely entered cultivation but it will be a wonderful addition to gardens in some of the climatically milder portions of North America.

Adiantum venustum.

A. venustum
Himalayan maidenhair

FRONDS: 8 to 12 inches long, arching, semievergreen

RHIZOME HABIT: creeping

AVAILABILITY: frequent

HARDINESS ZONES: 5 to 8

EASE OF CULTIVATION: easy

The Himalayan maidenhair has a rhizome which branches to form a low mat; the rachis is two to six inches long and black. The fronds are three to four inches wide with the blade oval or triangular, bipinnate to tripinnate. The segments are wedge-shaped, smooth, and toothed, with only one or two sori per segment.

A native of the Himalaya Mountains to China, the dwarf *A. venustum* is slow to start but, once established, spreads well, forming a broad, dense colony. It can be divided frequently but it is not at all invasive unless untended for several years. In fact, it is a wonderful plant.

The Himalayan maidenhair has become one of the all-time great ferns in my shaded, temperate garden. I acquired a small plant of *A. venustum* several years ago. Since that time it has been a real prize, and its blessings are even greater than expected. First, it is a gorgeous plant—the small, arching fronds with black stipes on a long-creeping rhizome make a pleasing, low mound of green in the garden. It is a strong grower, arching well and providing many new branches so divisions can be made regularly. The fronds can be used in flower arrangements for much of the year. The fronds, and even the fiddleheads, go nicely with flowers and other ferns in a vase in the house and stay well for two to three weeks. The fronds are semievergreen, remaining green well into the winter.

Yet another benefit revealed itself recently. Last October, just before company was coming for dinner, my wife, Carol, asked me to run outside and pot up a small plant of something for a table centerpiece. Of course I selected a fern, hurriedly digging a small section of *A. venustum* and stuffing it into a three-inch pot with a bit of garden soil. It did so well inside that we have kept it as a houseplant for over ten months with apparently no ill effects to the plant. It resides in our living room, not close to the window. We water it three times a week but give it no supplemental humidity, and it still shows no signs of browning tips or decline in any way. It put up new fronds until December, then suspended new growth due to the short day length. In late February it resumed its growth (indoor ferns generally begin their annual comeback in late February or early March in New York). We are delighted to add this to our list of outstanding home "fernishings" and to find that *A. venustum* is such a versatile and accommodating plant.

ARACHNIODES (syn. *Leptorumohra*, *Polystichopsis*)

This mostly Asian genus has leathery fronds that are broadly triangular to pentagonal, and mostly two- to four-times pinnate; the basal pinnae generally have long basal basiscopic pinnules. The rhizome is short-creeping, forming compact colonies. Bristle tips generally adorn the segments, and the sori are round with kidney-shaped indusia.

Arachniodes is composed of about thirty species of temperate and subtropical regions, and is closely allied to *Dryopteris* and *Polystichum*. Most species occur in eastern Asia, but two species are found at high elevations in tropical America. The species range from hardy to only semihardy, and they enjoy shaded, moist, rich soil. Few species of *Arachniodes* are found in cultivation at this time, but other species should be tested since they are all attractive.

A. aristata
East Indian holly fern
FRONDS: 1 to 2½ feet long, erect-arching, evergreen
RHIZOME HABIT: short-creeping
AVAILABILITY: frequent
HARDINESS ZONES: 6 to 8
EASE OF CULTIVATION: moderate

The lustrous, dark green foliage of this species is its real attraction. The leathery blade is bipinnate to tripinnate and pentagonal, the basal pinnae strongly developed on the basiscopic side, and the segments are bristle-toothed. It is native to much of southern and eastern Asia.

Arachniodes aristata.

This is a very handsome plant with its fine dissection and lustrous dark green blade.

A. cavalerii

FRONDS: 20 to 40 inches long, erect-arching, semievergreen
RHIZOME HABIT: short-creeping to ascending
AVAILABILITY: infrequent
HARDINESS ZONES: 5 to 8
EASE OF CULTIVATION: moderate

A native to Japan, Taiwan, China, and Indochina, this fern has a broadly oval, bipinnate, leathery blade.

A. denticulata

FRONDS: 10 to 20 inches long, arching, semievergreen
RHIZOME HABIT: ascending
AVAILABILITY: rare
HARDINESS ZONES: 7 to 8
EASE OF CULTIVATION: moderate

The fronds are triangular to pentagonal, four-times pinnate at the base, with the basal pair of pinnae strongly developed basiscopically. The segments are oblong, with a wedge-shaped base. The stipe and rachis have sparse, hairlike scales. This species is widespread at high elevations in Latin America, from Mexico to Brazil, and found occasionally in the West Indies.

Arachniodes denticulata is not commonly cultivated but can be coaxed to survive in milder regions. It is notable for its very finely dissected, lustrous, dark green fronds.

Arachniodes denticulata.

A. maximowiczii (syn. *Dryopteris maximowiczii*)

FRONDS: 3 to 3½ feet long, erect, deciduous
RHIZOME HABIT: ascending
AVAILABILITY: rare
HARDINESS ZONES: 6 to 9
EASE OF CULTIVATION: moderate

The blade is broadly triangular with basal pinnae each as large as the rest of the upper frond, and the basiscopic pinnules are greatly exaggerated. It resembles *A. standishii*, but the pinnae and segments are farther apart, giving the fronds a lacy appearance. It occurs in Japan and Korea.

A. miqueliana (syn. *Leptorumohra miqueliana*)

FRONDS: 1 to 3 feet long, arching, deciduous
RHIZOME HABIT: long-creeping
AVAILABILITY: infrequent
HARDINESS ZONES: 5 to 8
EASE OF CULTIVATION: easy

The long-creeping rhizome soon makes a respectable stand of this very attractive fern. The thin-textured fronds are three- to four-times pinnate and broadly triangular or pentagonal, the basal pair of pinnae strongly developed basiscopically. It is native to Japan, Korea, and China.

A. simplicior

FRONDS: 1 to 3 feet long, arching, semievergreen
RHIZOME HABIT: short-creeping

Arachniodes simplicior var. *variegata*.

Arachniodes miqueliana.

AVAILABILITY: frequent
HARDINESS ZONES: 6 to 9
EASE OF CULTIVATION: easy

The blade is bipinnate and very leathery-waxy. It comes from Japan and China.

A. s. var. *major*. The blade is broadly oval and bipinnate to tripinnate-pinnatifid, the terminal pinna broadest at the base and gradually merging into the upper lateral pinnae.

This resembles *A. aristata* superficially, but the segments and fronds are larger. At least some material sold under this name is really *Dryopteris formosana*.

A. s. var. *variegata* (syn. *A. aristata* var. *variegata*), variegated holly fern. This is usually said to be a variety of *A. aristata* but the segments are much larger than those of that species. This is one of the most remarkable of the hardy ferns. Not only is it gorgeous with its dark green, waxy segments with a yellow-green band running along the pinna axis, but it is erect and stiff through the summer and well into the winter, at least through the first several hard freezes in December, and is hardier than *A. aristata*. On the other hand, it is very late awakening in the spring, ours not showing itself until early June in New York.

A. standishii
Upside-down fern
FRONDS: 1 to 3 feet long, erect-arching, semievergreen
RHIZOME HABIT: short-creeping

Arachniodes standishii.

AVAILABILITY: frequent

HARDINESS ZONES: 4 to 9

EASE OF CULTIVATION: easy

This is the largest of the commonly cultivated species of *Arachniodes* and seems to be the hardiest. The blade is oval-triangular and tripinnate. It is not as leathery as *A. aristata* and *A. simplicior*. The common name derives from the larger veins being very prominent on the upper surface, appearing more like those typical of the lower surface. It is also upside-down in the sense that the acroscopic basal pinnules of each pinna are larger than the basiscopic ones, which is just the reverse of the condition found in most species of the genus. It is heavily fertile, the sori protected by arched, kidney-shaped indusia, but the spores do not mature until late fall. It is a native of Japan and Korea.

ASPLENIUM, Spleenwort

The spleenworts are most suitable for moist, shaded rock gardens of both an acidic and calcareous nature. The small, one- to three-times pinnate fronds spring from compact horizontal or ascending rhizomes and the sori are elongate on one side of the vein, covered by an indusium. *Asplenium* is among the larger fern genera, with seven hundred species, most of which are tropical epiphytes. The temperate species occur mostly on rocks and are evergreen.

Hybridization is frequent between species of *Asplenium* and with species of closely allied genera, such as *Phyllitis*, *Ceterach*, and *Camptosorus*. Some of the hybrids are fertile and in turn cross with their parents and other species to make an interesting network of relationships.

The plants require good drainage, and do well in vertical plantings in rock crevices. Water carefully so that the crowns do not rot, and beware of slugs, which can be a real problem for spleenworts and their relatives.

A. adiantum-nigrum
Black spleenwort
FRONDS: 6 to 12 inches long, erect-arching, semievergreen
RHIZOME HABIT: compact
AVAILABILITY: infrequent
HARDINESS ZONES: 8 to 9
EASE OF CULTIVATION: moderate
This species is rare in the Rocky Mountains but common in Europe, Asia, and Africa. It can be distinguished by its shiny, rich green, narrowly triangular, bipinnate to tripinnate blade and the shiny black stipe. The rachis is green. This species is generally not easy to establish nor is it a strong grower but this may be due to the fact that the cultivated material comes from Europe rather than the western United States, which may be hardier. It likes a vertical planting with good drainage, with some limestone and humus.

A. × alternifolium (= A. septentrionale × trichomanes subsp. trichomanes)
FRONDS: 2 to 3 inches long, erect-arching, evergreen
RHIZOME HABIT: ascending
AVAILABILITY: rare
HARDINESS ZONES: 6 to 8
EASE OF CULTIVATION: moderate
This delightful but rare little hybrid is native to Europe and West Virginia,

Asplenium × alternifolium.

and is worthy of a place in a noncalcareous rock garden. Its very small size necessitates a place in the front of the garden and keeping other plants away so it doesn't get lost among them. It is pale green in color; the fronds are once-pinnate and narrowly lanceolate.

A. billotii (syn. *A. obovatum* subsp. *lanceolatum*)
Lanceolate spleenwort
FRONDS: 4 to 12 inches long, erect, evergreen
RHIZOME HABIT: ascending
AVAILABILITY: rare
HARDINESS ZONES: 5 to 8
EASE OF CULTIVATION: difficult
This very attractive spleenwort resembles *A. adiantum-nigrum* but the blade is more lance-shaped (instead of triangular) and only bipinnate. The pinnae are somewhat crisped, and the sori are nearer to the pinna margin than the midveins. It is a rare plant in the wild, found near the coasts in the British Isles. The species is difficult to establish and grow, partly because of the great love slugs have for it.

A. bradleyi
Bradley's spleenwort
FRONDS: 3 to 10 inches long, erect, semievergreen
RHIZOME HABIT: ascending
AVAILABILITY: rare
HARDINESS ZONES: 6 to 8
EASE OF CULTIVATION: moderate
The fronds are narrowly oblong and pinnate-pinnatifid to bipinnate. This little fern is the fertile hybrid between *A. montanum* and *A. platyneuron*, and is intermediate in form between them. It is found on sandstone cliffs and ledges in the eastern United States and can be grown in crevices in an acidic rock garden.

A. darioides
FRONDS: 1 to 5 inches long, erect, evergreen
RHIZOME HABIT: short-creeping
AVAILABILITY: rare

Asplenium fissum.

Asplenium darioides.

HARDINESS ZONES: 6 to 8

EASE OF CULTIVATION: moderate

This small attractive species has leathery, triangular, tripinnate fronds with very small, rounded to wedge-shaped segments. It is native to southern Argentina, and Chile.

A. *fissum*

FRONDS: 2 to 8 inches long, erect, evergreen

RHIZOME HABIT: short-creeping

AVAILABILITY: rare

HARDINESS ZONES: 6 to 8

EASE OF CULTIVATION: moderate

The fronds are lance-shaped, tripinnate to quadripinnate, with small, linear segments, giving an open, lacy look. It occurs on limestone in central and southeastern Europe.

A. *fontanum*

Smooth rock spleenwort, Fountain spleenwort

FRONDS: 4 to 8 inches long, erect, deciduous

RHIZOME HABIT: compact

AVAILABILITY: infrequent

HARDINESS ZONES: 5 to 8

EASE OF CULTIVATION: moderate

A native of the Alps and Himalayas, this is a most desirable dwarf species with narrow, lance-shaped fronds. The blade is bipinnate-pinnatifid.

It resembles a miniature lady fern, and is good for shady, narrow crevices in rock gardens, especially in limestone. We had it for a few years in zone 4 at the Cary Arboretum of the New York Botanical Garden. As regards most spleenworts, watch out for slugs.

A. hallbergii
Hallberg's spleenwort
FRONDS: 6 to 10 inches long, erect, deciduous
RHIZOME HABIT: ascending
AVAILABILITY: rare
HARDINESS ZONES: 8 to 9
EASE OF CULTIVATION: moderate

This little treasure closely resembles *A. monanthes* but differs in having minute papillae along the shoulders of the stipe and rachis groove, and the sori are in three to four pairs per pinna rather than limited to the lower edge of the pinna. Native to high elevations of central Mexico to Guatemala.

A. monanthes
Single-sorus spleenwort
FRONDS: 8 to 14 inches long, erect, semievergreen
RHIZOME HABIT: ascending
AVAILABILITY: rare
HARDINESS ZONES: 7 to 9
EASE OF CULTIVATION: moderate

The very slender, stiffly erect fronds are only one half to one inch wide and are once-pinnate with many pairs of pinnae. The pinnae are oblong, with

Asplenium hallbergii.
(PHOTO BY JOSEPH BEITEL)

Asplenium monanthes.

one to two sori located only on the basiscopic edge of the pinna. This species occurs on or among shaded rocks in the southwestern and southeastern United States, tropical America, Africa, and Hawaii.

Asplenium monanthes is distinct in its linear blade and many pinnae. It resembles *A. platyneuron* but the pinnae are smaller and the sori usually limited to the lower edge of the pinnae. It is not commonly cultivated, but it would be good to test it in the milder parts of the United States.

A. montanum
Mountain spleenwort
FRONDS: 3 to 5 inches long, arching, evergreen
RHIZOME HABIT: ascending
AVAILABILITY: rare
HARDINESS ZONES: 4 to 7
EASE OF CULTIVATION: moderate

This little rock fern has its stipe making up about half of the frond length. The blade is oblong-triangular, bipinnate at the base, pinnate-pinnatifid in the upper parts, and leathery and shiny. The mountain spleenwort occurs on shaded, acidic rocks in the eastern United States. In the shaded rock garden it must be tucked tightly in rock crevices.

A. onopteris
Acute-leaved spleenwort
FRONDS: 6 to 10 inches long, arching, deciduous
RHIZOME HABIT: compact
AVAILABILITY: rare
HARDINESS ZONES: 6 to 9

Asplenium montanum. (PHOTO BY BARBARA HALLOWELL)

Asplenium montanum sori. (PHOTO BY BARBARA HALLOWELL)

Asplenium onopteris.

EASE OF CULTIVATION: moderate

This closely resembles *A. adiantum-nigrum*, differing largely by the finely attenuated pinna tips and the more broadly triangular blade, being nearly as wide as it is long. Some attractive, more extreme forms are elongated in all their parts. It is native to Europe, especially the Mediterranean region.

A. pekinense
Beijing spleenwort
FRONDS: 4 to 10 inches long, arching, deciduous
RHIZOME HABIT: ascending
AVAILABILITY: rare
HARDINESS ZONES: 5 to 9
EASE OF CULTIVATION: moderate

The lustrous, dark green fronds are narrowly oblong, bipinnate, and two to three inches wide. It occurs in Japan, Korea, China, and the Himalayas and is common on banks and rocks in woodlands around Beijing and should be hardy to zone 5 in North America.

A. platyneuron
Ebony spleenwort
FRONDS: 8 to 18 inches long, sterile prostrate, fertile erect, evergreen
RHIZOME HABIT: short-creeping to ascending
AVAILABILITY: frequent
HARDINESS ZONES: 4 to 8
EASE OF CULTIVATION: moderate

Asplenium platyneuron. (Photo by F. Gordon Foster)

Asplenium platyneuron sori. (Photo by F. Gordon Foster)

The slender, once-pinnate fronds have a very short stipe, only about one sixth of the frond length. The stipe and rachis are a glossy, dark reddish brown, the pinnae oblong, auricled, and dark green. The fronds are somewhat dimorphic, the sterile ones short and arching, the fertile ones erect. *Asplenium platyneuron* is found on dryish soil and both acid and calcareous rocks in open woods in eastern North America. It is not difficult to grow in gritty humus among rocks. Be careful not to overwater as it is particularly sensitive in this regard.

Asplenium platyneuron hybridizes with *A. montanum* to form *A. bradleyi* (page 94), with *A. trichomanes* to form the very rare *A.* × *virginicum*, and with *Camptosorus rhizophyllus* to form *Asplenosorus ebenoides* (page 104).

The pinnae are sometimes deeply incised with several forms known:

A. platyneuron (imbricated form). The pinnae are crowded and overlapping. This form has been found occasionally in the Northeast.

A. p. f. *bacculum-rubrum*. This is named for Baton Rouge, Louisiana. The pinnae are elongate and the margins irregularly coarsely toothed, looking like an extreme form of f. *incisum*. This too is largely native to the southern United States.

A. p. f. *hortonae*. This very rare form has the pinnae deeply cut into lobes (the blade pinnate-pinnatifid). It has been found a few times in the Northeast but lacks spores and has not reached general cultivation.

A. p. f. *incisum*. The pinnae are lightly incised, giving a delicate appearance to the plant. Incised forms occur most frequently in the southern states.

A. resiliens

Black-stemmed spleenwort

FRONDS: 6 to 12 inches long, erect, evergreen
RHIZOME HABIT: ascending
AVAILABILITY: rare
HARDINESS ZONES: 6 to 9
EASE OF CULTIVATION: moderate

The fronds are very slender and once-pinnate with a very short stipe, resembling *A. platyneuron* but with smaller pinnae that are more rounded at their tips, and the stipe and rachis are black. *Asplenium resiliens* occurs on calcareous rocks in the southern United States, West Indies, and Mexico to South America. It is not commonly cultivated but does well in a limestone rock garden.

A. ruta-muraria

Wall rue, Wall rue spleenwort

FRONDS: 2 to 5 inches long, erect-arching, evergreen
RHIZOME HABIT: short-creeping or ascending
AVAILABILITY: rare
HARDINESS ZONES: 4 to 7
EASE OF CULTIVATION: difficult

This tiny plant has an oval-triangular, bipinnate blade with wedge-shaped segments that are narrowed at their base. It is common on limestone cliffs in northern North America, Europe, and Asia.

It needs to have a sloping or vertical location among rocks. It is not easy to establish.

A. septentrionale

Forked spleenwort

FRONDS: 3 to 6 inches long, erect-arching, evergreen
RHIZOME HABIT: ascending
AVAILABILITY: rare
HARDINESS ZONES: 4 to 8
EASE OF CULTIVATION: difficult

This mountain fern can be found up to three thousand feet above sea level. Its fronds are irregularly forked, not pinnately divided. The leathery blade consists of one to three slender, grasslike pinnae, in which the stipe is much

Asplenium ruta-muraria.

Asplenium septentrionale.

longer than the blade. It occurs in crevices of noncalcareous cliffs in the western United States, West Virginia, Europe, and Asia.

Asplenium septentrionale is a candidate for a granite or shale rock garden or in walls. In Europe it crosses with *A. trichomanes* to form *A. × alternifolium* (page 93), the alternate-leaved spleenwort, another fine small plant for rock gardens or walls.

A. trichomanes
Maidenhair spleenwort
FRONDS: 4 to 7 inches long, arching, evergreen
RHIZOME HABIT: short-creeping or ascending
AVAILABILITY: common
HARDINESS ZONES: 2 to 9
EASE OF CULTIVATION: moderate

This is one of the loveliest of the spleenworts and the easiest to grow. The small fronds are once-pinnate, about one half inch wide, with many oblong pinnae and a dark stipe and rachis. It occurs in shaded rock crevices and is

Asplenium trichomanes sori. (PHOTO BY F. GORDON FOSTER)

Asplenium trichomanes.

Asplenium trichomanes 'Cristatum'

Asplenium
trichomanes 'Incisum'.

widespread in North America, Europe, and Asia. There are two subspecies: subspecies *trichomanes* is more delicate, its fronds more arching, and occurs on noncalcareous rocks; subspecies *quadrivalens* has a stouter rachis and stipe, is thicker textured and more erect, and occurs on calcareous rocks. The latter is the most commonly grown and establishes easily in vertical rock crevices or slopes. This is one of the best small ferns for the rock garden. Well-rooted plants are necessary for success, however.

A. t. 'Cristatum'. This dainty fern has the frond apex forking more than once in a tight crest, and the pinnae are extremely small, appearing like greenish pearls on the black rachis. The crests do not show well for two to three years. A good percentage come true from spores.

A. t. 'Incisum'. This plant has very narrow fronds, deeply cut segments, and does not always produce spores. The original find of this was barren and could be propagated only by division. Fortunately, some plants are fertile (A. t. 'Incisum Moule'), and come true from spores. The young plants show their character after two years.

A. t. 'Ramosum'. This cultivar is heavily crested with the frond divided lower on the rachis than in 'Cristatum'.

A. tripteropus
FRONDS: 3 to 10 inches long, arching, evergreen
RHIZOME HABIT: ascending
AVAILABILITY: rare

Asplenium tripteropus.

Asplenium viride.

HARDINESS ZONES: 6 to 9

EASE OF CULTIVATION: moderate

This small plant closely resembles *A. trichomanes* but roots at the tip of the frond. It is found on limestone cliffs in Japan, Korea, and China. It is well worth trying.

A. viride

Green spleenwort

FRONDS: 4 to 7 inches long, erect-arching, evergreen

RHIZOME HABIT: ascending

AVAILABILITY: rare

HARDINESS ZONES: 2 to 5

EASE OF CULTIVATION: difficult

This is an exquisite fern with a vivid green stipe and rachis. The blade is linear, once-pinnate, and thin-textured. It occurs only on shaded calcareous rocks in northern North America, Europe, and Asia.

Asplenium viride resembles *A. trichomanes* in its small size and once-divided blade but is distinguished by its green rachis. It is more challenging to grow and may be difficult to get established. It likes the crevice habitat of limestone rocks.

ASPLENOSORUS

This is the name applied to hybrids between species of *Camptosorus* and *Asplenium*. They are compact plants with erect or ascending rhizomes. Most are small plants, less than twelve inches tall, combining the characteristics of the long, narrow blade of the walking fern and the once- to twice-pinnate blade of the spleenworts. Most of these hybrids are sterile with abortive spores but a few are fertile.

Because of their small size, they are ideal for moist, shaded rock gardens and terrariums. Slugs are fond of them, though, so care must be taken to protect the plants from these marauders.

A. crucibuli
FRONDS: 6 to 16 inches long, erect, evergreen
RHIZOME HABIT: ascending
AVAILABILITY: infrequent
HARDINESS ZONES: 5 to 8
EASE OF CULTIVATION: moderate

The fronds are linear, once-pinnate at the base and pinnatifid above, with round to oblong pinnae at the base of the blade, while the terminal quarter of the blade is undivided and taillike.

The species name means "of the melting pot" because the two presumed parental species, *Camptosorus sibiricus* of eastern Asia and *Asplenium platyneuron* of North America, do not occur together in nature. Rather, this hybrid arose accidentally in a flat of *Camptosorus sibiricus* being grown in an Ohio greenhouse that was brought to my attention by Charles Gleaves. Curiously, this hybrid has well-formed viable spores, so it can be propagated readily.

A. ebenoides
Scott's spleenwort
FRONDS: 6 to 12 inches long, erect, evergreen
RHIZOME HABIT: ascending
AVAILABILITY: frequent
HARDINESS ZONES: 5 to 8
EASE OF CULTIVATION: moderate

This is probably the best-known fern hybrid in America and combines the characteristics of its parents, *Camptosorus rhizophyllus* and *Asplenium platyneuron*. The blade is narrowly lance-shaped and once-pinnate, with narrowly triangular pinnae on the lower half of the blade, often of irregular lengths; the terminal quarter to half of the blade is undivided and occasionally roots at the apex. The apices of some of the pinnae are slender also, rarely forming babies at their tips. The spores are abortive in all natural populations except one, in

Asplenosorus ebenoides.

Trigeneric cross of *Asplenium*, *Camptosorus*, and *Phyllitis*, the hybrid between *Asplenosorus ebenoides* and *Phyllitis scolopendrium*.

central Alabama. Spores from those plants have been used to propagate this hybrid, which forms a fine plant for terrariums and rock gardens. It grows on shaded, calcareous, moss-covered rocks in eastern North America.

Asplenosorus ebenoides was the first hybrid in America to be re-created in a laboratory (in 1902), and the process was described recently by Leslie Duthie of the Norcross Wildlife Sanctuary (*Fiddlehead Forum* 17: 34–35, 1990, "Re-creating Scott's Spleenwort").

The fertile form of *Asplenosorus ebenoides* has crossed with *Phyllitis scolopendrium* in cultivation to form a trigeneric cross, with equal genetic contributions by *Asplenium*, *Camptosorus*, and *Phyllitis* (see Hybridization, page 67).

A. kobayashi (syn. *Asplenium kobayashi*)

FRONDS: 4 to 14 inches long, erect, evergreen
RHIZOME HABIT: ascending
AVAILABILITY: rare
HARDINESS ZONES: 5 to 8
EASE OF CULTIVATION: moderate

This hybrid between *Asplenium incisum* (bipinnate) and *Camptosorus sibiricus* (undivided) is once-pinnate, and is found in Japan. It somewhat resembles *A. ebenoides* and is its Asian counterpart.

A. pinnatifidus (syn. *Asplenium pinnatifidum*)

Lobed spleenwort
FRONDS: 4 to 8 inches long, arching, evergreen
RHIZOME HABIT: ascending
AVAILABILITY: rare

HARDINESS ZONES: 5 to 8

EASE OF CULTIVATION: moderate

This is the fertile hybrid between *Asplenium montanum* and *Camptosorus rhizophyllus*. The blade is linear and pinnately lobed (pinnatifid), occasionally rooting at the tip. It occurs on shaded, mossy, noncalcareous rocks of the eastern United States.

Asplenosorus pinnatifidus in turn backcrosses with *Asplenium montanum* to form *A.* × *trudelii* and crosses with *A. platyneuron* to form the very rare *A.* × *kentuckiensis*, and with *Asplenium trichomanes* to form *A.* × *herb-wagneri*.

ATHYRIUM, Lady fern

Athyrium, along with *Dryopteris* and *Polystichum*, forms the backbone of the fern garden. It is a temperate genus of 180 species that are all terrestrial and deciduous. The rhizome is short-creeping or erect, resulting in a handsome crown or compact clump of erect or gracefully arching fronds. The feathery, one to three times divided fronds are generally medium-sized and thin-textured. Lady ferns frequently exhibit reddish color in the stipe and rachis; sometimes there are green- and red-stalked forms in the same species. On the underside of the fronds the sori and their indusia are elongate along the veins, oblong or hooked over the veins in a J-shape, or, rarely, rounded with a kidney-shaped indusium.

The name "lady fern" has long been applied to the athyriums, in particular *A. filix-femina*, but the reason behind the name is lost. It may well be due to the delicate fronds, especially in contrast to the more coarse cutting of the male fern (*Dryopteris filix-mas*). As a mnemonic device, it has been suggested that the arching sori resemble the eyebrows of a fair maiden. Still others waggishly point out that the extreme variability of the lady fern is not unlike a woman's changing mind, but I have been advised not to pursue this.

Athyrium is one of the most dependable genera in shaded temperate gardens with rich, moist soil. Nearly all the species are strong growers and hardy to zone 5 or 6. The European lady fern, *A. filix-femina*, one of our most popular and vigorous species, has given rise to literally hundreds of cultivars, many of which make excellent and distinctive garden plants. Most of these forms, however, do not breed true from spores. Increasingly available are some excellent species from Japan and other parts of Asia, where the genus is especially rich in species diversity.

Athyrium alpestre occurs among rocks in the mountains near Seattle.

Athyrium alpestre.

The species of *Athyrium* are, on the whole, rather delicate plants and the fronds are easily broken. The stipes and rachises are brittle and snap when a dog or child runs through the fern garden. The lady ferns, like most ferns, have little strengthening in the frond, in contrast to the dryopterises and polystichums, which have special fibers in the stipe and rachis that make them fairly tough. These special tissues can be seen when you break off a stipe and look at the dark sheath around each conducting bundle.

A. alpestre (syn. A. distentifolium)
Alpine lady fern
FRONDS: 16 to 30 inches long, erect, deciduous
RHIZOME HABIT: compact
AVAILABILITY: rare
HARDINESS ZONES: 5 to 9
EASE OF CULTIVATION: moderate to difficult

This largely alpine gem has a stout, erect rhizome with the fronds clumped into a vaselike crown. Its lacy blade is oval-triangular, bipinnate-pinnatifid to tripinnate-pinnatifid, and not strongly tapering at the base. In contrast to the sori of other lady ferns, its sori are round and very small, with the indusium minute or lacking. The alpine lady fern occurs in moist wooded or alpine slopes in northwestern North America, eastern Canada, Iceland, Europe, and Asia.

Plants from Europe and Asia are shorter and more compact and more readily cultivated than North American plants (var. *americanum*), which tend to fade after a few years in the garden.

Athyrium angustum.

Athyrium bourgaei.

A. angustum (syn. A. filix-femina var. angustum)
Northern lady fern

FRONDS: 16 to 36 inches long, erect, deciduous

RHIZOME HABIT: short-creeping

AVAILABILITY: frequent

HARDINESS ZONES: 2 to 9

EASE OF CULTIVATION: easy

The northern lady fern is one of the most common ferns of northeastern North America. The rhizome is short-creeping, resulting in a diffuse crown of fronds. The blade is bipinnate-pinnatifid, and not strongly tapering at the base. The elongate sori are often hooked over the veins. This species is native to moist, rich woods.

Athyrium angustum is sometimes considered a variety of *A. filix-femina* but has a creeping rather than erect rhizome and the base of the blade is not strongly reduced. Some plants have green leaf stalks, others have red ones (forma *rubellum*).

A. arcuatum

FRONDS: 1 to 3 feet long, arching, deciduous

RHIZOME HABIT: compact

AVAILABILITY: rare

HARDINESS ZONES: 6 to 8

EASE OF CULTIVATION: moderate

The triangular blade is bipinnate-pinnatifid and six to twelve inches wide. This and *A. bourgaei* (its blade three to seven inches wide and tapering slightly at the base) occur at six- to nine-thousand-foot elevation in Mexico, and are both closely related to *A. filix-femina*. I would like to see both species tried in some of the milder zones of North America.

A. asplenioides (syn. A. filix-femina var. asplenioides)
Southern lady fern
FRONDS: 16 to 36 inches long, erect, deciduous
RHIZOME HABIT: short-creeping
AVAILABILITY: infrequent
HARDINESS ZONES: 4 to 9
EASE OF CULTIVATION: easy

This is much like *A. angustum* but the blade is broader and more triangular. The spores are different, too, but that is impossible to distinguish without microscopic study. As the common name implies, it occurs in the southeastern United States north to New Jersey and makes a fine addition to the fern garden.

A. crenulato-serrulatum (syn. Cornopteris crenulato-serrulata, Dryopteris crenulato-serrulata)
Crenate lady fern
FRONDS: 18 to 30 inches long, arching, deciduous
RHIZOME HABIT: short-creeping
AVAILABILITY: rare
HARDINESS ZONES: 5 to 8
EASE OF CULTIVATION: easy

This native of Japan, Korea, and Manchuria is distinct in having its basal pair of pinnae bent forward, and their basal pinnules much reduced. The rhizome is creeping, sending up large, graceful fronds. The stipe is as long as the blade, which is broadly triangular and bipinnate-pinnatifid. Unlike most other lady ferns, it has round sori, resembling those of *Dryopteris*. How can you tell it is not a *Dryopteris*? If you cut across the lower part of the stipe, you will see two ribbon-shaped conducting bundles, characteristic of *Athyrium* and its relatives (see Appendix, Relationships, page 331), whereas *Dryopteris* and its friends have several (five to nine) small, round bundles.

A. cyclosorum
Western lady fern
FRONDS: 2½ to 8 feet long, erect-arching, deciduous
RHIZOME HABIT: compact
AVAILABILITY: infrequent
HARDINESS ZONES: 5 to 8
EASE OF CULTIVATION: easy

The western lady fern is the largest of the lady ferns, with its fronds reaching eight feet in height. The blade is bipinnate-pinnatifid and tapers greatly at the base, with a relatively short stipe. The sori vary from the typical J-shape to round. This is sometimes considered a variety of *A. filix-femina* but is distinct in its large, fleshy fronds and round sori.

Athyrium cyclosorum is a handsome plant, somewhat lighter green and more fleshy than *A. angustum* and *A. asplenioides,* and though it does not reach the large size seen in its native western North America, nonetheless it is still an impressive addition to eastern gardens. I have it growing in my New York garden, where it is easily four feet tall, still our largest *Athyrium.*

A. filix-femina
European lady fern
FRONDS: 1 to 2 feet long, erect, deciduous
RHIZOME HABIT: erect or ascending
AVAILABILITY: common
HARDINESS ZONES: 4 to 8
EASE OF CULTIVATION: easy

This extremely widespread and abundant species of Europe and Asia has beautiful, feathery fronds which are lance-shaped, bipinnate-pinnatifid, and thin-textured. The stipe and rachis are green or red, with dark brownish scales on the stipe. The sori are J-shaped, typical of most athyriums.

Athyrium filix-femina is quite easy to grow, but appreciates shelter from wind because the fronds are easily broken. Although generally grown in shade, it is adaptable to sunny situations if the soil is kept moist. Unlike most of the American species of lady ferns, it has an erect rhizome. Reginald Kaye (1968) points out that "As the crowns get older, they tend to grow out of the ground and roots have farther to grow to reach the soil. Dividing the crowns and replanting them level with the soil with the addition of compost results in renewed vigor."

This is probably the most variable species in the world, with more than three hundred named English forms. They range in size from three inches to four feet tall, the degree of dissection varying from pinnate-pinnatifid to four or five times pinnate. *Athyrium filix-femina* is quite reliable in the garden, both it and its cultivars being strong growers. Some plants are not stable and revert to the wild form. I have had plants of 'Frizelliae' and 'Fieldiae', for example, that were fine specimens when planted, but soon I found fronds that were more typical of the species and I thought I had a mixture of varieties. It turned out that later fronds did not all have the features I expected.

There is an increasing number of forms available in America. Not all of the ones cited below are on the market, but they are chosen to show the range of variation in this single remarkable species. For a more comprehensive discussion of the variation and varietal names, see Reginald Kaye, "Variation in *Athyrium* in the British Isles," *British Fern Gazette* 9(1965): 193–204. In this paper Kaye lists seventy-two varieties known to be in cultivation in England at that time (though not all publicly available). Relatively few of them have reached American shores.

Crested forms: These have forkings of the frond tip, pinnae and pinnule tips, or the rachis.

A. f.-f. 'Acrocladon' is a highly branched type with fronds twelve inches long or less, forming a mass of slender tips. It is very rare and propagated only by division.

A. f.-f. 'Corymbiferum'. Fronds are heavily crested, forming bunched tassels (dense clusters of forkings) at the tips of the frond and the pinnae. Reportedly, it can be grown from spore to a mature, spore-producing plant within one year. Plants are two to three feet tall.

Athyrium filix-femina 'Acrocladon'.

Athyrium filix-femina 'Corymbiferum'.

Athyrium filix-femina 'Grandiceps'.

Athyrium filix-femina 'Multifidum'.

Athyrium filix-femina 'Percristatum'.

A. f.-f. 'Cristatum' has flat, fanlike crests on the frond apex and the pinna tips, the crests usually in one plane. Both green- and red-stalked forms are common. There are many subtle variations of this form.

A. f.-f. 'Grandiceps'. Extra-large crests wider than the frond itself decorate the tip of the frond.

A. f.-f. 'Multifidum'. Long fingers on slender pinnules, often called 'Waterfall'.

A. f.-f. 'Percristatum'. The two- to three-foot-long fronds have the frond tip, pinna tips, and even the pinnules crested.

Cruciate forms: The pinnae are forked at their bases with the halves crisscrossing with those of adjacent pinnae.

A. f.-f. 'Cruciatum'. The pinnae are cruciate as described above, with fronds twelve to twenty inches long.

A. f.-f. 'Cruciatum Congestum' has very stiff, narrow fronds reaching only twelve inches in length.

A. f.-f. 'Fieldiae'. The linear fronds are up to three feet long and only two to three inches wide, with the pinnae greatly shortened. It is in the group of 'Victoriae' but with shorter and broader pinna halves.

Athyrium filix-femina 'Victoriae'.

Athyrium filix-femina 'Congestum'.

A. *f.-f.* 'Victoriae'. This is the most spectacular of all fern cultivars in its magnificent frond architecture. It is really the "Queen of Green." The fronds are two to three, or even to four feet long in the original plant and three to four inches wide, arching, with drooping, crested frond and pinna tips. The pinnae are very slender, only one half inch or less wide, and forked in the cruciate manner but in a most dramatic fashion. Half of each pinna ascends at a 45-degree angle from the rachis and the other half descends at right angles to the first, thus creating the typical crisscross architecture, but the excitement doesn't stop there. The pinnae are not held in a single plane; the ascending pinnae are tipped down (away from you as you face the top of the blade) and the descending pinnae are tipped up (toward you), so viewed from the end of the frond, the pinnae form an × configuration. Furthermore, the pinnules themselves tend to be cruciate as well (percruciate). The segments tend to be forked (not all of them make it), but they are so small that they do not overlap adjacent pinnules.

There are both green- and red-stalked forms. Unfortunately, spore sowings give highly variable results with only a very low percentage coming true to form. Some of the offspring are very attractive, varying in degree of cruciateness, cresting, and width of pinnae, but most have a mixture of cruciate and normal pinnae on the same frond and are not worth saving. Thus, a true 'Victoriae' with perfect crisscrossing is valuable and to be prized.

Dwarfed forms:

A. *f.-f.* 'Caput-medusae' has fronds four to eight inches long with densely crested, parsleylike foliage, a congested ball of cresting on a bare stipe, like the head of Medusa with its snakes. I was visiting a garden in England and was so taken by the foliage in these miniature lady ferns that I went to take

Athyrium filix-femina 'Frizelliae'.

Athyrium filix-femina 'Gemmatum'.

Athyrium filix-femina 'Minutissimum'.

a picture of one and found that it indeed was parsley. The offspring of spore sowings from this uncommon form result in a mixture of cristate and corymbiferous forms.

A. f.-f. 'Congestum' is three to six inches tall with densely overlapping pinnae and shortened rachis but no cresting. Spore propagation is fairly reliable but it is usually barren. This tends to get lost in a garden bed but is used to good effect in a rock garden.

A. f.-f. 'Congestum Grandiceps' reaches twelve inches in height, with a large terminal crest and crested pinnae.

A. f.-f. 'Fancy Fronds'. This dwarf fimbriate form is only six to eight inches tall with delicate, finely dissected fronds with a small apical crest.

A. f.-f. 'Frizelliae' (tatting fern) has narrow fronds twelve to eighteen inches long with pinnae reduced to beadlike balls. It often reverts, sending out broader fronds like those more typical of *A. filix-femina*. The spores generally do not breed true.

A. f.-f. 'Frizelliae Capitatum' and 'Frizelliae Cristatum' are few to many times forked at the frond tip. They can be very graceful and reach eighteen inches in length.

A. f.-f. 'Gemmatum'. This has dense, tasseled crests on the pinnae and frond apex. Spores do not come true, so division is necessary.

A. f.-f. 'Minutissimum' is a perfect miniature form of the species, three to six inches long, without crests. This is ideal for the front of a border or in the rock garden. Rich soil tends to make the plants grow larger. Unlike many forms of lady fern, this cultivar is fairly reliable from spore.

Finely dissected (plumose) forms:

A. f.-f. 'Clarissima' (syn. *A. f.-f.* 'Fimbriatum Cristatum'). This is a most elegant variety with long, arching fronds to four feet long and two feet wide. The finely cut fronds with hairlike segments have a light, golden green color. It is barren and must be propagated by division, which is agonizingly slow. Sometimes prothallial outgrowths grow from the sori, but further development of these structures and their sexual reproduction produce irregular offspring. This is a perfect candidate for reproduction by tissue culture.

A. f.-f. 'Kalothrix'. The name means "beautiful hair" in Greek, alluding to the extremely fine division of the fronds, the segments tapering to hairlike tips.

A. f.-f. 'Plumosum' is a group with many beautiful forms. The fronds are two to three feet long, three to four times pinnate, and appear feathery and graceful with a yellowish green color. Crested forms tend to be less finely divided and are called "subplumose."

Under close greenhouse culture some of the plumose forms develop bulbils in the axils of the pinnae and at the sori in place of sporangia, especially on late-season fronds. Druery found this condition on 'Plumosum Divaricatum', and Lowe on 'Plumosum Axminster'. Such fronds can be pegged on a moist sand-peat mixture until plantlets develop.

Athyrium filix-femina 'Clarissima'.

Athyrium filix-femina 'Kalothrix'.

Athyrium filix-femina
'Plumosum
Axminster'.

Athyrium filix-femina 'Plumosum
Bolton'.

Athyrium filix-femina 'Plumosum
Cristatum Bolton'.

*Athyrium filix-
femina*
'Plumosum
Cristatum
Coke'.

*Athyrium filix-
femina*
'Plumosum
Superbum
Druery'.

A. *f.-f.* 'Plumosum Axminister' is extra-feathery but not crested. This is a parent of the 'Superbum' varieties produced by Druery.

A. *f.-f.* 'Plumosum Penny'. This is a robust, lacy form developed in the 1950s in England.

A. *f.-f.* 'Plumosum Superbum Druery'. A rare but magnificent flatly crested form.

Miscellaneous variations:

A. *f.-f.* 'Vernoniae'. This very distinct form has the pinnae crisped and broadly triangular, with overlapping, undulating pinnules ending in slender tassels. The fronds are two to three feet long.

Athyrium japonicum.

Athyrium filix-femina 'Vernoniae Cristatum'.

A. f.-f. 'Vernoniae Cristatum' is a crested variety.

A. *filix-femina* ✕ *niponicum* 'Pictum'
Giant painted fern
FRONDS: 20 to 40 inches long, erect-arching, deciduous
RHIZOME HABIT: short-creeping
AVAILABILITY: frequent
HARDINESS ZONES: 4 to 9
EASE OF CULTIVATION: easy

The fronds are lance-shaped, not strongly tapering at the base, bipinnate-pinnatifid, of soft gray-green shades with burgundy centers to the segments. The stipe makes up about one third of the frond length and is green at the base becoming reddish at the rachis, with tan scales.

This is another medium-sized lady fern of unknown origin that looks very much like a large Japanese painted fern, but I am still unsure of its name. It is frequently called the hybrid between the Japanese painted fern (*Athyrium niponicum* 'Pictum') and *A. filix-femina*. It does indeed have the size and dissection of *A. filix-femina* and the general coloration of the painted fern, but the spores are well-formed, i.e., it is probably not a hybrid, and the stipe scales are pale rather than dark as in the lady fern. I suspect it is a distinct Asiatic species, but efforts to identify it have not been conclusive. Nevertheless, it is a very handsome plant, a good grower, and well worth having in your garden.

A. japonicum (syn. *Deparia japonica, Diplazium japonicum, Lunathyrium japonicum*)

Black lady fern

FRONDS: 10 to 24 inches long, erect-arching, deciduous

RHIZOME HABIT: short-creeping

AVAILABILITY: rare

HARDINESS ZONES: 6 to 9

EASE OF CULTIVATION: easy

This species has striking blackish green, nearly fleshy fronds. The rhizome is short-creeping and branching so it can be easily divided periodically. Late to arise in the spring, the fiddleheads with their slender, pale scales are a welcome sight in June in my garden, after nearly all the other ferns are in full leaf. The blade is broadly lance-shaped and pinnate-pinnatifid with the segments rounded. The sori are arranged in a herringbone pattern, as in *A. thelypteroides*. It occurs in southern and eastern Asia.

A. niponicum (*A. goeringianum* in hort., *A. iseanum* in hort.)

FRONDS: 8 to 20 inches long, arching, deciduous

RHIZOME HABIT: compact to short-creeping

AVAILABILITY: common

HARDINESS ZONES: 4 to 9

EASE OF CULTIVATION: easy

This is the wild type of the Japanese painted fern, and is native to eastern Asia. The blade is oval and bipinnate with toothed segments, green with a reddish rachis and pinna bases.

Athyrium niponicum 'Pictum'.

Athyrium niponicum.

Athyrium niponicum 'Pictum' sori.

Athyrium niponicum. The pale swellings are young crosiers and mark the growing tips of the rhizome.

A. n. 'Pictum' (*A. goeringianum* 'Pictum' in hort., *A. iseanum* 'Pictum' in hort.), Japanese painted fern. With its tricolored fronds, this is one of the most popular ferns in cultivation in America today. The spectacular blade is triangular, bipinnate to bipinnate-pinnatifid, with a burgundy rachis and pinna midribs, and zones of gray and darker green on the pinnae. The best color is developed on plants in light shade. Too much sun washes out the color. It was previously known as *A. goeringianum* and *A. iseanum*, but it has been found that those names apply to other species.

To say that this fern does very well in a shaded, moist garden where the soil is loose and the rhizome and roots can spread well is one of the great understatements of fern horticulture. Under good conditions it will keep sending up fronds all summer and into the fall, so it appears pleasing all season. The rhizome is short-creeping and branches freely, providing many growing tips in each plant, generally doubling or tripling in a single year. Full plants can be dug up and divided into eight to fifteen plants, each with three or four growing points. You can keep dividing such a clump until there is a single growing tip, but the resulting plants would be very small, and it takes greater care to cut a fern into such small divisions. For coarse division, on the other hand, I merely use the spade to cut through the middle of the plant and then again to give four plants, and each will surely have several growing tips. For finer division and to better see what you are doing, use a sharp knife to divide it. This is a fern that keeps on giving.

There are several color forms of this lively fern with differing degrees of red or gray or even metallic tones. There is also said to be a dwarf variety. A crested form has a crested and drooping frond tip.

Athyrium otophorum.

A. *otophorum*
Eared lady fern
FRONDS: 12 to 18 inches long, erect, deciduous
RHIZOME HABIT: erect
AVAILABILITY: common
HARDINESS ZONES: 5 to 9
EASE OF CULTIVATION: easy

Athyrium otophorum is a dramatic addition to the garden, with its triangular, flat, almost plasticlike, pale green, young fronds with burgundy stipes and rachises. Even the crosiers are a dark maroon. Mature fronds are a medium dusky gray-green but keep the dark red frond axes. It is native to Japan and China, and one of the essential ferns for those interested in the Oriental Connection. Occasionally *Athyrium otophorum* is called English painted fern, but this is a great misnomer.

A. *spinulosum*
Spinulose lady fern
FRONDS: 1½ to 2½ feet long, arching, deciduous
RHIZOME HABIT: creeping
AVAILABILITY: rare
HARDINESS ZONES: 4 to 8
EASE OF CULTIVATION: easy

This gorgeous plant has broadly triangular fronds on a long stipe, with the lower pinnae especially large and curving upward toward the frond tip. The creeping rhizome produces fronds at a distance from one another, the fronds delicately cut, bipinnate-pinnatifid to tripinnate, with both red- and green-stalked forms. It comes from southern and eastern Asia.

Athyrium thelypteroides. (PHOTO BY
BARBARA HALLOWELL)

Athyrium thelypteroides sori.

A. *thelypteroides* (syn. *Diplazium acrostichoides*, *Deparia acrostichoides*)

Silvery spleenwort, Silvery glade fern
FRONDS: 1½ to 4 feet long, erect-arching, deciduous
RHIZOME HABIT: short-creeping
AVAILABILITY: common
HARDINESS ZONES: 4 to 9
EASE OF CULTIVATION: easy

The lower surface of the blade becomes silvery from the whitish juvenile sori arranged in a herringbone pattern, contrasting beautifully with the brilliant green upper surface. The stipe and rachis are green, appearing hairy due to abundant narrow scales and some fine hairs. The fronds are pinnate-pinnatifid tapering markedly at base, the segments squarish or rounded, and with numerous hairs. The silvery spleenwort occurs in damp woods and rich soil, often near water in eastern North America and eastern Asia.

There are two forms of margin: one has the segments nearly smooth-margined and round-tipped, the other has the segments toothed and slightly pointed at the tip.

A. *vidalii*

FRONDS: 1 to 2 feet long, arching, deciduous
RHIZOME HABIT: erect
AVAILABILITY: rare
HARDINESS ZONES: 5 to 9
EASE OF CULTIVATION: easy

This graceful fern has colorful new growth. The fronds are bipinnate, the segments toothed to shallowly lobed. It is native to Taiwan, Korea, and Japan.

Azolla filiculoides.

AZOLLA FILICULOIDES (syn. *A. rubra*), Mosquito fern

FRONDS: 1/32 inch long, floating, evergreen
RHIZOME HABIT: creeping
AVAILABILITY: infrequent
HARDINESS ZONES: 5 to 10
EASE OF CULTIVATION: easy

These are small floating ferns with minute, round, overlapping opposite leaves. The plants often turn reddish in cold weather. The leaves are minute and bilobed, with a green upper lobe and colorless lower lobe, with the cavity bearing a blue-green alga (*Anabaena*). Sporocarps are borne in pairs on the stem.

It is difficult to distinguish the seven species of the genus except by details of the minute sporocarps and, unfortunately, the plants are only rarely fertile. Most of the species are natives of tropical regions. *Azolla filiculoides* occurs on open quiet water or bare mud in western North America and New York, and from Mexico to South America. This would be an interesting addition for a small pond or pool in hardiness zones 6 to 9, but the plants can be invasive in frost-free areas.

BLECHNUM, Hard fern

This largely tropical genus includes relatively few species of horticultural merit for a temperate garden. The rhizome is long-creeping to compact and erect, scaly, often stoloniferous and forming large stands. The fronds are small to medium-sized (rarely large), mostly pinnatifid to pinnate, with the margin entirely to finely toothed. Young fronds are usually reddish, maturing to green, and monomorphic or dimorphic. The blade is naked, occasionally with small scales on the midveins, mostly leathery. The distinctive feature of the genus is the location of the sori along the midvein, with an indusium opening toward the midvein.

Of the nearly two hundred species of *Blechnum*, only two occur in north-temperate regions and several are south-temperate.

They prefer moist, acid soils, generally in the milder parts of North America, but a couple will survive to zone 6. Some other species in New Zealand may be hardy in North America, and more should be tested, especially on the humid West Coast.

B. amabile

FRONDS: 2½ to 4 feet long, arching, evergreen

RHIZOME HABIT: creeping

AVAILABILITY: rare

HARDINESS ZONES: 8 to 10

EASE OF CULTIVATION: moderate

The fronds are monomorphic, the pinnae linear, long-tipped, and rounded at their bases. The species is native to southern and eastern Asia and the South Pacific.

B. auriculatum

FRONDS: 1 to 2 feet long, erect-arching, deciduous

RHIZOME HABIT: crown

AVAILABILITY: rare

HARDINESS ZONES: 8 to 9

Blechnum auriculatum.

EASE OF CULTIVATION: moderate

The fronds are two to four inches wide and monomorphic. The sori are parallel to the midvein but not right next to it as in all other species of *Blechnum*. The stipe is short, only about one quarter of the frond length. The pinnae are slender and stalkless, flared to form auricles above and below at the base, somewhat clasping the rachis. *Blechnum auriculatum* is native to Peru, Chile, Argentina, Brazil, and Uruguay.

B. australe

FRONDS: 12 to 18 inches long, sterile arching, fertile erect, evergreen
RHIZOME HABIT: creeping to ascending
AVAILABILITY: rare
HARDINESS ZONES: 8 to 9
EASE OF CULTIVATION: moderate

The fronds are tufted and dimorphic, one and a half to five inches wide, much like *B. spicant* but the frond is tapering to the base. This native of South Africa is hardy in the Seattle area and one of several ferns of that region that might be tested for growing in the milder regions of North America.

B. capense
Palmleaf fern

FRONDS: 2 to 4 feet long, dimorphic, sterile arching, fertile erect, evergreen
RHIZOME HABIT: short-creeping
AVAILABILITY: rare
HARDINESS ZONES: 8 to 9
EASE OF CULTIVATION: moderate

The long, palmlike fronds reach a length of ten feet in the wild, mostly one to four feet in cultivation. The blade is once-pinnate, dimorphic, and lanceolate, the sterile pinnae are linear, pointed, lustrous, and finely toothed. The fertile fronds are taller than the sterile. *Blechnum capense* is native to Australia and New Zealand, growing at elevations as high as four thousand feet in the latter country.

There is considerable confusion in the identification of blechnums in cultivation. Some plants claimed to be of this species are grown in the Seattle area.

Blechnum cordatum (with *Phyllitis scolopendrium* in background).

B. cordatum (B. chilense, B. magellanicum, B. tabulare, all of hort.)
FRONDS: 1 to 2 feet long, arching, evergreen
RHIZOME HABIT: long-creeping or ascending
AVAILABILITY: rare
HARDINESS ZONES: 7 to 9
EASE OF CULTIVATION: moderate

The fronds are once-pinnate and broadly oval, with narrow, leathery pinnae. The fertile fronds are erect, with linear pinnae. It is native to southern South America.

Blechnum cordatum spreads to cover a large area. It is established in many gardens in England but is not generally planted in America.

B. niponicum
Japanese deer fern
FRONDS: Sterile 8 to 14 inches long, prostrate; fertile 12 to 20 inches long, erect; evergreen
RHIZOME HABIT: ascending
AVAILABILITY: rare
HARDINESS ZONES: 6 to 9
EASE OF CULTIVATION: moderate

The sterile fronds lie flat on the ground with long slender frond tips, while the fertile fronds are erect. It is similar to *B. spicant* but the sterile fronds are broader than those of that species. A native of Japan.

B. penna-marina

Little hard fern

FRONDS: 4 to 8 inches long, erect-arching, evergreen

RHIZOME HABIT: creeping

AVAILABILITY: common

HARDINESS ZONES: 5 to 8

EASE OF CULTIVATION: easy

This small creeping fern has slender, pinnatifid fronds. The sterile fronds are laxly erect-arching, with rounded, dark green, leathery segments, whereas the fertile fronds are stiffly upright with short, linear pinnae. The fronds are generally four to eight inches tall and there is a dwarf form only two to four inches tall.

Blechnum penna-marina is native to alpine, wet grasslands in Australia, New Zealand, and Chile. It makes an excellent ground cover or an edging by rocks. *B. p.-m.* subsp. *alpinum* (syn. *Blechnum alpinum*, *Lomaria alpina*) from southern South America has pinnae more crowded than the species, its fertile fronds without a long stipe, but many botanists do not consider it distinct from the species.

B. p.-m. 'Cristatum'. The frond apex is crested.

B. spicant

Deer fern, Hard fern

FRONDS: Sterile 8 to 20 inches long, prostrate; fertile 16 to 36 inches
    long, erect; evergreen

Blechnum penna-marina.

Blechnum penna-marina 'Cristatum'.

Blechnum spicant.

RHIZOME HABIT: ascending
AVAILABILITY: common
HARDINESS ZONES: 5 to 8
EASE OF CULTIVATION: easy

The large, flat rosette of elegant, dark green, leathery, stiff, pinnatifid sterile fronds and the fountain of erect fertile fronds from the center of this fern are a common sight, both in the wild and in gardens in the Northwest. The sterile fronds are very slender with numerous linear segments closely set like the teeth of a comb, tapering to the frond base. *Blechnum spicant* occurs in moist coniferous forests in northwestern North America and Europe. It appreciates deep humus but needs strictly acidic conditions. It produces lush growth in shade but will grow in full sun in the Pacific Northwest with sufficient moisture.

There are several forms. For more details on them, see Rush: "Variation in *Blechnum spicant*," *Pteridologist* 1(1984): 42.

B. s. 'Anomalum'. The fertile fronds have pinnae nearly as broad as the sterile pinnae.

B. s. 'Bipinnatifidum' has bipinnatifid fronds, and the pinnae are about one quarter inch wide and cut about halfway to the midvein.

B. s. 'Crispum' has irregularly wavy margins.

B. s. 'Cristatum'. The fronds are six to twelve inches long, once-pinnate, with crested tips.

Blechnum spicant crosiers.

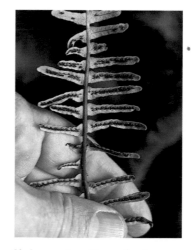

Blechnum spicant 'Anomalum'.

Blechnum spicant 'Crispum'.

Blechnum spicant 'Rickard's Serrate'.

B. s. 'Imbricatum' is a dwarf variety with fronds to twelve inches long, with overlapping pinnae that look like overlapping shingles. This form may appear when plants are under stress.

B. s. 'Lineare'. This bizarre form is very little divided. It has short pinnae at the blade base, but the terminal three quarters of the frond is barely lobed.

B. s. 'Redwoods Giant'. This form, from northern California, is larger in all dimensions.

B. s. 'Rickard's Serrate' has pinnae about one half inch wide and deeply incised, cut nearly to the midrib. There is little space between the pinnae, which are slightly curved in the direction of the frond tip.

BOMMERIA HISPIDA, Copper fern

FRONDS: 4 to 10 inches long, erect-arching, deciduous
RHIZOME HABIT: short-creeping
AVAILABILITY: rare
HARDINESS ZONES: 7 to 10
EASE OF CULTIVATION: moderate
This small fern of rocky situations has hairy, pentagonal fronds, which are pinnate-pinnatifid, and the basal pinnae with their basiscopic pinnules are greatly elongated. The stipe is long, being three quarters of the leaf length, and the sori run along the veins near their ends without an indusium.

The copper fern grows on dry, rocky ledges in the southwestern United States and northern Mexico. In cultivation it requires a loose, gritty soil and rather dry conditions, including a sunny situation, and must be watered sparingly. The plants are treated similarly to *Cheilanthes* species.

Bommeria hispida.

BOTRYCHIUM, Grape fern

The botrychiums are hardly recognizable as ferns to the amateur. The stem is subterranean, erect, and fleshy, with thick, fleshy roots. Usually there is one frond (rarely two) with two distinct parts: an arching, divided sterile blade (one to four times pinnate) and an erect fertile part (two to three times divided) with a loose sporangial cluster, usually taller than the sterile blade, arising from the base of the sterile blade or from lower on the stipe, at or below ground level. The sporangia are large and round. The fronds are deciduous or evergreen; the species which are evergreen come up in late summer and die down the following summer.

The grape ferns usually grow in pastures, grassy meadows, and open second-growth woodlands; many are very small and are a challenge to find, much less to cultivate, and the slugs love them. There are about fifty species, mostly of temperate regions of North America, Europe, and Asia.

Botrychium and *Ophioglossum* spores germinate in the dark under the ground. The gametophytes develop in association with a fungus that presumably aids the plant in its nutrition. This mycorrhizal (literally "fungus" and "root") association is carried over into the roots of the sporophyte plant as well, and soil lacking the fungus makes it difficult for the transplanted plants to survive for long. Transplants often live for a year or two or three, diminishing in size each year and then dying. Transplants are rarely successful, and any such action should not be accompanied by great expectation.

Botrychium dissectum.

B. dissectum (syn. B. obliquum)
Dissected grape fern
FRONDS: 4 to 8 inches long, arching, evergreen
RHIZOME HABIT: erect, subterranean
AVAILABILITY: infrequent
HARDINESS ZONES: 4 to 8
EASE OF CULTIVATION: difficult

This grape fern has leathery leaves which are triangular and bipinnate, tripinnate at the base. The segments are long, somewhat pointed, and several times as long as wide. New fronds appear in the summer and often turn bronze-colored in the winter. The fertile stalk arises from the base of the stipe, at or below ground level. It is interesting to look for these little plants in moist woods and meadows. *Botrychium dissectum* is native to eastern North America.

There are two forms, f. *dissectum* with finely toothed segments and f. *obliquum* with smooth-margined segments, that may occur side by side.

B. virginianum
Rattlesnake fern
FRONDS: 6 to 20 inches long, erect-arching, deciduous
RHIZOME HABIT: erect, subterranean
AVAILABILITY: infrequent
HARDINESS ZONES: 4 to 9
EASE OF CULTIVATION: difficult

The fronds are broadly triangular, bipinnate to tripinnate with segments pointed, toothed, very thin-textured, and usually papery when dry. The fertile

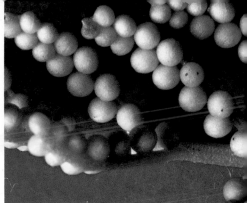

Botrychium virginianum. (PHOTO BY F. GORDON FOSTER)

Botrychium virginianum sporangia. (PHOTO BY F. GORDON FOSTER)

stalk arises from the base of the blade. It grows in moist, rich woods over much of North America, Europe, and Asia.

CAMPTOSORUS, Walking fern

Closely related to *Asplenium*, the well-known walking fern is characterized by small, slender, undivided fronds with long-attenuate tips that root to form new plants. This often results in large colonies. The sori with indusia are elongate in an irregular pattern; in fact, the genus name means "crooked sorus."

The genus has but two species, one of eastern North America and one of eastern Asia. Both species of *Camptosorus* hybridize with species of *Asplenium*, the hybrids being placed in *Asplenosorus*. The walking ferns prefer moist, shady, moss-covered limestone or other calcareous rocks. Slugs find them especially

Camptosorus rhizophyllus. (PHOTO BY JOSEPH BEITEL)

Camptosorus rhizophyllus sori. (PHOTO BY F. GORDON FOSTER)

appetizing. The walking fern should be grown from spores, but unfortunately, all known plants for sale are taken from the wild.

C. rhizophyllus (syn. *Asplenium rhizophyllum*)
Walking fern

FRONDS: 5 to 10 inches long, arching, evergreen
RHIZOME HABIT: ascending
AVAILABILITY: frequent
HARDINESS ZONES: 4 to 8
EASE OF CULTIVATION: moderate

The long, slender fronds have heart-shaped bases. A native of eastern North America, the plants can be established outdoors in a moist, limestone rock garden (or among acid rocks with lime chips around them). They do best if the rocks are really wet and mossy, allowing the frond tips to root and new plants to become started. Once established, plants can stand dry conditions for a short time, but prolonged drought is detrimental. Plants are often damaged by slugs and snails.

C. sibiricus (syn. *Asplenium ruprechtii*)
Asian walking fern

FRONDS: 3 to 6, rarely to 10 inches long, arching, evergreen
RHIZOME HABIT: ascending
AVAILABILITY: rare
HARDINESS ZONES: 4 to 8
EASE OF CULTIVATION: moderate

The blade is linear to linear-lance-shaped and only one quarter to one half inch wide; the base is tapering, not cordate or auricled as in *C. rhizophyllus*, and smaller than that species. It is native to Japan, Korea, Manchuria, northern China, and eastern Siberia.

Camptosorus sibiricus hybridizes with species of *Asplenium* naturally to form intermediates with long, sometimes rooting tips. It also has crossed accidentally in cultivation to form the fertile hybrid *Asplenosorus crucibuli* (page 104), which makes a fine plant for rock gardens or terrariums.

CETERACH

Closely allied to *Asplenium* and included in that genus by some botanists, *Ceterach* is notable for forming rosettes of small, pinnatifid fronds. The rhizome is compact and ascending. The rounded to oblong pinnae have sori, with indusia, which are elongate along the veins, often obscured by the dense scale cover on the lower blade surface.

There are five species native to warm to temperate climates, on limestone, largely of Europe and Asia.

C. dalhousiae (syn. *Asplenium alternans*, *Ceterachopsis dalhousiae*)

FRONDS: 2 to 6 inches long, arching, evergreen
RHIZOME HABIT: erect
AVAILABILITY: rare
HARDINESS ZONES: 8 to 9
EASE OF CULTIVATION: moderate

The blade is pinnatifid with six to thirteen pairs of lobes and, as a distinguishing mark, naked, in contrast to *C. officinarum*'s dense covering of scales. This species has an interesting distribution pattern, occurring in moist, rocky limestone ravines of southern Arizona, northern Mexico, and the Himalayas.

Ceterach dalhousiae requires well-drained soil and frost protection. It has been used as a terrarium plant but should be tried more often outdoors in milder climates. It has been reported hardy in Massachusetts.

C. officinarum (syn. *Asplenium ceterach*)

Rusty-back fern, Scaly spleenwort
FRONDS: 3 to 8 inches long, arching, evergreen
RHIZOME HABIT: erect
AVAILABILITY: infrequent
HARDINESS ZONES: 5 to 8
EASE OF CULTIVATION: moderate

This dwarf, evergreen fern has pinnatifid fronds with the lobes green to blue-green above, densely scaly and silvery below. The blade margin is usually slightly curled upward to show the silvery scales—a very attractive contrast. On mature fronds the scales turn a rusty color. The plant lies flat on the ground as a rosette. When dry, it curls up but quickly spreads again when

moisture is restored. The sori are elongate along the veins but are usually obscured by the dense scale covering.

The rusty-back fern is a common sight in Europe, usually found growing on the mortar of old walls. It is also found in western Asia and northern Africa on limestone outcroppings. It should be cultivated more, with the little rosettes tucked into crevices of a limestone rockery. It establishes easily both on soil and limestone in light shade.

Hybrids between this species and species of *Asplenium* are placed in the hybrid genus *Asplenoceterach*, but these are not cultivated.

CHEILANTHES, Lip fern, Cloak fern

The lip ferns and cloak ferns are well adapted to dry habitats and deserve to be more widely cultivated in sunny rock gardens, especially in drier warm regions of the United States. Even though they are small plants, they are quite diverse and very attractive. The fronds range from once-pinnate to a lacy five times divided. In color they exhibit a wide array of shades of green to blue to gray, and they are often hairy, scaly, or white-waxy on the lower surface to help reduce water loss. The rhizome is short- or long-creeping, occasionally ascending. The sori are near the blade margin, usually with the margin inrolled as a "false indusium" (lip ferns), or along the veins without any sort of indusium (cloak ferns). *Cheilanthes* is a large genus of about two hundred species, mostly natives of warm, dry, rocky regions, with many species in Mexico and the southwestern United States.

Often the genus *Notholaena* has been separated from *Cheilanthes* on the basis of the sori running along the veins near their tips and the margin undifferentiated, but this characteristic seems to be artificial and unreliable as a distinguishing generic feature. There are several natural species groups within

Cheilanthes, but at what level they should be recognized is still one of the major questions in fern taxonomy. Current botanists tend to treat these as distinct genera, including *Astrolepis*, *Argyrochosma*, *Pentagramma*, and a redefined *Notholaena*, but here I will keep them all within *Cheilanthes*.

For rock gardens, plant them in rock crevices or between large stones. Some require acidic rocks, others calcareous. Good drainage is essential. Use a loose mixture of humus with abundant coarse sand, grit, and gravel, and take care not to overwater as the crowns may rot. Once established, *Cheilanthes* can survive long dry periods, especially if their roots can be kept cool by planting among rocks. They may even lose their fronds without dying. They are usually difficult to obtain but are easy to grow from spores.

C. alabamensis

Alabama lip fern

FRONDS: 8 to 20 inches long, erect-arching, deciduous

RHIZOME HABIT: short-creeping

AVAILABILITY: infrequent

HARDINESS ZONES: 7 to 10

EASE OF CULTIVATION: moderate

A black, naked stipe subtends the narrowly oblong, bipinnate-pinnatifid blade, and the segments are often pointed. The upper and lower surfaces are naked or have scattered short hairs beneath. The indusium is continuous along the margin. *Cheilanthes alabamensis* is found on calcareous rock slopes in the southern United States, northern Mexico, and Jamaica. It occurs north to Tennessee and Arkansas, so it should be hardy in many areas of the South. It can be used in a limestone rock garden with good drainage.

Cheilanthes alabamensis.

C. argentea

FRONDS: 4 to 6 inches long, erect, deciduous
RHIZOME HABIT: short-creeping
AVAILABILITY: rare
HARDINESS ZONES: 5 to 7
EASE OF CULTIVATION: moderate

This charming little gem from eastern Asia has triangular to pentagonal fronds with a reddish black stipe half the frond length. The blade is green above and white below with white wax glands. The basal pinnae are exaggerated basiscopically to make the frond star-shaped. The sori are continuous along the margin, the sporangia appearing black when mature.

Cheilanthes argentea is common on dry limestone rocks in its native lands. We saw it growing on mortared walls near our hotel in Beijing. It is not common in cultivation, but judging from the Beijing climate, *C. argentea* should do well in at least some parts of North America.

C. beitelii (syn. *Astrolepis beitelii*)

Beitel's cloak fern
FRONDS: 10 to 24 inches long, erect, semievergreen
RHIZOME HABIT: short-creeping
AVAILABILITY: rare
HARDINESS ZONES: 9 to 10
EASE OF CULTIVATION: moderate

In this species the fronds are held stiffly erect, and are once-pinnate with the many pinnae shallowly lobed. The pinnae are a rich dark green to bluish green above, and densely tan-scaly below. The sporangia follow the veins but

The undersurface of the frond of *Cheilanthes argentea* is covered with a white wax.

Cheilanthes beitelii.

are mostly hidden by the dense scale cover. It is frequent on open, acidic, rocky slopes of southern and central Mexico.

Cheilanthes beitelii closely resembles *C. sinuata* but has broader, more robust pinnae.

C. bonariensis (syn. *Notholaena aurea*)

Golden cloak fern

FRONDS: 8 to 24 inches long, erect, deciduous

RHIZOME HABIT: short-creeping

AVAILABILITY: frequent

HARDINESS ZONES: 8 to 9

EASE OF CULTIVATION: easy

The fronds are linear and erect with many pairs of deeply lobed pinnae. A few delicate hairs adorn the upper surface of the pinnae, but the lower surface is densely covered with long white to tan hairs. *Cheilanthes bonariensis* is found among acidic rocks in the southwestern United States and much of tropical America. Apparently it is hardy in the Seattle area, at least through moderate winters.

C. covillei

Coville's lip fern

FRONDS: 4 to 12 inches long, erect-arching, deciduous

RHIZOME HABIT: short-creeping

AVAILABILITY: rare

HARDINESS ZONES: 7 to 8

EASE OF CULTIVATION: moderate

The stipe is brown to purplish, clothed with pale lance-shaped scales, and is one third to one half of the frond length. The blade is oblong to triangular and tripinnate. A distinctive feature is its round, beadlike segments, with the upper surface naked and the lower surface covered with broad, triangular, white to pale reddish brown scales. The indusium is continuous along the margin. It occurs among granitic and sandstone rocks in the southwestern United States and northwestern Mexico.

C. dealbata (syn. *Argyrochosma dealbata*, *Notholaena dealbata*)

Powdery cloak fern

FRONDS: 2 to 6 inches long, arching, deciduous

RHIZOME HABIT: short-creeping
AVAILABILITY: rare
HARDINESS ZONES: 6 to 9
EASE OF CULTIVATION: moderate

This is one of the most distinct of all the *Cheilanthes* species. The triangular blade is four to five times divided and the lower surface has a white, waxy covering, but the frond is otherwise glabrous. The slender chestnut brown stipe is at least half the frond length. The sporangia follow the veins and look like pepper sprinkled against white wax. The species occurs on limestone cliffs in the central United States. It ranges north to Missouri and Kansas, so it should be hardy in other parts of the country.

C. distans

Woolly cloak fern

FRONDS: 4 to 10 inches long, erect, deciduous
RHIZOME HABIT: short-creeping
AVAILABILITY: rare
HARDINESS ZONES: 8 to 10
EASE OF CULTIVATION: moderate

A lovely tufted fern, it has a bipinnate-pinnatifid blade that is fluffy below with dense hairs, fewer hairs above. The sporangia follow the veins. It occurs on dry, acidic rocks in full sun in Australia, New Zealand, and New Caledonia.

C. eatonii

Eaton's lip fern

FRONDS: 4 to 16 inches long, erect, deciduous
RHIZOME HABIT: short-creeping
AVAILABILITY: infrequent
HARDINESS ZONES: 6 to 8
EASE OF CULTIVATION: moderate

The blade is oblong-lance-shaped and tripinnate to tripinnate-pinnatifid, with white curly hairs on the upper surface, dense rusty hairs and lance-shaped scales underneath. The stipe is brown and one third to one half the frond length, with narrow scales and hairs. The indusium is continuous along the margin. It occurs on calcareous and noncalcareous rocks in Virginia, the southwestern United States, and northern Mexico.

C. feei
Slender lip fern
FRONDS: 5 to 10 inches long, arching, deciduous
RHIZOME HABIT: ascending
AVAILABILITY: rare
HARDINESS ZONES: 5 to 8
EASE OF CULTIVATION: difficult

The bipinnate-pinnatifid fronds are clothed with long white to tan hairs, sparsely so above, densely below. The indusium is continuous along the margin. It occurs on calcareous and noncalcareous rocks and cliffs in the central and western United States.

C. fendleri
Fendler's lip fern
FRONDS: 6 to 12 inches long, erect, deciduous
RHIZOME HABIT: long-creeping
AVAILABILITY: frequent
HARDINESS ZONES: 5 to 8
EASE OF CULTIVATION: easy

The blades are narrowly oval and tripinnate with round segments. The upper surface is glabrous, the lower surface covered with white to red-brown, lance-shaped scales. The stipe is chestnut brown, scaly, and comprises half the frond length. The indusium is continuous along the margin. It is found among igneous rocks in the southwestern United States and northern Mexico.

Cheilanthes fendleri is a strong grower in gardens of the Northwest, often forming extensive colonies.

Cheilanthes fendleri.

C. formosa

FRONDS: 4 to 12 inches long, erect, deciduous
RHIZOME HABIT: compact, horizontal
AVAILABILITY: rare
HARDINESS ZONES: 8 to 10
EASE OF CULTIVATION: moderate

The blade is three to four times pinnate with small, distinct, bluish green, oval segments and a dark stipe and rachis. It closely resembles some species of *Pellaea*. The species is native to dry, calcareous regions of Mexico and Guatemala and is good for rock gardens in milder parts of North America.

C. gracillima

Lace fern
FRONDS: 4 to 10 inches long, arching, evergreen
RHIZOME HABIT: short-creeping
AVAILABILITY: rare
HARDINESS ZONES: 7 to 8
EASE OF CULTIVATION: moderate

The blade is oblong, bipinnate with oblong segments whose upper surfaces have a few stellate scales, and dense cinnamon hairs and very narrow scales underneath. The stipe is dark brown, usually more than half the frond length, and nearly naked or with linear scales. The indusium is continuous along the margin. *Cheilanthes gracillima* occurs on igneous rocks in the northwestern United States and adjacent Canada.

C. jonesii (syn. *Notholaena jonesii*)

Jones's cloak fern
FRONDS: 2 to 6 inches long, erect-arching, deciduous
RHIZOME HABIT: short-creeping
AVAILABILITY: rare
HARDINESS ZONES: 8 to 9
EASE OF CULTIVATION: moderate

The blade is narrowly oblong and bipinnate with the segments smooth-margined or slightly lobed and lacking any hairs or scales. The chestnut brown stipe is glabrous and accounts for one third to one half the frond length. *Cheilanthes jonesii* occurs on calcareous or igneous rock ledges in the southwestern United States.

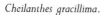
Cheilanthes gracillima.

Cheilanthes kaulfussii.

C. kaulfussii
Glandular lip fern

FRONDS: 4 to 16 inches long, erect, deciduous
RHIZOME HABIT: short-creeping to erect
AVAILABILITY: rare
HARDINESS ZONES: 8 to 9
EASE OF CULTIVATION: moderate

The delicate, tripinnate to tripinnate-pinnatifid blade is broadly pentagonal with the basal pinnae greatly exaggerated basiscopically. All surfaces are covered with glandular hairs, giving a sticky feel to the fronds. The slender, purplish brown stipe is more than half the frond length. The sori are round, protected by a slightly modified lobe margin. *Cheilanthes kaulfussii* occurs on noncalcareous rocky slopes from Texas to South America.

C. lanosa
Hairy lip fern

FRONDS: 6 to 16 inches long, erect, deciduous
RHIZOME HABIT: short-creeping
AVAILABILITY: frequent
HARDINESS ZONES: 5 to 8
EASE OF CULTIVATION: moderate

The loose clumps of this attractive species have narrowly oblong, bipinnate-pinnatifid blades, whose upper surfaces have sparse straight or lax reddish hairs and underneath have woolly hairs similar to those above. The chestnut brown stipe has arching hairs and comprises one quarter to one third the frond length. *Cheilanthes lanosa* occurs on calcareous and noncalcareous rocky slopes in the eastern, southern, and midwestern United States.

Cheilanthes
lanosa.

Cheilanthes
lindheimeri.

This small rock fern makes a fine addition to the sunny or lightly shaded rockery. It prefers acidic or neutral soil but tolerates a little lime. It likes a dry, well-drained, sunny rock garden in areas of low rainfall. It is the easiest of the eastern species to establish.

C. lendigera

FRONDS: 8 to 14 inches long, erect, deciduous
RHIZOME HABIT: short- to long-creeping
AVAILABILITY: rare
HARDINESS ZONES: 8 to 10
EASE OF CULTIVATION: easy

The fronds are three to four times divided and are distinct in their tiny, beadlike segments. The indusium is broad, nearly covering the entire lower segment surface, and the frond clothing is of hairs only. *Cheilanthes lendigera* is native to dry, acidic, rocky regions of the southwestern United States south to Ecuador.

C. lindheimeri

Lindheimer's lip fern, Fairy swords
FRONDS: 8 to 14 inches long, erect, semievergreen
RHIZOME HABIT: long-creeping
AVAILABILITY: rare
HARDINESS ZONES: 8 to 9
EASE OF CULTIVATION: moderate

This is one of the most striking dryland ferns by virtue of its silvery fronds with white, curly hairs on the upper surface. The blade is oblong and tripinnate to quadripinnate with beadlike segments. In addition to the hairs on the upper surface, the lower surface is densely covered with matted rusty hairs and scales. The stipe is about half or more of the frond length and dark

Cheilanthes myriophylla.

Cheilanthes
newberryi.
(Photo by
Judith Jones)

brown with scales and woolly hairs. The indusium is continuous along the margin. The species occurs at the moist base of igneous rocks in the southwestern United States and northern Mexico.

C. myriophylla
Beaded lip fern
Fronds: 8 to 18 inches long, erect-arching, semievergreen
Rhizome habit: short-creeping
Availability: rare
Hardiness zone: 9
Ease of cultivation: easy

This is a very attractive fern with bright green and very finely divided fronds. The blade is lance-shaped and four times divided with beadlike segments, whose upper surface is smooth or has sparse twisted white hairs, the lower surface being obscured by white to tan scales. It occurs among various types of rock in the mountains from Mexico to Argentina.

C. newberryi (syn. *Notholaena newberryi*)
Cotton fern, Newberry's cloak fern
Fronds: 3 to 8 inches long, erect, deciduous
Rhizome habit: short-creeping
Availability: rare
Hardiness zones: 8 to 9
Ease of cultivation: moderate

The name "cotton fern" is appropriate for this little fern with its stipe and blade clothed with a mass of fine, long, curled, matted hairs, white on the blade's upper surface, tan below. The segments are round and beadlike. It grows among acidic rocks in the mountains of southern California and Baja California.

C. notholaenoides
FRONDS: 10 to 16 inches long, erect, deciduous
RHIZOME HABIT: short- to long-creeping
AVAILABILITY: rare
HARDINESS ZONES: 8 to 10
EASE OF CULTIVATION: easy

The fronds are distinctly and rigidly bipinnate, and often a bluish green color. *Cheilanthes notholaenoides* is native to Texas and Mexico south to Argentina on dry, acidic, or calcareous, rocky slopes.

C. parvifolia (syn. *Notholaena parvifolia*, *Argyrochosma parvifolia*, *Pellaea parvifolia*)
Small-leaved cloak fern
FRONDS: 4 to 10 inches long, arching, deciduous
RHIZOME HABIT: short-creeping
AVAILABILITY: rare
HARDINESS ZONES: 8 to 9
EASE OF CULTIVATION: moderate

This gorgeous and unusual fern has a finely divided, bluish frond with a slightly zigzag rachis. The blade is broadly triangular and three to four times divided, the segments small, numerous, round or oblong, glabrous, and occurring on little stalks. The stipe is one third to one half the frond length. It occurs on limestone ledges and slopes in the southwestern United States and northern Mexico.

C. siliquosa (syn. *Aspidotis densa*)
Indian's dream
FRONDS: 4 to 8 inches long, erect, deciduous
RHIZOME HABIT: short-creeping
AVAILABILITY: rare

Cheilanthes siliquosa.

Cheilanthes
sinuata.

HARDINESS ZONES: 7 to 9

EASE OF CULTIVATION: moderate

The blade is triangular-oblong and bipinnate to tripinnate, and the pinnae are close and overlapping. The segments are long and slender, four to eight times long as wide. The brown glabrous stipe is one half to three quarters the frond length. The sori are continuous along the segment margin. *Cheilanthes siliquosa* is always associated with serpentine rocks in western North America and the Gaspé Peninsula of eastern Canada.

This pleasant little fern forms a tidy bed in a serpentine rock garden, but its requirement of selenium-bearing rock makes its cultivation difficult.

C. sinuata (syn. *Astrolepis sinuata, Notholaena sinuata*)
Wavy cloak fern

FRONDS: 6 to 18 inches long, erect, semi evergreen

RHIZOME HABIT: short-creeping

AVAILABILITY: infrequent

HARDINESS ZONES: 8 to 9

EASE OF CULTIVATION: moderate

The stout stipe is clothed with white scales and comprises only about one eighth the frond length. The blade is linear and pinnate-pinnatifid, the pinnae cutting one third to one half the way from the margin to the midvein, with three to six pairs of lobes per pinna. The upper surface has a few white dissected scales, and the lower surface is covered with brown or white scales. The sporangia follow the veins, immersed in the scales and mostly hidden by them. The species occurs on limestone rocks and slopes from the southwestern United States to southern South America and Hispaniola.

Cheilanthes tomentosa.

Cheilanthes
wrightii.

C. tomentosa
Woolly lip fern
FRONDS: 8 to 14 inches long, erect, deciduous
RHIZOME HABIT: short-creeping
AVAILABILITY: frequent
HARDINESS ZONES: 6 to 8
EASE OF CULTIVATION: easy

The blade is oblong to linear and bipinnate-pinnatifid to tripinnate. The upper surface has white curly hairs, and the lower surface has a dense mat of white, gray, or brown hairs and very narrow scales. The brown stipe is one third to one half the frond length and is covered with tan hairs and narrow scales. The indusium is continuous along the margin. *Cheilanthes tomentosa* occurs among a wide range of rock types, both calcareous and acidic, in the southern United States and northern Mexico.

C. wrightii
Wright's lip fern
FRONDS: 3 to 6 inches long, erect, deciduous
RHIZOME HABIT: short-creeping
AVAILABILITY: rare
HARDINESS ZONES: 8 to 9
EASE OF CULTIVATION: easy

The blade is narrowly oblong, bipinnate, and glabrous. The stipe is chestnut brown and one third to one half the frond length. The sori are small and discontinuous along the margin, protected only by the segment teeth or folded back lobes. The species occurs on igneous rocks and slopes in the southwestern United States and northern Mexico. It grows quickly and easily from spores.

CONIOGRAMME, Bamboo fern

The bamboo ferns are so named for their lance-shaped pinnae that resemble the leaves of bamboo. These are medium-sized ferns with once- to twice-pinnate fronds, the basal pinnae often with large basiscopic pinnules, looking much like a giant *Pteris cretica*. The sporangia are distributed along the veins and lack an indusium. There are about twenty species native to Africa, southern and eastern Asia, and Polynesia.

For more information, see Rush, "Choice Ferns: *Coniogramme*," *Pteridologist* 1 (1984): 40–41.

C. intermedia
FRONDS: 2 to 4 feet long, arching, semievergreen
RHIZOME HABIT: creeping
AVAILABILITY: rare
HARDINESS ZONES: 8 to 10
EASE OF CULTIVATION: moderate
The fronds have five to eight pairs of pinnae and a linear pinna at the tip. The basal pair has two to three pairs of pinnules, and the pinna margins are toothed. This lovely fern is common in the woods of eastern Asia.

C. japonica
FRONDS: 2 to 4 feet long, erect-arching, semievergreen
RHIZOME HABIT: short-creeping
AVAILABILITY: rare
HARDINESS ZONES: 8 to 10
EASE OF CULTIVATION: moderate
The fronds are much like those of *C. intermedia* but with netted veins rather than free veins. This native of the low mountain woods in Japan, China, Korea, and Taiwan needs a sheltered site in our milder regions as the fronds break easily in the wind. It prefers a woodland type of soil or is lovely used as a waterside plant. Some have found it slow to establish, though it is capable of eventually colonizing large areas. There is a variegated form with a yellow band down the center of each pinna.

C. omeiense
FRONDS: 2 to 4 feet long, arching, semievergreen
RHIZOME HABIT: short-creeping
AVAILABILITY: rare
HARDINESS ZONES: 8 to 10
EASE OF CULTIVATION: moderate
This native of China closely resembles *C. intermedia*. It grows well in moist woodland soil.

C. o. var. *lancipinna* is a spectacular fern with a most unusual form of variegation—narrow streaks of white extend from the midvein to the pinna margin.

CRYPTOGRAMMA, Rock brake

The rock brakes are small, glabrous plants with slightly to strongly dimorphic fronds. The rhizomes are compact and creeping or clustered and ascending or erect, and the fronds are pinnate-pinnatifid to quadripinnate. The sori are protected by the recurved margin. The eight or more species are all natives of cliffs and rock outcrops in rocky woodlands to alpine scree habitats. *Cryptogramma* species are all delightful gems for the rock garden but are not easy to keep in cultivation.

C. acrostichoides
Parsley fern, American rock brake
FRONDS: Sterile 3 to 8 inches long, erect, wintergreen, dying back in spring of second year; fertile 4 to 10 inches long, deciduous in autumn after spores are shed
RHIZOME HABIT: ascending
AVAILABILITY: infrequent
HARDINESS ZONES: 2 to 8
EASE OF CULTIVATION: moderate
The clustered fronds are oval-triangular and bipinnate to tripinnate, leathery, and parsleylike. The fertile fronds are taller and have slender segments, with the margin curved over the sori. It occurs in rocky woodlands, open rocky barrens, and alpine slopes of western North America. It can be cultivated

Cryptogramma acrostichoides.

in cool climates with mild winters in rock gardens or trough gardens in strictly acidic conditions.

C. crispa
Parsley fern, Asiatic rock brake
FRONDS: 3 to 8 inches long, erect, deciduous
RHIZOME HABIT: ascending to erect
AVAILABILITY: rare
HARDINESS ZONES: 2 to 8
EASE OF CULTIVATION: difficult

This closely resembles *C. acrostichoides* and differs in having a softer texture, deciduous sterile fronds, and sterile fronds that are often quadripinnate. It grows on strictly acidic formations in Europe.

C. sitchensis
FRONDS: Sterile 3 to 8 inches long, erect, wintergreen; fertile 4 to 10 inches long, erect, deciduous
RHIZOME HABIT: ascending to erect
AVAILABILITY: rare
HARDINESS ZONES: 2 to 8
EASE OF CULTIVATION: difficult

This lacy fern is related to *C. acrostichoides* but is more finely divided and has a broadly triangular, tripinnate to quadripinnate blade. It is a native of Alaska and the Yukon and grows in cool, acidic, rocky situations.

Cryptogramma stelleri.

C. stelleri
Slender cliff brake
FRONDS: 3 to 6 inches long, erect-arching, deciduous
RHIZOME HABIT: creeping
AVAILABILITY: rare
HARDINESS ZONES: 3 to 5
EASE OF CULTIVATION: difficult

The sterile fronds are broadly lance-shaped, pinnate-pinnatifid to barely bipinnate, and thin-textured, whereas the fertile fronds are taller, narrowly lance-shaped, fully bipinnate, and the segments more slender than those of the sterile. *Cryptogramma stelleri* grows on cool, moist, shaded calcareous rock ledges in northern North America and Asia.

This choice delicate plant is very attractive but difficult to get established from spores.

CYATHEA, Tree fern

Nothing is more elegant than the graceful trunk and broadly arching crown of large, lacy leaves of the tree ferns. Unfortunately, they are limited to a few moist, essentially frost-free areas of North America—southern Florida and coastal California. Although the vast majority of its six hundred species occur in the wet tropics, some are found at high elevations in Southeast Asia and Central America and in southern temperate locales that experience occasional frost, and thus may be candidates for further testing in sheltered gardens in North America. In addition to shelter from wind, they also need above average humidity and damp, rich soil. Most species are not difficult to raise from spores, but the spores seem to be short-lived.

The stem is an erect, scaly trunk three to eight inches in diameter. The fronds range from eight to fifteen feet in length, arching from the stem apex, and they are bipinnate to tripinnate. The sori are round and located on the lower blade surface. The indusium surrounds the sorus from below like a sack, or is cup- or saucer-shaped, or is completely lacking.

Another genus of tree ferns, *Dicksonia*, has a stouter trunk, stiffer fronds, long hairs clothing the crown and stipe bases, and sori within clam-shaped indusia along the blade margin.

C. *cooperi* (syn. *Sphaeropteris cooperi*, often misidentified as C. *australis*)

Australian tree fern

FRONDS: to 15 feet long, arching

TRUNK: to 40 feet tall, 6 inches in diameter

AVAILABILITY: common

HARDINESS ZONES: 9 to 10

EASE OF CULTIVATION: moderate

The trunk and stipe have conspicuous whitish scales with chestnut brown spine teeth along the margin. The trunk has oval leaf scars from the fallen fronds. The indusium covers the sorus like a sack, shattering at maturity. This native of Australia is by far the most widely cultivated species of tree fern. It can take light frosts; prolonged frosts may kill the fronds and recovery may be slow. It is the fastest growing of cultivated tree ferns, shooting up one to three feet per year, and in warm, humid climates C. *cooperi* spreads quickly by spores. Introduced to Hawaii, it has become a weed and has taken over parts of the natural forests.

Cyathea cooperi.

The undersurface of the frond of *Cyathea dealbata* has a covering of white wax.

C. dealbata
Silver fern, Ponga
FRONDS: to 15 feet long, arching
TRUNK: to 30 feet tall, 8 inches in diameter
AVAILABILITY: infrequent
HARDINESS ZONES: 9 and 10
EASE OF CULTIVATION: moderate

This is one of the most dramatic of the tree ferns, the fronds having a pure white undersurface. This native of New Zealand is one of the national symbols of that country, along with the kiwi. The crown and stipe bases are clothed with lustrous, dark brown scales, and the indusium surrounds the sorus when young, at maturity appearing as a cup.

C. fulva
FRONDS: to 15 feet long, arching
TRUNK: to 40 feet tall, 8 inches in diameter
AVAILABILITY: rare
HARDINESS ZONES: 9 and 10
EASE OF CULTIVATION: moderate

The crown and stipe bases are covered with chestnut brown scales. The indusium encloses the sorus in a sacklike manner, shattering at maturity. *Cyathea fulva* occurs in wet forests to over ten thousand feet elevation from Mexico to Colombia, and it should be tested in areas of light frost in the southern United States and coastal California.

Cyathea medullaris.

Cyathea princeps.

C. medullaris
Black tree fern
FRONDS: to 15 feet long, arching
TRUNK: to 60 feet tall in the wild, 8 inches in diameter
AVAILABILITY: infrequent
HARDINESS ZONES: 9 and 10
EASE OF CULTIVATION: moderate

This tall tree fern has a black trunk and characteristic hexagonal leaf scars from the fallen leaves. The black stipes are clothed with scales with spiny margins, and the indusium surrounds the sorus, splitting irregularly. *Cyathea medullaris* is native to New Zealand.

C. princeps
FRONDS: 6 to 8 feet long, arching, deciduous
TRUNK: to 60 feet tall in the wild, 12 inches in diameter
AVAILABILITY: rare
HARDINESS ZONES: 9 to 10
EASE OF CULTIVATION: moderate

This magnificent tree fern is native to Mexico and Central America. It is a close relative of the Australian tree fern (*C. cooperi*), resembling it in the dense stipe and rachis covering of pale, toothed scales, the delicate indusia surrounding the sorus, and the rapid growth of the trunk (often one to two feet per year in optimal conditions).

It has been grown out-of-doors in central England but with some protection.

CYRTOMIUM, Holly fern

The holly fern gets its name from its beautiful, leathery, hollylike pinnae. It has a stout ascending rhizome with large tan scales. The fronds are arranged in a circle, medium-sized, once-pinnate, with often auricled pinnae tapering to a point. The veins are netted and the sori are round with a round, centrally attached indusium. There are twelve species in eastern Asia. *Cyrtomium falcatum* has become naturalized in the southern United States, and some species are hardy in protected areas north to Massachusetts. They thrive in shaded, rich soil. Especially important for their survival is good drainage so the plants do not get too wet and rot during the winter.

    Cyrtomium is closely related to *Polystichum*; both have umbrella-shaped indusia and leathery blade texture, but *Cyrtomium* has broader pinnae and netted veins.

C. *caryotideum*
FRONDS: 1 to 2½ feet long, arching, evergreen
RHIZOME HABIT: erect crown
AVAILABILITY: frequent
HARDINESS ZONES: 6 to 10
EASE OF CULTIVATION: easy

This bold, handsome fern has larger and fewer pinnae than does the more familiar *C. falcatum*. The fronds are a beautiful pale gray-green, not as glossy as *C. falcatum*, and have three to six pairs of large pinnae, a large terminal pinna with toothed margins, and a prominent auricle sticking up from the base of each pinna. This Asian beauty is native to Japan, China, India, and Hawaii.

C. *falcatum*
Japanese holly fern
FRONDS: 1 to 2½ feet long, arching, semievergreen
RHIZOME HABIT: erect crown
AVAILABILITY: common
HARDINESS ZONES: 6 to 10
EASE OF CULTIVATION: easy

The Japanese holly fern has a beautiful and distinctive shape, its few fronds forming a vaselike crown. The fronds are four to seven inches wide and a

Cyrtomium caryotideum.

Cyrtomium falcatum.

Cyrtomium falcatum sori. (PHOTO BY F. GORDON FOSTER)

beautiful glossy dark green with four to ten pairs of pinnae, which are usually auricled. The pinnae usually have a coarsely toothed margin like that of holly. *Cyrtomium falcatum* is grown extensively in the southern and southwestern parts of the United States, becoming locally naturalized in those areas, and is hardy north to New York. As the common name implies, it is a native of Japan, and is also found naturally in Korea, Taiwan, China, Malaysia, India, eastern and southern Africa, and Hawaii. The leathery, glossy foliage makes it tolerant of dry atmospheres and it is commonly grown as a houseplant. It does well north to zone 6, and is borderline in zone 5. We had it for several years, hanging on to life, but not developing to its potential in our New York garden, and it eventually died during a moderate winter. A protected location might have enabled it to survive longer. The addition of commercial fertilizer at half the usual dosage improves its color and growth. It is a moderate to rapid grower when it is happy. Fronds of some plants have a sort of hammered finish, while others are smooth and glossy.

There are several forms in cultivation:

C. f. 'Butterfieldii', with deeply serrated margins.

C. f. 'Mayi'. The tips of the pinnae are crested, and the tip of the frond is often forked and crested.

C. f. 'Rochfordianum'. The margins are coarsely fringed. This is the variety most widely sold as holly fern.

C. fortunei

FRONDS: 1½ to 2½ feet long, erect, semievergreen
RHIZOME HABIT: erect crown
AVAILABILITY: common
HARDINESS ZONES: 5 to 10
EASE OF CULTIVATION: easy

This is our hardiest species of *Cyrtomium*. The blade is dull green, not as lustrous or dark green or leathery as in *C. falcatum*. It makes a handsome plant nevertheless. There are twelve to twenty-six pairs of pinnae and the pinna apex has minute, sharply pointed teeth. The unrolling crosiers are especially striking with their pale pea green pinnae and scattered black scales on the stipe and rachis.

Cyrtomium fortunei is native to Japan, Korea and China. It has also escaped and become naturalized in the United States north to South Carolina. It is hardier than *C. falcatum* and has been cultivated out-of-doors in New York and Massachusetts. *Cyrtomium fortunei* can be distinguished from *C. falcatum* by the greater number of pinnae which are paler green, duller, and with fewer teeth on the margin and no auricles on the pinnae.

C. f. var. *intermedia* has fewer pinnae (ten to twelve pairs) than the typical variety. The pinnae are more lance-shaped, more rounded at the base, and do not curve upward toward the frond tip.

Cyrtomium fortunei.

Cyrtomium lonchitoides. (PHOTO BY JUDITH JONES)

Cyrtomium macrophyllum.

C. lonchitoides

FRONDS: 12 to 15 inches long, erect, evergreen
RHIZOME HABIT: compact
AVAILABILITY: infrequent
HARDINESS ZONES: 6 to 9
EASE OF CULTIVATION: easy

This species resembles *C. fortunei* but has broader pinnae with wavy margins. It is a native of China.

C. macrophyllum

Large-leaved holly fern
FRONDS: 1 to 2½ feet long, arching, semievergreen
RHIZOME HABIT: compact
AVAILABILITY: frequent
HARDINESS ZONES: 6 to 10
EASE OF CULTIVATION: easy

Cyrtomium macrophyllum fronds have two to eight pairs of pinnae which are yellowish green in color with a large terminal leaflet. The pinnae are smooth-margined and without an auricle. This species is native to Japan, Taiwan, China, and the Himalayas.

CYSTOPTERIS, Fragile fern, Bladder fern

The small, delicate fragile ferns deserve a place in the rock garden or at the front of the border. The rhizome is short- to long-creeping. The stipes are extremely brittle and easily broken, but they are soon replaced. The blades are bipinnate to tripinnate-pinnatifid and of a light green color. The sori are small and round on the lower surface, protected by an indusium arising, hoodlike, from the base of the sorus. The genus has about twenty species, all deciduous, of temperate regions of the world. Some species have little bulblets, looking like green peas, which drop off to produce new plants.

Recent detailed work showed that the widespread *C. fragilis* in North America is actually a complex of several species and their sterile and fertile hybrids.

Several species of *Cystopteris* are extremely useful in the garden. In spite of their fragile nature, the rhizomes grow well in a variety of soils and send out new fronds all through the growing season. They give a light touch to the garden. Fragile ferns are among the earliest ferns up in the spring, although the crosiers are so small they can easily go unnoticed. They do best in a loose, rich, moist soil.

C. bulbifera

Bulblet bladder fern, Berry fern

FRONDS: 1½ to 3 feet long, arching, deciduous

RHIZOME HABIT: short-creeping

AVAILABILITY: common

HARDINESS ZONES: 3 to 8

EASE OF CULTIVATION: easy

The blade is bipinnate-pinnatifid and very narrowly triangular, the basal pinnae are the longest. Round pealike bulblets are produced on the lower surface of the frond along the rachis and pinna midribs. These fall off readily and quickly germinate into plantlets. *Cystopteris bulbifera* is usually found on or among wet limestone rocks in the northeastern to midwestern United States and southern Canada, and the southwestern United States.

This distinct species hybridizes with *C. fragilis* to form *C. laurentiana* (page 157), and with *C. protrusa* to form *C. tennesseensis* (page 161). Both hybrids are fertile and have at least a few scaly bulblets, and blades that are broadest at the base.

The bulblet bladder fern is easily grown. It does not need limestone or especially wet conditions to flourish. The bulblets fall in profusion and quickly result in a nice patch of yellow-green fronds.

C. b. var. *crispa* is distinguished from the typical *C. bulbifera* by the smaller fronds (six to fourteen inches) and wavy margin. It was discovered in the wild near Falls Village, Connecticut, and is easily cultivated, especially among limestone rocks.

Cystopteris bulbifera.

Cystopteris bulbifera var. *crispa.*

Cystopteris fragilis.

C. fragilis

Fragile fern, Brittle bladder fern

FRONDS: 5 to 16 inches long, erect-arching, deciduous

RHIZOME HABIT: compact

AVAILABILITY: frequent

HARDINESS ZONES: 2 to 9

EASE OF CULTIVATION: easy

The rhizome is compact, with its tip not projecting noticeably beyond the stipe bases. The blade is lance-shaped and bipinnate-pinnatifid. It occurs on moist woods and cliffs in much of northern and western North America and Europe. It is easy to grow and adaptable for general garden use but appreciates some lime.

Plants from Scotland with overlapping pinnae are sometimes considered a distinct species, *C. dickieana*, which is sometimes cultivated.

Cystopteris fragilis crosses with *C. montana* in Europe to form *C. × alpina.*

C. laurentiana

St. Lawrence bladder fern

FRONDS: 6 to 18 inches long, erect-arching, deciduous

RHIZOME HABIT: short-creeping

AVAILABILITY: rare

HARDINESS ZONES: 2 to 4

EASE OF CULTIVATION: easy

This is the fertile hybrid between *C. bulbifera* and *C. fragilis*. The blade is oval or lance-shaped as in *C. fragilis* but has bulblets on the lower surface, although they are smaller and fewer than those of *C. bulbifera* and irregular in size and shape. This species is found on ledges and cliffs, often calcareous, in the Northeast, west to Wisconsin.

C. montana
Mountain fragile fern
FRONDS: 6 to 18 inches long, erect-arching, deciduous
RHIZOME HABIT: long-creeping
AVAILABILITY: rare
HARDINESS ZONES: 2 to 4
EASE OF CULTIVATION: moderate

Cystopteris montana looks much like *Gymnocarpium dryopteris* with its broadly triangular blade and long-creeping rhizome with the stipe one half to three quarters the frond length, and the fronds one to two inches apart. The blade is tripinnate-pinnatifid at the base, the basal pinnae nearly as large as the rest of the blade above. The basal pinnae have their basiscopic pinnules longer than the acroscopic ones. *Cystopteris montana* occurs in wet woods, rocks, and meadows, rarely in northern North America (mostly Canada to Alaska), more frequently in northern Europe and Asia.

It is a choice plant but is rare and difficult to acquire.

C. protrusa
Woodland fragile fern, Southern fragile fern
FRONDS: 6 to 18 inches long, erect, deciduous
RHIZOME HABIT: short-creeping
AVAILABILITY: infrequent
HARDINESS ZONES: 5 to 9
EASE OF CULTIVATION: easy

This fern closely resembles *C. fragilis* but grows on soil rather than limestone rocks and its rhizome is more creeping, with the growing tip protruding well beyond the fronds. It is a strong grower, the rhizome branching abundantly to form colonies that are easily divided. It often turns brown in midsummer but sends up new fronds that last until frost. It occurs in moist woodlands

Cystopteris protrusa.

over much of the eastern United States, but it is more common in the southeastern states.

C. reevesiana (syn. C. fragilis var. tenuifolia)
Southwestern fragile fern
FRONDS: 8 to 18 inches long, erect-arching, deciduous
RHIZOME HABIT: short-creeping
AVAILABILITY: rare
HARDINESS ZONES: 5 to 10
EASE OF CULTIVATION: easy
This recently described species is similar to *C. fragilis* and *C. protrusa* but the blade is broadly triangular and the rhizome apex does not extend far beyond the stipe bases. The fronds are lance-shaped and bipinnate pinnatifid to tripinnate-pinnatifid, with a dark stipe. It grows very well in New York gardens. It is found on soil or on a variety of rock types from southern Utah and Colorado to Texas and Mexico.

C. tennesseensis
Tennessee bladder fern
FRONDS: 6 to 18 inches long, arching, deciduous
RHIZOME HABIT: short-creeping
AVAILABILITY: rare
HARDINESS ZONES: 5 to 8
EASE OF CULTIVATION: easy
This very light green plant is the hybrid between *C. bulbifera* and *C. protrusa*. It looks like a short version of *C. bulbifera*. It is broadest at the blade base like that species but the buds are smaller and fewer. It occurs on limestone ledges and cliffs, but also on the mortar of old walls and bridge foundations

Cystopteris tennesseensis.

in the southeastern United States. *Cystopteris tennesseensis* makes a great garden plant. It is a delightful pale green, and makes enough offspring from the buds that there are soon additional plants.

C. tenuis (syn. *Cystopteris fragilis* var. *mackayi*)
Slender fragile fern
FRONDS: 5 to 16 inches long, erect-arching, deciduous
RHIZOME HABIT: short-creeping
AVAILABILITY: rare
HARDINESS ZONES: 4 to 8
EASE OF CULTIVATION: easy
The pinnae are at times held upward at an angle toward the blade apex and *C. tenuis* is usually larger than *C. fragilis* but is often difficult to distinguish from it. That species occurs mostly on cliffs, whereas *C. tenuis* grows usually on rocks and soil. It occurs primarily in northeastern North America, but also in a few locations in the western states.

DENNSTAEDTIA, Cup fern

In spite of their running habit, the dennstaedtias can be used to good advantage in many garden situations. The medium-sized, soft, feathery fronds bear sori along the margin in minute cuplike structures. The genus is composed of about fifty species found mostly in tropical wet forests, but a few are found in temperate regions—one in eastern North America and two in Japan. The tropical species are much larger than the temperate ones, with the fronds reaching nine feet in length.

Forming large colonies, these lacy-looking ferns have great appeal because of their attractively divided fronds. They need plenty of room and are good for estates and municipal gardens because they require little maintenance. *Dennstaedtia* prefers well-drained, slightly acid loam.

D. davallioides
Lacy ground fern
FRONDS: 2 to 4 feet long, erect-arching, semievergreen
RHIZOME HABIT: long-creeping
AVAILABILITY: rare

HARDINESS ZONES: 9 to 10

EASE OF CULTIVATION: easy

The lacy ground fern, a native of Australia, has very delicately cut fronds which are triangular, medium green, and tripinnate. The rachis and veins have scattered whitish hairs. This wide-ranging fern is easy to control and requires little care. It likes shady conditions and will not take extended periods in the sun.

D. hirsuta (syn. *Microlepia hirsuta, M. pilosella*)

FRONDS: 7 to 18 inches long, erect-arching, deciduous

RHIZOME HABIT: short-creeping

AVAILABILITY: rare

HARDINESS ZONES: 6 to 8

EASE OF CULTIVATION: easy

The leaves of *D. hirsuta* have a triangular to lance-shaped blade which is pinnate-pinnatifid and soft and hairy all over. It is native to Japan, China, Korea, and Manchuria and should do beautifully in North America but is not yet cultivated here.

D. punctilobula

Hay-scented fern, Boulder fern

FRONDS: 15 to 30 inches long, erect-arching, deciduous

RHIZOME HABIT: long-creeping

AVAILABILITY: common

HARDINESS ZONES: 3 to 8

EASE OF CULTIVATION: easy

This common North American fern has beautiful, hairy fronds which are bipinnate to bipinnate-pinnatifid, oval-oblong in outline, yellow-green in color, and thin-textured. The stipe is one quarter to one third the frond length and shining red-brown shading to brown, and the sori are cylindrical in shape. *Dennstaedtia punctilobula* is found in open, sandy meadows or thinly wooded slopes. It tends to spread too rapidly for use in smaller gardens but is attractive and carefree in large gardens where there is plenty of room for it to spread. It goes beautifully with large rocks, softening their harsh lines and filling in vacant spaces, and filling in areas that might otherwise be difficult to manage. Though it is delicate-looking, the hay-scented fern is able to thrive in light shade or open sun and spreads rapidly by means of its slender, branching, underground rhizome and can survive, once established, in fairly dry soil.

Dennstaedtia punctilobula. (PHOTO BY F. GORDON FOSTER)

Here you can see the hairs on the rachis of *Dennstaedtia punctilobula.* (PHOTO BY BARBARA HALLOWELL)

This species grows so readily that it is one of the few North American ferns that rarely is on a list of protected species. I have not found its rapid growth a problem. The haylike smell is evident when fresh fronds are brushed, coming from gland-tipped whitish hairs which cover the fern. Being a strong grower, the hay-scented fern is very useful in the right situation. It is very adaptable to all soil conditions and can be grown in barren, strongly to moderately acid soil and also in fairly dry situations. In the fall it turns a soft yellow color.

D. wilfordii
FRONDS: 6 to 18 inches long, erect, deciduous
RHIZOME HABIT: creeping
AVAILABILITY: rare
HARDINESS ZONES: 6 to 8
EASE OF CULTIVATION: easy

This attractive and distinctive *Dennstaedtia* has the sterile frond smaller than the fertile one; both are glabrous, lance-shaped and very narrow, only one to three inches wide with the pinna tips being slender and attenuate. Although not yet cultivated in North America, this native from Japan, Korea, China, and Manchuria could be very useful since it is such a strong grower.

Dennstaedtia wilfordii resembles *Cystopteris protrusa* since both have small, delicate, naked fronds and wide-creeping rhizomes, but differs from it in the cuplike sori along the blade margin.

DICKSONIA, Tree fern

These spectacular tree ferns have stout, erect, woody trunks, the stem itself being only three to four inches in diameter but bearing a mantle of roots that expand the overall trunk diameter to eight to twenty-eight or more inches. The trunk apex and the frond bases are clothed with long, dark golden or reddish brown hairs. The fronds are large, and the stipe hairy. The blade is bipinnate-pinnatifid to tripinnate and stiff, with sparse hairs. The sori are located in clamlike indusia along the margin of the blade.

The twenty-five species of the genus occur mostly in the temperate South Pacific, although a few are found in high-elevation tropical America, and is grown in southern and western England and Scotland and coastal Ireland where there are fewer than twenty frosts a year along with high rainfall and humidity. There is an outstanding display of these and other tree ferns at Golden Gate Park in San Francisco. Dicksonias should be tested in gardens farther north with some extra winter protection; it would be well worth experimenting to determine the climatic limits of these magnificent specimens in cultivation. They are slow growers but do well if they have high humidity and rich, moist soil. They can tolerate some sun if they have consistent soil moisture. The young roots are produced in the crown and must grow down the trunk, so drought greatly impedes growth. In hot weather daily spraying of the trunk with water is beneficial to encourage root development.

D. antarctica
Soft tree fern, Tasmanian tree fern
FRONDS: 6 to 8 feet long, arching crown, evergreen
TRUNK: 10 to 30 feet tall, 12 to 28 inches in diameter, including root
    mantle

Dennstaedtia punctilobula sori. (PHOTO BY F. GORDON FOSTER)

Dicksonia antarctica grove at Logan, Scotland. (PHOTO BY JUDITH JONES)

AVAILABILITY: frequent
HARDINESS ZONES: 9 to 10
EASE OF CULTIVATION: moderate

The fronds of this stately tree fern have short, brown to yellow stipes with hairs one to two inches long. The pinnae are smaller toward the base of the blade, with hairs scattered on the lower sides of the axes. The fronds are soft to the grasp, and old fronds are persistent, making a skirt on the trunk.

A native of Australia and Tasmania, *D. antarctica* is a majestic, popularly cultivated tree fern, especially in coastal California. Older specimens can be transplanted easily.

D. fibrosa

FRONDS: 3 to 5 feet long, arching, evergreen
TRUNK: 6 to 20 feet tall, 10 to 12 inches in diameter, including root
    mantle
AVAILABILITY: frequent
HARDINESS ZONES: 8 to 10
EASE OF CULTIVATION: moderate

This species is very similar to *D. antarctica* except that *D. fibrosa* has stiffer, more erect fronds (the fronds are harsh and prickly to the grasp), and the trunk is more slender.

This attractive tree fern from New Zealand has a large arching crown of dark green, leathery fronds. It is very adaptable, easily grown, and likes cool, moist conditions. With protection it has survived harsh winters in Seattle.

D. squarrosa

FRONDS: 4 to 6 feet long, arching, evergreen
TRUNK: 6 to 12 feet tall, 3 to 8 inches in diameter, including root
    mantle
AVAILABILITY: rare
HARDINESS ZONES: 9 to 10
EASE OF CULTIVATION: moderate

This species is distinct in having a very slender trunk. The stipes are dark, comprise one third the frond length, and are clothed with black hairs. The fronds are harsh and prickly to the grasp, and old fronds fall from the crown. Established plants produce underground rhizomes that send up additional trunks.

DIPLAZIUM

Closely related to *Athyrium*, *Diplazium* is distinct from it by being largely tropical and having at least some of the sori, which are elongate along the veins, back to back on the same vein. The rhizome is short-creeping to erect, and the fronds are medium-sized to large with an undivided to tripinnate blade. The leaves are thin to leathery and naked to short-pubescent, sometimes scaly.

Diplazium is a genus of about four hundred species native to wet tropical forests of low to medium elevation. Only a few species occur in temperate regions, and some tropical species may be used in moist, shaded gardens in milder, humid parts of North America.

D. australe
FRONDS: 3 to 4 feet long, erect-arching, deciduous
RHIZOME HABIT: erect
AVAILABILITY: rare
HARDINESS ZONES: 8 to 10
EASE OF CULTIVATION: easy
This native of Australia and New Zealand has an erect rhizome that eventually becomes a short trunk. The fronds are oval-triangular, bipinnate to tripinnate-pinnatifid, and thin-textured; the segments are about one inch long and one quarter inch wide and have a toothed margin.

D. pycnocarpon (syn. Athyrium pycnocarpon)
Narrow-leaved spleenwort, Glade fern
FRONDS: 1½ to 3½ feet long, sterile erect-arching, fertile erect, deciduous
RHIZOME HABIT: short-creeping
AVAILABILITY: common
HARDINESS ZONES: 4 to 9
EASE OF CULTIVATION: easy
Diplazium pycnocarpon is distinct in its tall, narrow (only six to twelve inches wide), once-pinnate, dimorphic fronds. The sterile fronds are slightly arching and shorter than the taller, erect, fertile fronds. The pinnae are one half inch wide and smooth-margined, while the stipe and rachis are green and naked

Diplazium pycnocarpon sori.

The fertile and vegetative fronds of
Diplazium pycnocarpon.

or only sparsely hairy. The fertile fronds appear late in the summer, with the sori long and straight in a herringbone pattern that nearly covers the lower surface of the frond. It is frequently found in moist woodlands in eastern North America.

The glade fern is easy to grow and does well in shade and moist, rich soil, the short-creeping rhizome branching frequently to make it readily divisible.

D. sibiricum (syn. Athyrium crenatum)

FRONDS: 1 to 1½ feet long, arching, deciduous
RHIZOME HABIT: creeping
AVAILABILITY: rare
HARDINESS ZONES: 5 to 8
EASE OF CULTIVATION: easy

This *Diplazium* has a stipe half the frond length, with brown scales; the frond has a triangular blade which is bipinnate-pinnatifid to tripinnate with the lower pinnae turned down and forward. The plant has no scales or hairs and is native to Siberia, China, Manchuria, Korea, and Japan.

D. subsinuatum (syn. D. lanceum)

FRONDS: 4 to 18 inches long, erect, evergreen
RHIZOME HABIT: short-creeping
AVAILABILITY: rare
HARDINESS ZONES: 9 to 10
EASE OF CULTIVATION: easy

This delightful small *Diplazium* forms slowly arching clumps. The fronds

Diplazium tomitaroanum.

are dark green, about one inch apart and one half to one inch wide, undivided, and narrowly lance-shaped with smooth margins and no scales or hairs.

A native of Japan, Taiwan, China, Korea, and northern India, this fern is well-suited to planting in a small pot or the rock garden. It likes shade and rich soil.

Diplazium subsinuatum is similar to *D. tomitaroanum* but the fronds of the former have unlobed margins.

D. tomitaroanum (syn. *D. lanceum* var. *crenatum*, *D. subsinuatum* var. *crenatum*)

FRONDS: 6 to 16 inches long, erect, evergreen
RHIZOME HABIT: short-creeping
AVAILABILITY: rare
HARDINESS ZONES: 9 to 10
EASE OF CULTIVATION: easy

This dwarf fern which likes a pocket in the rock garden has very compact growth. The small fronds are produced closely together, giving a matted appearance. The blade has deep round lobes. It is slow-growing and good for containers. Some unusual cultivars are grown in Japan and China.

DOODIA MEDIA, Common rasp fern

FRONDS: 8 to 12 inches, erect, evergreen
RHIZOME HABIT: short-creeping

Doodia media.

AVAILABILITY: infrequent
HARDINESS ZONES: 8 to 10
EASE OF CULTIVATION: moderate

This relative of *Woodwardia* is small in size. The fronds are erect, pinnatifid, and leathery, with a coarse, firm, prickly texture, and are usually pink-tinged when young. The veins are netted and the sori occur slightly away from the midvein in a broken chain.

Native to Australia, New Zealand, and New Caledonia, *D. media* is easy to grow and adaptable in cultivation. This delightful little fern grows in arching clumps by way of underground runners. It is ideal as a ground cover or in shaded rock gardens with rich, acidic soil. It will tolerate some sun if it has consistent soil moisture, and is easily propagated by division.

DRYOPTERIS, Wood fern, Shield fern, Buckler fern

The wood ferns have presented us with more species for the garden than any other fern genus. The rhizome is stout, either short-creeping or as an erect crown, and conspicuously scaly. The scales, especially dense on the fiddleheads and on the stipe bases of mature fronds, are tan, gold, black, or brown. Many species are striking for their vase-shaped arrangement of fronds. The fronds are usually medium-sized and erect or arching, and many species are evergreen. The sori are round with a kidney-shaped indusium.

Dryopteris contains 225 species, occurring in moist, shady woodlands or swamps of temperate regions around the world. The genus is especially well represented in eastern Asia and the Himalayas.

Most *Dryopteris* species are called wood ferns, shield ferns, or, in England, buckler ferns. In this book I will use "wood fern" to avoid confusion with *Polystichum* species, some of which are also called shield ferns. The "shield" and "buckler" refer to the shape of the indusium—kidney-shaped in *Dryopteris*, round and centrally attached in *Polystichum*—which are reminiscent of a warrior's shield.

Hybridization is common among the dryopterises in the wild. In some cases the progeny become fertile and act as distinct species. In North America north of Mexico there are only nine basic species, but these have given rise to six fertile hybrids and twenty-seven sterile hybrids. To show the intermediacy of characteristics in the hybrids, the New York Botanical Garden's hardy fern collection has representatives of the North American *Dryopteris* hybrids planted between the parental species. Because many are sterile, the availability of the hybrids is limited to finding them in the wild or dividing garden plants. Some of the better ones are prime candidates for propagation by tissue culture.

Many species of *Dryopteris* have special garden merit and several species have given rise to an impressive number of beautiful varieties. All of the dryopterises are more or less strong-growing, sturdy plants with few problems in the garden. They prefer moist, rich, well-drained woodland soil. Although a few species naturally occur in swamps, they do not require such wet habitats to do well in the garden. The great variability in size, from five inches to five feet, makes it easy to find the right *Dryopteris* for every garden.

D. aemula

Hay-scented wood fern
FRONDS: 6 to 24 inches long, arching, semievergreen
RHIZOME HABIT: compact crown
AVAILABILITY: infrequent
HARDINESS ZONES: 6 to 8
EASE OF CULTIVATION: easy

This fern's name comes from the scent of new-mown hay given off when old fronds are crushed. This is caused by the presence of minute glands present on both blade surfaces. The fronds, which have distinctly drooping tips and are a bright green color, reach two feet in height. The triangular, bipinnate blade has the lowest pinnae enlarged basiscopically, with drooping frond tips and pinnules turning up, giving a distinctive crimped frond texture, and having lance-shaped brownish scales below. The stipe is as long as the blade and is dark purplish brown with a matte finish at the base, grading to green higher up. This fern prefers high year-round humidity and should be grown in a well-drained situation in rocky woodlands or rock gardens.

It is slow-growing and needs a long growing season, which confines it in nature to oceanic areas, such as its native Scotland to northern Spain and the Azores.

D. affinis (syn. D. borreri, D. pseudomas)

Golden-scaled male fern, Scaly male fern

FRONDS: 2 to 3 feet (to 5 feet) long, erect, semievergreen

RHIZOME HABIT: erect crown

AVAILABILITY: common

HARDINESS ZONES: 4 to 8

EASE OF CULTIVATION: easy

The fronds may reach five feet in the wild. Stipes and rachises are shaggy with golden brown scales. The blade is lance-shaped, pinnate-pinnatifid, and leathery, with a lustrous surface. *Dryopteris affinis* is similar to *D. filix-mas* in its form and dissection, but is distinguished by its stipe scales and more leathery blade texture, with a small dark spot at the base of each pinna at the junction of the rachis on the lower surface. There are five structural forms ("morphotypes") of this species in England, differing in details of blade shape, segment teeth, and indusium form. *Dryopteris affinis* occurs on acid to calcareous soils throughout Europe and Asia.

Dryopteris affinis is one of the great ferns for the garden. Not only is it easy to grow, but it is highly adaptable. It does well in the shaded garden with other ferns, but also can tolerate a considerable amount of sun. The plants make multiple crowns, which can and should be separated. It is apogamous (the prothalli developing directly into plants without fertilization) as are its

Dryopteris affinis crosiers.

Dryopteris affinis 'Crispa Gracilis'.

Dryopteris affinis 'Cristata'.

hybrids, so they are readily propagated by spores, and all its varieties come true. There are many cultivated forms, with unbelievable variation, ranging in size from six inches to four feet in height, with many degrees and forms of cresting.

D. a. 'Congesta Cristata'. Very small with congested crested fronds six to nine inches tall.

D. a. 'Crispa Gracilis' is a striking congested dwarf form.

D. a. 'Cristata', also called 'The King'. This handsome and spectacular plant is the most popular form of *D. affinis*. The gracefully arching fronds are two to four feet tall and about six inches wide, with a fine terminal crest and tightly crested pinna tips.

D. a. 'Cristata Angustata' is similar to 'The King' but narrower, two to three inches wide, one and one half to two feet tall.

D. a. 'Grandiceps' has a heavy terminal crest.

D. a. 'Polydactyla' is similar to 'The King' but is a little broader in form and the crests occur in long fingerlike tassels rather than wide fans.

D. a. 'Revolvens' has the blade margins curving downward. The fronds are three feet tall.

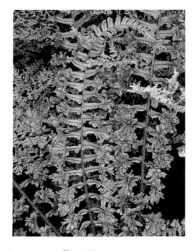

Dryopteris affinis 'Polydactyla'.

Dryopteris affinis 'Cristata Angustata'.

Dryopteris affinis 'Grandiceps'.

D. a. 'Stableri' is a distinct, three-foot-tall, erect variety with short pinnae and narrow fronds. It closely resembles *D. filix-mas* 'Barnesii' but differs in the pinnules being squared and not oval and minutely toothed.

D. a. 'Stableri Crisped' differs from the preceding in having a wavy margin.

D. amurensis
Amur wood fern
FRONDS: 1 to 2 feet long, erect, evergreen
RHIZOME HABIT: short-creeping
AVAILABILITY: rare
HARDINESS ZONES: 4 to 8
EASE OF CULTIVATION: easy

The delicate, pentagonal, much-dissected fronds are similar to those of a small *D. dilatata*, including the very long basal basiscopic pinnules. This rare wood fern occurs in coniferous woods in Japan and eastern Russia. It needs consistent moisture to grow well.

D. arguta
Western wood fern, Coastal wood fern, California wood fern
FRONDS: 1 to 3 feet long, erect-arching, evergreen
RHIZOME HABIT: short-creeping
AVAILABILITY: rare
HARDINESS ZONES: 8 to 9
EASE OF CULTIVATION: easy

Dryopteris arguta.

Dryopteris affinis 'Stableri'.

The scales of the rhizome and stipe are light brown. The blade is lance-shaped, with a short stipe, one quarter to one third the frond length. The leathery blade is pinnate-pinnatifid, the pinnules tapering toward the tip, with fine, arching teeth. It occurs on sparsely wooded slopes from southern California to southern British Columbia.

D. × *australis* (= *D. celsa* × *ludoviciana*)
Dixie wood fern
FRONDS: 4 to 5 feet long, erect, semievergreen
RHIZOME HABIT: short-creeping
AVAILABILITY: rare
HARDINESS ZONES: 5 to 9
EASE OF CULTIVATION: easy

Dryopteris × *australis* is one of the great ferns for the garden. It is four to five feet tall, fairly slender, and a lustrous dark green. The fertile terminal quarter of the frond has slightly smaller segments than does the strictly vegetative lower part of the frond, but is not as distinctly different from the vegetative parts as in *D. ludoviciana*. Although *D.* × *australis* produces sporangia, the spores are abortive. Since only rarely will a plant develop from the sowing of spores, this is one of my candidates for tissue culture propagation. The short-creeping rhizome branches frequently enough to permit regular division. This sterile hybrid is found in scattered populations from Louisiana to Virginia, but it is fully hardy and a strong grower in New York.

Dryopteris ×
australis.

Dryopteris × *australis*, close-up.

D. bissetiana (syn. D. varia var. setosa)
Beaded wood fern
FRONDS: 1 to 2 feet long, arching, evergreen
RHIZOME HABIT: short-creeping
AVAILABILITY: frequent
HARDINESS ZONES: 5 to 8
EASE OF CULTIVATION: easy

Dryopteris bissetiana is one of the most delightful of the *Dryopteris* species. The small, rounded, leathery segments give a distinct beaded appearance to the frond. The plant remains green all winter but is one of the latest to send up new fronds, which emerge in early summer. The spores are not produced until fall. The rhizome is stout, and the fronds are triangular and bipinnate-pinnatifid. The first basiscopic pinnule of the basal pinna is enlarged. A mixture of narrow blackish scales and small tan scales gives a mottled appearance to the stipe and rachis. The rounded, oblong segments are somewhat curved and have one sorus per segment. The beaded wood fern occurs on moist, wooded slopes in Japan, Korea, and China.

D. × boottii (= D. cristata × intermedia)
Boott's wood fern
FRONDS: 1½ to 3 feet long, erect, deciduous
RHIZOME HABIT: short-creeping
AVAILABILITY: frequent
HARDINESS ZONES: 3 to 7
EASE OF CULTIVATION: easy

This sterile hybrid is intermediate in cutting and form between its parents, and has the distinctive minute glandular hairs of *D. intermedia*. The tall, narrow fronds have the "open venetian-blind" pinnae of *D. cristata*, but are more deeply cut than those of that species. This is a common hybrid where the parents are found growing together in eastern North America.

Dryopteris × boottii makes a fine garden plant and is occasionally offered for sale. The short-creeping rhizome is easily divided.

D. campyloptera
Mountain wood fern, Spreading wood fern
FRONDS: 2 to 3 feet long, erect-arching, deciduous
RHIZOME HABIT: short-creeping

Dryopteris bissetiana.   *Dryopteris* × *boottii.*   *Dryopteris campyloptera.*

AVAILABILITY: infrequent
HARDINESS ZONES: 4 to 7
EASE OF CULTIVATION: easy

The mountain wood fern is a magnificent plant with three to four times divided, broadly triangular to pentagonal fronds. One of its outstanding features is the lowest pair of pinnae, with the basiscopic pinnules three to five times as long as the acroscopic pinnules on the same pinna. The scales of the rhizome and stipe are light brown, and the stipe is about one half the frond length. The blade is thin-textured, glabrous, or with some glands. It is a frequent fern of moist, deciduous woods and occurs among rocks the length of the Appalachian Mountains and north to Labrador.

Dryopteris campyloptera is the fertile hybrid of *D. expansa* × *intermedia*. In the garden it is happy even in partial sun.

D. carthusiana (syn. D. spinulosa)

Spinulose wood fern, Toothed wood fern
FRONDS: 1 to 3 feet long, erect-arching, deciduous
RHIZOME HABIT: ascending crown
AVAILABILITY: frequent
HARDINESS ZONES: 2 to 7
EASE OF CULTIVATION: easy

The rhizome and stipe scales are light brown, the blade narrowly oval to triangular and bipinnate-pinnatifid. *Dryopteris carthusiana* has been confused with *D. intermedia* but differs in having several lower pairs of triangular pinnae, deciduous fronds that yellow in the fall, and a totally smooth blade lacking glandular hairs. The spinulose wood fern is common in swamps and wet woods in northern North America, Europe, and Asia.

This species is easy to grow in rich woodland soil and can also succeed in swampy and boggy situations or along streams, either in full shade or partial sun.

Dryopteris carthusiana hybridizes frequently in eastern North America with *D. cristata* to form *D.* × *uliginosa* and with *D. intermedia* to form *D.* × *triploidea*, but, although these are good growers in the garden, they are not distinct enough to merit cultivation other than as collector's items.

D. caucasica

FRONDS: 2 to 3 feet long, erect-arching, deciduous
RHIZOME HABIT: erect crown
AVAILABILITY: rare
HARDINESS ZONES: 5 to 8
EASE OF CULTIVATION: easy

This closely resembles *D. filix-mas* (of which it is one of the parents) but has paler color and its segments are more toothed. This and other Caucasian species should be excellent candidates for temperate gardens.

D. celsa
Log fern

FRONDS: 3 to 4 feet long, erect, semievergreen
RHIZOME HABIT: short-creeping
AVAILABILITY: infrequent
HARDINESS ZONES: 5 to 9
EASE OF CULTIVATION: easy

The log fern is the fertile hybrid between *D. goldiana* and *D. ludoviciana*. The fronds are intermediate in width between its parents, wider than *ludoviciana* but narrower than *goldiana*, and have the shiny blade surface of the former. The blade is pinnate-pinnatifid, oblong, and of firm texture. Rhizome and stipe scales are generally dark, especially in the center, like those of *D. goldiana*. The stipe is about one third the frond length. It occurs on rotting logs and in rich soils in the swamps and wet woods of the southeastern United States, with scattered populations north to Michigan and New York.

I like this in the garden for its rich, dark green color and the long, slender pinna tips. Like most other species of *Dryopteris*, it prefers moist, acid soil.

Dryopteris celsa.

Dryopteris championii.

The hybrids of *D. celsa* with *D. cristata* and *D. goldiana* are rare but excellent garden plants.

D. championii

Champion's wood fern

FRONDS: 1 to 3 feet long, erect-arching, evergreen
RHIZOME HABIT: short-creeping
AVAILABILITY: infrequent
HARDINESS ZONES: 5 to 8
EASE OF CULTIVATION: easy

Dryopteris championii is another of my favorite ferns. It is a strong grower, and remains handsome, neat, dark green, rather glossy, and leathery all through the winter. Whereas nearly all species of *Dryopteris* have fronds that lie down in the winter, this one remains erect and cheery, right through the snow. Apparently to make up for its long winter's work, it sleeps in until early June in New York when the black-scaled crosiers arise. New fronds are a gorgeous apple green, gradually maturing to their typical lustrous dark green.

The blade is bipinnate, broadly oval to triangular. Red-brown scales cover the stipe and rachis. The segments are smooth-margined, mostly with two basal lobes and looking like little daggers; the segment margins curve down slightly. *Dryopteris championii* is native to Japan, Korea, and China.

D. chinensis

FRONDS: 8 to 18 inches long, erect-arching, deciduous
RHIZOME HABIT: short-creeping

AVAILABILITY: rare
HARDINESS ZONES: 5 to 8
EASE OF CULTIVATION: easy

This lovely oriental import has a pentagonal, thin-textured frond that is three times divided. The basiscopic basal pinnules are greatly exaggerated. The stipe, rachis, and costae have scattered brown scales. It occurs in Japan, Korea, China, and Manchuria.

D. clintoniana
Clinton's wood fern
FRONDS: 2 to 4 feet long, erect, semievergreen
RHIZOME HABIT: short-creeping
AVAILABILITY: infrequent
HARDINESS ZONES: 3 to 8
EASE OF CULTIVATION: easy

Clinton's wood fern is another robust *Dryopteris* that is a good plant for the moist, shady garden. The leathery fronds are narrowly oblong and pinnate-pinnatifid. It occurs in swamps and wet woods in northeastern North America.

This handsome species is the fertile hybrid between *D. goldiana* and *D. cristata*. The fronds are much narrower than those of *D. goldiana* and the basal pinnae are broadly triangular, like those of *D. cristata*. The fronds have fewer, but more lance-shaped pinnae that are not as strongly turned to the horizontal as in *D. cristata*.

D. commixta
FRONDS: 1½ to 3 feet long, arching, semievergreen
RHIZOME HABIT: crown
AVAILABILITY: rare
HARDINESS ZONES: 6 to 8
EASE OF CULTIVATION: easy

The blade is rather broad and pinnate-pinnatifid. The ten to fifteen pairs of pinnae are slenderly lance-shaped and shallowly lobed. This fern is native to Japan and related to *D. atrata*.

D. complexa (= D. affinis × filix-mas; syn. D. tavelii)
FRONDS: 2 to 3 feet long, erect-arching, semievergreen
RHIZOME HABIT: erect crown

Dryopteris clintoniana.

Dryopteris complexa.

AVAILABILITY: frequent
HARDINESS ZONES: 4 to 8
EASE OF CULTIVATION: easy

This is intermediate between its parents in frond cutting and texture. It is a handsome, vigorous plant, taking the best characteristics of both parents. It is frequent in Europe and Asia.

D. coreano-montana (syn. D. sichotensis)

FRONDS: 2 to 4 feet long, erect-arching, semievergreen
RHIZOME HABIT: crown
AVAILABILITY: infrequent
HARDINESS ZONES: 5 to 8
EASE OF CULTIVATION: easy

This attractive, pale green fern has a dense covering of glossy scales on the stipe, and the blade is pinnate-pinnatifid to bipinnate. It resembles a large specimen of *D. oreades*. *Dryopteris coreano-montana* occurs in Japan, Korea, and northeastern China.

D. crassirhizoma (syn. D. buschiana)

Thick-stemmed wood fern
FRONDS: 2 to 3½ feet long, erect-arching, semievergreen
RHIZOME HABIT: erect crown
AVAILABILITY: infrequent
HARDINESS ZONES: 5 to 8
EASE OF CULTIVATION: easy

Dryopteris crassirhizoma.

Dryopteris crassirhizoma crosiers.

As the name implies, this handsome fern has a massive crown (four inches across) with abundant brown scales nearly one inch long on the crown and stipe. The fronds are pinnate-pinnatifid, with thirty-five or more pairs of closely set pinnae on very short stipes. The thin-textured blade is broadest above the middle, tapering to the base. The vase-shaped crown of large fronds makes this a good plant for a single specimen focal point in the garden. In the fall the large fronds take the season literally and seem to go down overnight, lying flat on the ground, yet remaining mostly green through the winter. It is widespread in eastern Asia.

D. cristata
Narrow swamp fern, Crested wood fern
FRONDS: 1 to 3 feet long, erect, evergreen
RHIZOME HABIT: short-creeping
AVAILABILITY: frequent
HARDINESS ZONES: 3 to 7
EASE OF CULTIVATION: easy

Dryopteris cristata is a common resident of marshes, bogs, and swamps, often rising above the water from little hummocks. The rhizome and stipe are clothed with light brown scales, and the blade is narrowly oblong and pinnate-pinnatifid. The pinnae are narrowly triangular, being broadest near the rachis, and the basal pinnae are only about one inch long. This species is unique in having the stiffly erect fertile fronds with the pinnae turned at right angles to the plane of the frond, like open venetian blinds. The shorter sterile leaves are evergreen and more arching. It is common in northern and eastern North America, and rare in Europe.

The plant is very distinct but not at all crested. Linnaeus must have had

Dryopteris cristata.

Dryopteris cycadina.

The young bronze foliage of *Dryopteris decipiens.*

a peculiar specimen or was mistaken when he gave this fern its name.

Although in the wild it grows in rather wet places, in the garden it can be planted with other ferns in moist, rich soil. But if you have a stream or pond, *D. cristata* may attain a greater size when planted in the wetter soil.

D. cycadina (*D. atrata* in hort., *D. hirtipes* in hort.)

Black wood fern, Shaggy wood fern

FRONDS: 1½ to 3 feet long, erect, semievergreen

RHIZOME HABIT: short-creeping

AVAILABILITY: common

HARDINESS ZONES: 5 to 8

EASE OF CULTIVATION: easy

The common names derive from the dense covering of slender, black scales on the stipe and rachis. The stiff, leathery fronds are once-pinnate. The pinnae are narrowly lance-shaped, shallowly toothed, and auricled, and the lower pinnae point downward. *Dryopteris atrata* is found in Japan, Taiwan, China, and northern India.

D. decipiens

FRONDS: 1 to 2 feet long, erect-arching, deciduous

RHIZOME HABIT: crown

AVAILABILITY: infrequent

HARDINESS ZONES: 5 to 8

EASE OF CULTIVATION: easy

Dryopteris dilatata. Dryopteris dilatata sori. Dryopteris dilatata 'Recurved Form'.

The colorful young foliage of this once-pinnate wood-fern enlivens the fern garden in the early summer. The fresh bronze pinnae resemble those of *D. erythrosora*, but the frond shape and dissection are more akin to that of a small *D. filix-mas*. The fifteen to eighteen pairs of pinnae are slender and shallowly lobed, with the pinna tips gently curving toward the frond apex. The stipe base is densely clothed with purplish brown scales. The species hails from Japan and China.

D. dilatata (syn. D. austriaca)
Broad wood fern
FRONDS: 2 to 3½ feet long, erect-arching, deciduous
RHIZOME HABIT: crown
AVAILABILITY: common
HARDINESS ZONES: 4 to 8
EASE OF CULTIVATION: easy

The broad wood fern gets its name from its broadly triangular fronds, which are most easily seen in young plants. In more mature plants the blade shape is more broadly lance-shaped or oval. Fronds are two to three times divided, often with the margins turned under, and the basal pinnae are much longer on the basiscopic side. The blade is a deep rich green, almost a blue-green at times, and thin-textured.

This species is quite variable and, depending on age and habitat, the fronds may reach a length of four or even five feet in the wild in Europe and Asia. It does best in acidic deciduous or coniferous woodland soil with lots of organic matter, but it is very adaptable and a vigorous grower.

Lowe (1890) listed thirty-seven varieties but there are few today.

D. d. 'Crispa Whiteside' is somewhat lighter in color than the species and has crisped foliage.

D. d. 'Cristata' has crested frond and pinna tips.

D. d. 'Grandiceps'. A very dense tassel terminates the frond, and the broad pinnae are also crested.

D. d. 'Jimmy Dyce' has bluish green fronds that stand stiffly upright.

D. d. 'Lepidota Cristata' ('Grandiceps' of hort.) is a finely dissected, minutely crested form. The fronds are twelve to eighteen inches long and bipinnate, while the stipe and rachis have reddish brown scales.

D. d. 'Recurved Form'. The segment margins are curved downward.

D. erythrosora
Autumn fern
FRONDS: 1½ to 2 feet long, arching, evergreen
RHIZOME HABIT: short-creeping
AVAILABILITY: common
HARDINESS ZONES: 5 to 8
EASE OF CULTIVATION: easy

This colorful fern is distinguished by its bronze young foliage and the bright red indusia covering the young sori. The young fronds are glossy

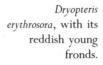
Dryopteris erythrosora.

Dryopteris erythrosora, with its reddish young fronds.

coppery pink and hold that color until they are mature, when they change to a deep glossy green in early summer. It is one of the most frequently cultivated of the Asian dryopterises, and one of the best. This plant remains erect all through the winter, bright green in color. The fronds are triangular and bipinnate, and the segments have curved teeth. Small scales decorate the undersurface of the midveins and pinna rachises. Some plants have white indusia rather than red. The species is native to Japan, China, and Taiwan.

D. e. 'Prolifica' has narrower segments than the species, and occasional plantlets are produced on the upper surface along the rachis. It seems to be more touchy and not as hardy as the species, but some growers have had no difficulty with it.

D. expansa (syn. *D. assimilis*, *D. dilatata* var. *alpina*)
Arching wood fern, Northern wood fern
FRONDS: 16 to 30 inches long, arching, deciduous
RHIZOME HABIT: crown
AVAILABILITY: infrequent
HARDINESS ZONES: 3 to 8
EASE OF CULTIVATION: easy

This is a small to moderately large fern with broad, finely dissected fronds. The fronds are pentagonal, with the pinnules of the basal pinnae quite long on the basiscopic side. There are about five pairs of thin-textured pinnae. *Dryopteris expansa* is found rather sparsely in the mountains of eastern Canada, the Pacific Northwest, and Europe. In alpine habitats (and perhaps rock gardens) it achieves a much smaller size, sometimes to only six inches. It also likes damp, rocky, acidic woodlands where it has consistently moist, cool conditions.

Dryopteris expansa is a variable species, making it difficult to identify at times. It is similar to *D. dilatata* and *D. campyloptera* in form (*D. expansa* is a

Dryopteris expansa, with its long, downward-pointing pinnules.

parent of *D. campyloptera*, along with *D. intermedia*), but differs in its broader, more oval frond form and more delicate texture.

D. filix-mas
Male fern
FRONDS: 2 to 4 feet long, erect, deciduous
RHIZOME HABIT: crown
AVAILABILITY: frequent
HARDINESS ZONES: 4 to 8
EASE OF CULTIVATION: easy

This large fern is one of the best-known of the wood ferns, giving us many easily grown varieties for garden cultivation. The scales of the rhizome and stipe are light brown. The blade is narrowly lance-shaped and pinnate-pinnatifid with a short stipe less than one quarter the frond length. The thin-textured pinnules are parallel sided and blunt-tipped with a few inconspicuous incurved teeth. As in a few other dryopterises, the sori are located nearer the midvein than the margin. *Dryopteris filix-mas* occurs in cool, moist, rocky woods in western and northeastern North America, Europe, and Asia. It is abundant in Europe where it is found everywhere—along roads, foundations, and even naturalized in industrial areas. In eastern North America it is a rare fern of calcareous, rocky slopes and moist woods. These plants are probably not the same as the European material. The western North American material occurs on granitic and volcanic rocks in open woods, and appears to be the same as the European material. More study is needed on this varied group, and a common garden with representatives of the different regions and habitats growing together would be helpful.

Dryopteris filix-mas is commonly confused with *D. affinis*, which is more

Dryopteris filix-mas.

Dryopteris filix-mas sori.

leathery, darker green, semievergreen, and with a dark spot at the base of the pinnae on the underside.

Like *D. affinis*, *D. filix-mas* is very handsome in a woodland setting where it has room to show off, but it is also quite sun-tolerant. The fronds persist awhile into the winter but turn brown in colder regions. The crown multiplies and can be divided regularly. Don't be bashful about taking off the new plants. If you don't do it, you lose the symmetry of the main plant and it becomes a large clump, which, however, can be attractive.

British plants have given rise to many cultivated forms and are fairly reliable from spore. Lowe (1890, p. 282) listed sixty-nine varieties. Some of the varieties are found today under both *D. filix-mas* and *D. affinis*.

D. f.-m. 'Barnesii' is a magnificent, slender, stiffly erect plant with toothed margins. It stands three feet tall and is only about four inches wide—a very distinct variety. The pinnae are short, oval-triangular, and deeply pinnatifid with toothed margins.

D. f.-m. 'Cristata' includes several forms with crested pinna tips.

D. f.-m. 'Cristata Martindale' has small crests on all pinnae and the frond apex, with the pinnae slightly curving upward toward the frond apex.

D. f.-m. 'Decomposita' is a beautiful variety with the pinnae almost fully pinnate and with toothed pinnules.

D. f.-m. 'Digitata Dadds' has long-fingered crests on the pinna tips and is easily confused with *D. f.-m* 'Linearis Polydactyla'.

Dryopteris filix-mas 'Barnesii'.

Dryopteris filix-mas 'Cristata'.

Dryopteris filix-mas 'Linearis'.

Dryopteris filix-mas 'Grandiceps'.

Dryopteris filix-mas
'Linearis Polydactyla'.

D. f.-m. 'Grandiceps'. This is a strong grower with a large arching terminal crest and narrow pinnae that are finely crested.

D. f.-m. 'Linearis' is a tall variety with slender segments, so slender in fact that the sori stick out from the sides when seen from above. The fronds are three feet long, and have a leathery, crisped texture.

D. f.-m. 'Linearis Congesta' is a small version of 'Linearis', only six to nine inches tall, with finely divided fronds. It is ideal for small spaces in the rock garden.

D. f.-m. 'Linearis Cristata' differs from 'Linearis' in having crested pinnae and frond tips.

D. f.-m. 'Linearis Polydactyla'. The pinnae are very slender, and they and the frond tip are multiforked. The segments may be depauperate and some even missing.

D. f.-m. 'Nana' is a small form only six inches long.

D. formosana
Formosan wood fern
FRONDS: 1½ to 3 feet long, erect-arching, semievergreen
RHIZOME HABIT: crown

Dryopteris formosana.

Dryopteris formosana, with its very long, downward-pointing pinnules.

AVAILABILITY: rare

HARDINESS ZONES: 6 to 9

EASE OF CULTIVATION: easy

This oriental *Dryopteris* has bipinnate fronds that are broadly ovate and abruptly long-tipped. The stipe is about half the frond length and rather scaly. *Dryopteris formosana* is quite distinct in having very long basal basiscopic pinnules, giving a pentagonal form to the blade and the appearance of an *Arachniodes*. It is native to Japan and Taiwan.

D. goldiana

Goldie's wood fern, Giant wood fern

FRONDS: 3 to 4 feet long, arching, deciduous

RHIZOME HABIT: short-creeping

AVAILABILITY: frequent

HARDINESS ZONES: 3 to 8

EASE OF CULTIVATION: easy

Goldie's wood fern is the largest of our native *Dryopteris* species. It is distinguished by the large, oblong-triangular, pinnate-pinnatifid blade that tapers abruptly at the tip. The segments are of firm texture, the sori lie nearer the midvein than the margin, and it has dark brown scales on the rhizome and stipe base. It occurs in cool, moist woods, often near water, in northeastern North America.

This species, with its short-creeping rhizome, makes an attractive, compact stand of broad, arching fronds, and the fiddleheads, shaggy with brownish scales, are a highlight of the spring garden.

Dryopteris goldiana crosses with several other species, forming some excellent

Dryopteris goldiana pinnae.

Dryopteris goldiana sori. (PHOTO
BY BARBARA HALLOWELL)

Dryopteris hondoensis.

hybrids for the garden, e.g., with D. *cristata* and D. *ludoviciana* to form the
widespread fertile hybrids D. *clintoniana* (page 180) and D. *celsa* (page 178),
respectively, and rarely with D. *celsa*, D. *clintoniana*, D. *intermedia*, and D.
marginalis to form sterile hybrids.

D. hondoensis
FRONDS: 1 to 2½ feet long, erect-arching, evergreen
RHIZOME HABIT: crown
AVAILABILITY: rare
HARDINESS ZONES: 4 to 8
EASE OF CULTIVATION: easy

The blade is narrowly to broadly oval, bipinnate to bipinnate-pinnatifid,
and somewhat leathery. The rachis and other frond axes are sparsely brown-
scaly below. The segments are oblong and rounded at their tips. *Dryopteris
hondoensis* comes from moist forests of Japan.

D. intermedia (syn. D. spinulosa var. intermedia)
Evergreen wood fern, Glandular wood fern, Fancy fern
FRONDS: 1½ to 3 feet long, erect-arching, evergreen
RHIZOME HABIT: crown
AVAILABILITY: frequent
HARDINESS ZONES: 3 to 8
EASE OF CULTIVATION: easy

Dryopteris intermedia.

Dryopteris lacera in early summer.

Dryopteris lacera in late summer, with its deciduous fertile tip.

"Fancy fern" is a good name for this species because of its finely dissected blade. The stipe has light brown scales and is one quarter to one third the frond length. The thin-textured blade is oval to narrowly triangular and bipinnate-pinnatifid to tripinnate. *Dryopteris intermedia* is similar to *D. carthusiana* but is evergreen, only the basal pinna pair is triangular (the other pinnae are narrow), and the basal basiscopic pinnule on the basal pinna is usually shorter than the next pinnule. In addition, *D. intermedia* has minute glands, resembling tiny hatpins, that are visible with a 10-power hand lens. These glands are all over the blade, especially on the lower surface. This fern is very common in moist, shaded woods and on rocky slopes in eastern North America.

This is a very strong grower and is beautiful as a specimen plant or planted in a mass. It does very well in a moist, shady woodland garden in acid to neutral soil. In the wild it also occupies dryish sites on slopes and among rocks.

Dryopteris intermedia hybridizes with several other species, including

D. carthusiana (*D.* × *triploidea*), *D. cristata* (*D.* × *boottii*), *D. campyloptera, D. celsa* (*D.* × *separabilis*), *D. clintoniana* (*D.* × *dowellii*), *D. expansa, D. goldiana,* and *D. marginalis.* The first two are common, the others rare. All are good garden plants.

D. lacera
FRONDS: 1 to 2 feet long, erect-arching, semievergreen
RHIZOME HABIT: crown

AVAILABILITY: infrequent

HARDINESS ZONES: 5 to 8

EASE OF CULTIVATION: easy

This distinctive fern from Korea, China, and Japan has a lance-shaped to triangular blade, apple green in color. The pinnae are pinnate at the frond base, pinnatifid higher on the frond, and naked on both surfaces. The segments are oblong, nearly smooth-margined, and slightly oblique or curved toward the pinna tip. Curiously, the fronds are fertile only in the terminal one third of the frond. The fertile segments are smaller and the fertile pinnae are often deciduous from the rest of the frond. The light green color and leathery texture add to its beauty. In nature it occurs on exposed, hilly areas, along mountain streams, and in moist woodlands.

D. laeta (syn. D. goeringiana, Athyrium goeringianum)

FRONDS: 1 to 2 feet long, arching, semievergreen

RHIZOME HABIT: compact

AVAILABILITY: infrequent

HARDINESS ZONES: 5 to 8

EASE OF CULTIVATION: easy

Dryopteris laeta is another beautiful, light green, oriental fern with triangular fronds. It has about eight pairs of thin-textured pinnae, with the stipe about half the frond length. This species resembles *D. dilatata* but is less dissected and less toothed, and the basiscopic pinnules are not long. It is native to Japan, Korea, Manchuria, and northern China.

The name *Athyrium goeringianum* has been mistakenly applied to the Japanese painted fern.

D. lepidopoda

FRONDS: 1 to 2 feet long, erect-arching, semievergreen

RHIZOME HABIT: crown

AVAILABILITY: rare

HARDINESS ZONES: 5 to 8

EASE OF CULTIVATION: easy

The scales are brown to black at the stipe base, the blade broadly lance-shaped and bipinnate, with the pinnae long-pointed. The segments have rounded tips and are slightly toothed. The basiscopic pinnules are not elongated. Sori are found on the upper two thirds of the frond. *Dryopteris lepidopoda* is native to the Himalayas, western China, and Taiwan.

Dryopteris lepidopoda is similar to *D. wallichiana* but has larger, narrower pinnules and red-gold colored young fronds.

D. ludoviciana
Southern wood fern
FRONDS: 2 to 4 feet long, erect, semievergreen
RHIZOME HABIT: short-creeping
AVAILABILITY: infrequent
HARDINESS ZONES: 6 to 9
EASE OF CULTIVATION: easy

The tall, slender, glossy, dark green fronds of *D. ludoviciana* make an impressive effect in the fern garden. The blade is leathery and pinnate-pinnatifid, with the basal pinnae triangular, and the stipe is only one quarter the frond length. Sori are borne only on the upper third or half of the frond, and the fertile pinnae and pinnules are much smaller and narrower than the sterile ones. *Dryopteris ludoviciana* occurs in wet woods, swamps, shaded limestone outcrops, and margins of cypress swamps of the southeastern United States.

As is true for other swamp-loving ferns, it is not necessary to provide abundant moisture to maintain this stately fern in the garden. Furthermore, it is not necessary to keep the plant in its native southern woodlands, for although it occurs naturally north to North Carolina, it can be grown considerably further north. We grew *D. ludoviciana* in the New York area successfully for several years until it died during an especially harsh winter. It is apparently not as hardy as its hybrid with *D. celsa* (*D.* × *australis*), which resembles it in having tall, lustrous fronds.

D. marginalis
Marginal wood fern, Leather wood fern (not Leatherwood fern as in some
  catalogs)
FRONDS: 1½ to 2½ feet long, erect-arching, evergreen
RHIZOME HABIT: erect crown
AVAILABILITY: frequent
HARDINESS ZONES: 2 to 8
EASE OF CULTIVATION: easy

This fern was named for its sorus position, the sori being situated very near the margin of the pinnules. The rhizome is a broad, erect crown at ground level, densely clothed with light brown scales, and is slow to branch,

The crown of *Dryopteris marginalis*.

Dryopteris marginalis.

Dryopteris marginalis sori, with the indusia curled up to expose the sporangia. (Photo by F. Gordon Foster)

so this species makes a large, single-crowned specimen. The stipe is one quarter to one third the frond length, with many pale brown scales, especially at the base. The blade is lance-shaped, bipinnate to bipinnate-pinnatifid, and leathery with the sori located near the margin. The fronds are evergreen, bluish green, and very attractive. It is a common fern of woods and rocky wooded slopes in northeastern North America.

The marginal wood fern is a sturdy plant, and highly recommended for cultivation.

D. × mickelii (= D. clintoniana × goldiana)
Mickel's wood fern
FRONDS: 4 to 5 feet long, erect, semievergreen
RHIZOME HABIT: short-creeping
AVAILABILITY: rare
HARDINESS ZONES: 4 to 8
EASE OF CULTIVATION: easy

I put this sterile hybrid in my list of great garden ferns. I prefer it to either of its parents. It is taller and more robust than *D. clintoniana* on the one hand, and more slender, shinier, and erect than *D. goldiana* on the other. Unfortunately, it does not produce viable spores so is not as readily available as *D. goldiana*, but its short-creeping, branching rhizome is easily divided. A specimen of this hybrid was planted in the Native Plant Garden at the New York

Botanical Garden in 1960, and now occupies a space about twelve feet across with more than two hundred growing tips. Hopefully, we can get this plant into tissue culture to enable its broader use as a garden plant. It occurs occasionally in swamps and wet woods in northeastern North America.

D. munchii
FRONDS: 18 to 30 inches long, arching, semievergreen
RHIZOME HABIT: erect crown
AVAILABILITY: rare
HARDINESS ZONES: 8 to 9, perhaps colder
EASE OF CULTIVATION: easy

The thin-textured blade is lance-shaped to triangular and bipinnate-pinnatifid, with the lower pinnae having longer pinnules on the basiscopic side than the acroscopic. It occurs but rarely in cool forests at 6,500 to 8,500 feet elevation in southern Mexico.

Dryopteris munchii has been grown in English gardens and may be hardy further north in the United States. This, *D. wallichiana*, and *D. pseudo-filix-mas* show that ferns of high-elevation tropical America are candidates for North American gardens.

D. nipponensis (syn. D. cystolepidota, D. erythrosora var. cystolepidota)
FRONDS: 1 to 2 feet long, arching, evergreen
RHIZOME HABIT: erect crown
AVAILABILITY: rare
HARDINESS ZONES: 6 to 9
EASE OF CULTIVATION: easy

This evergreen Japanese fern is very attractive. It has an erect rhizome and a broadly triangular blade, which narrows abruptly at the tip. As in *D. erythrosora*, the new fronds are tinged with red, but the pinnules are wider and more rounded at the tip. The comely fronds make this a desirable addition to the garden, though it is still rarely grown.

D. oreades (syn. D. abbreviata)
Mountain male fern, Dwarf male fern
FRONDS: 1 to 2 feet long, erect, evergreen

Dryopteris munchii.

Dryopteris oreades.

RHIZOME HABIT: short-creeping
AVAILABILITY: infrequent
HARDINESS ZONES: 4 to 8
EASE OF CULTIVATION: easy

This is a very hardy medium-sized fern with stiff, upright, pale gray-green, narrow fronds (about six inches wide). The lower pinnae curve forward out of the plane of the frond; the frond margin is crisped. The stipe is moderately covered with very pale gray-brown scales and the rhizome is much-branched. The sori are restricted to the inner part of pinnules in the upper one third of the frond, and the indusium is caplike. In its native Europe, *D. oreades* is exclusively a mountain plant and especially likes well-drained, rocky banks and talus slopes. It is not always possible to distinguish this from small plants of *D. filix-mas*. In the garden this plant likes a well-drained rock garden situation, although it is easily grown in the woodland garden as well.

D. o. 'Crispa'. The margins are even more wavy than is typical for the species.

D. o. 'Cristata'. The pinnae are crested at the tips.

D. o. 'Incisa Crispa' has the pinnules both cut and crisped.

D. polylepis
Scaly wood fern
FRONDS: 1½ to 3 feet long, arching, deciduous
RHIZOME HABIT: crown

AVAILABILITY: rare

HARDINESS ZONES: 6 to 8

EASE OF CULTIVATION: easy

The scaly wood fern from Japan has stipes that are stout, short, and scaly. The fronds are pinnate-pinnatifid and a narrowly inverted lance shape— broadest above the middle and tapering to base. There are twenty or more pairs of pinnae, and the segments are wavy margined. The sori are limited to the upper one third of the frond.

Dryopteris polylepis is similar to *D. crassirhizoma* except that it has narrower fronds and black lustrous scales rather than brown.

D. pseudo-filix-mas

Mexican wood fern, Mexican male fern

FRONDS: 2½ to 4 feet long, erect, semievergreen

RHIZOME HABIT: erect crown

AVAILABILITY: rare

HARDINESS ZONES: 5 to 8

EASE OF CULTIVATION: easy

This is a great garden fern from Mexico, fully hardy, forming a large crown. The stipe is one fifth to one third the frond length, and moderately clothed in scales. The blade is pinnate-pinnatifid except for the base, where the basal pinnae have enlarged, pinnatifid to pinnate basiscopic basal pinnules. The segments are rounded to pointed at the tip. This rare wood fern occurs in moist forests at high elevations in Mexico and Guatemala. It resembles *D. wallichiana*, with which it grows in Mexico, but the basal pinna pair is more lobed in *D. pseudo-filix-mas* and the segments more rounded.

The plant, unlike our native and European dryopterises, keeps sending out new fronds and producing new sori all through the growing season, and doesn't stop until there is a very hard frost in late fall.

D. purpurella (syn. D. erythrosora var. purpurascens)

FRONDS: 3 to 3½ feet long, arching, evergreen

RHIZOME HABIT: short-creeping

AVAILABILITY: frequent

HARDINESS ZONES: 5 to 9

EASE OF CULTIVATION: easy

This Japanese fern is an impressive plant similar to *D. erythrosora* in the distinctive bronze color of its young, developing fronds, but *D. purpurella* is

Dryopteris pseudo-
filix-mas.

Dryopteris remota.

larger and more broadly triangular in blade shape, and the stipe and rachis are a distinctive reddish purple. It is surely one of the most beautiful ferns in cultivation.

D. pycnopteroides
FRONDS: 1 to 2 feet long, erect, evergreen
RHIZOME HABIT: crown
AVAILABILITY: infrequent
HARDINESS ZONES: 6 to 9
EASE OF CULTIVATION: easy

A native of Japan, this distinctive lustrous, green fern is pinnate-pinnatifid with twenty-five to thirty pairs of long, slender pinnae.

D. remota (= D. affinis × expansa)
FRONDS: 2 to 3 feet long, erect, semievergreen
RHIZOME HABIT: erect crown
AVAILABILITY: frequent
HARDINESS ZONES: 4 to 8
EASE OF CULTIVATION: easy

This is one of my favorite ferns for the garden and is impressive-looking with its shaggy, golden-scaled stipe and delicately cut blade. It is a fertile hybrid, intermediate between the parents, with the slender pinnae and shaggy stipe of D. affinis and the thin texture of D. expansa. It is a strong grower and one of the few ferns to volunteer in my garden. Dryopteris remota is scattered but rare in Europe and western Asia.

Dryopteris sieboldii.

D. sieboldii
Siebold's wood fern
FRONDS: 1 to 2 feet long, sterile arching, fertile erect, semievergreen
RHIZOME HABIT: short-creeping
AVAILABILITY: frequent
HARDINESS ZONES: 6 to 8
EASE OF CULTIVATION: easy

Dryopteris sieboldii is quite different from the other species of the genus in having only two to five pairs of broad, leathery, undivided pinnae with a terminal pinna eight to twelve inches long. The vegetative fronds are arching, the fertile ones more erect with slightly narrower pinnae and with sori toward the margins. This distinctive species is native to Japan, Taiwan, and China.

Handsome but slow-growing, Siebold's wood fern barely survives in Massachusetts and New York, and is reluctant to come up in the spring (not until late June in New York). However, it does well and even volunteers itself in gardens in central Virginia.

D. submontana (syn. D. villarii)
Limestone wood fern, Rigid buckler fern
FRONDS: 8 to 24 inches long, erect-arching, deciduous
RHIZOME HABIT: ascending
AVAILABILITY: rare
HARDINESS ZONES: 6 to 8
EASE OF CULTIVATION: easy

This medium-sized fern from the mountains of Europe and northern Africa has stiffly upright, narrowly lance-shaped, bipinnate fronds. The color is a dull gray-green, with abundant yellowish glands on both surfaces, which make the fronds fragrant when bruised (they smell like balsam). The widely spaced pinnae are narrowly lance-shaped, one to two inches wide and six to eight inches long, with wavy margins. The large, round sori, also with glands, are limited to the upper half of the frond.

This is a distinctive *Dryopteris*, very hardy and easy to cultivate in a rock garden with abundant limestone. The leaves are said to die down with the first frost.

D. tokyoensis
Tokyo wood fern
FRONDS: 1½ to 3 feet long, erect, deciduous
RHIZOME HABIT: crown
AVAILABILITY: frequent
HARDINESS ZONES: 5 to 8
EASE OF CULTIVATION: easy

This slender wood fern is another of my favorites for its stiffly erect, narrow fronds. The blade is pinnate-pinnatifid and narrowly inversely lance-shaped, broadest above the middle and tapering to the base, four to six inches wide. There are twenty to forty pairs of narrowly lance-shaped pinnae, which are slightly auricled at the base and glabrous. The sori are large and abundant. *Dryopteris tokyoensis* is native to Japan and Korea.

This slender, vase-shaped plant makes a wonderful addition to the garden with its slender fronds and vigorous growth. Unfortunately, it branches slowly, so divisions are infrequent.

D. uniformis
FRONDS: 1 to 2½ feet long, erect, evergreen

Dryopteris tokyoensis.

A closeup of the pinnae of *Dryopteris tokyoensis*.

Dryopteris uniformis 'Cristata'.

Dryopteris uniformis 'Cristata' crosiers.

RHIZOME HABIT: erect crown
AVAILABILITY: infrequent
HARDINESS ZONES: 5 to 8
EASE OF CULTIVATION: easy

This appealing, medium-sized fern has bipinnate fronds which are oval-triangular, with long, finely toothed, narrow pinnules. The scales of the stipe and rachis are dark brown to black, and the sori are borne on the upper pinnae. *Dryopteris uniformis* occurs in the wooded mountains of Japan, Korea, and China.

D. u. 'Cristata'. The pinnae are crested and the rachis forks in the upper half. This is one of my favorite medium-sized ferns, with its beautiful dark, evergreen fronds and interesting forking and cresting. It spores abundantly and a few plants have volunteered in my garden.

D. wallichiana
Wallich's wood fern
FRONDS: 2 to 4 feet long, erect, semievergreen
RHIZOME HABIT: erect crown
AVAILABILITY: frequent
HARDINESS ZONES: 5 to 8
EASE OF CULTIVATION: moderate

When I see this fern, my mind drifts to the high mountains of southern Mexico, to dripping forests of moss-festooned oaks and lichen-laden pines, and through the drifting, chilling mists appear the abundant, blackish green vase-shaped crowns of *D. wallichiana*. The stipe is one quarter or less of the

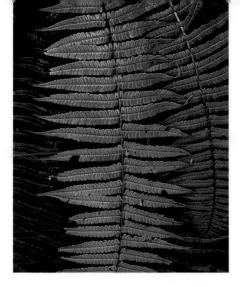

Dryopteris wallichiana.

The undersurface of the frond of *Dryopteris wallichiana*, with its scales and sori.

frond length, and densely clothed with reddish black scales, which also make the crosiers a spectacular sight. The pinnate-pinnatifid blade is oblong-lance-shaped, leathery, lustrous, dark green above, lighter below, and the basal pinnae somewhat smaller, without enlarged basal pinnules. The segments are oblong, and squarish at the tip.

Dryopteris wallichiana occurs at high elevations from Mexico to the South American Andes, West Indies, Africa, Asia, and Hawaii. There is considerable variation in populations from different parts of the world, with differences in the degree and color of scaliness, blade texture, and segment shape.

The rhizome seldom branches, so divisions are uncommon. This species does not do especially well in temperate areas with warm summers, such as around New York but will grow in nearby areas with more uniform coolness, such as the Pocono Mountains of eastern Pennsylvania.

EQUISETUM, Horsetail, Scouring rush

Rarely used as garden plants, the horsetails and scouring rushes can provide vertical lines and soft, feathery textures not found in other plant groups. The rhizome is subterranean, long-creeping, and highly branched, giving it a decidedly aggressive habit. The above-ground stems are green, erect, hollow, grooved, and jointed, generally with a large central canal and smaller peripheral canals. The leaves are nearly nonexistent; they are minute, white to black, whorled, and fused to form a sheath at the joints. The stem is either tall and unbranched or short with whorls of branches at the joints. The stem ridges are embedded with silica, making them very rigid in most species. The aerial stems are evergreen or deciduous. A cone at the tip of the stem contains the sporangia on the underside of closely fitted umbrellalike structures. The cones may be at the ends of the vegetative green stems or on special ephemeral stems that die down quickly in early spring as soon as the spores are shed. The spores are green and short-lived.

Equisetum is a genus of fifteen species, mostly of north temperate regions. The species hybridize frequently to form sterile (abortive-spored) intermediates. This ancient group is of the same age and evolutionary level as the ferns but is not related to them. In the wild, they occur on sand and gravel in waste places, railroad banks, roadsides, swamps, and meadows, often in the sun. Some species, such as *E. arvense*, can be decidedly aggressive, but even these can be used to advantage in the right location. Horsetails are a curiosity in the garden and give a distinct texture not available elsewhere.

Equisetums are tolerant of diverse soils as long as they are not too acid, and most species require full sun or only very light shade. They generally need good soil moisture, at least when they are getting established. Start equisetums in clay pots set in pans of water to keep them soggy. They are often difficult to transplant because of their deep roots, especially *E. telmateia*.

Propagation is best done by division, either of the rhizome or the aerial stems. If you divide the rhizome, cut the clump at its edge where active growth is taking place rather than the center, where there may not be as many growing tips. Pieces of aerial stems, including one or more joints, can be laid down horizontally in mud, or stuck into moist sand with a joint below ground level, where new shoots will originate. Horsetails can also be propagated by spores, but their spores are short-lived and thus not commonly available.

E. arvense
Field horsetail

AERIAL STEMS: 8 to 18 inches tall; sterile branched, fertile unbranched; erect, deciduous

RHIZOME HABIT: long-creeping

AVAILABILITY: frequent

HARDINESS ZONES: 1 to 7

EASE OF CULTIVATION: easy

This common species has two distinct kinds of aerial stems. The fertile stems are pinkish orange, fleshy, and unbranched, with a cone at the tip, coming up in early spring and lasting only a few days. The vegetative stems,

The vegetative stems of *Equisetum arvense*.

The fertile stems and early vegetative stems of *Equisetum arvense*.

on the other hand, are green, branched, tough, and last all summer. *Equisetum arvense* occurs in northern North America, Europe, and Asia.

The field horsetail can be aggressive and is recommended only for a confined space because of its propensity to travel widely. I saw a very attractive bed of it, bounded by sidewalks and a building foundation, on the campus of Hamilton College in upstate New York. I thought at the time that a very progressive landscape architect had planted it, but later I realized that the intended planting had died and the *Equisetum* had merely volunteered in a solid mass. What pity it was not intentional!

E. fluviatile
Water horsetail, Pipes
AERIAL STEMS: 2 to 3 feet tall, branched, erect, deciduous
RHIZOME HABIT: creeping
AVAILABILITY: rare
HARDINESS ZONES: 1 to 6
EASE OF CULTIVATION: easy

The aerial stems are tall and slender, sparsely branched, and have long, whiplike tips. *Equisetum fluviatile* grows in marshes and swamps, often rooted underwater with aerial stems sticking out of the water, and is native to northern North America, Europe, and Asia.

This species is very effective in the shallow water of a pond margin.

E. hyemale
Scouring rush, Evergreen scouring rush, Rough scouring rush
AERIAL STEMS: 2 to 4 feet tall, unbranched, erect, evergreen

Equisetum hyemale.

RHIZOME HABIT: creeping
AVAILABILITY: frequent
HARDINESS ZONES: 2 to 10
EASE OF CULTIVATION: easy

The aerial stems have ash-colored leaf sheaths with black bands at their upper and lower edges. The ridges feel rough because of the silica deposited in the cell walls, causing it to be used by early settlers and campers for cleaning cooking pots. It has also been valuable, even in recent years, in filing clarinet reeds. A cone is produced at the tip of the aerial stem, with a small black point on top. *Equisetum hyemale* occurs in northern North America, Europe, and Asia.

Curiously, this plant, strong-growing in the wild, is often difficult to transplant and establish. We have planted *E. hyemale* outside at the New York Botanical Garden in the past, and it has survived but not really done well. Last year we obtained nine plants of a robust form of *E. hyemale* from the West Coast, var. *californicum*. They were planted in a recently cleared bed in the rockery of Lyndhurst, the Jay Gould estate now in the National Trust, located in Tarrytown, New York. Gray Williams, the coordinator of the Taconic Garden Club project of restoring the beds, was skeptical about introducing this scouring rush. I assured him that *Equisetum* species usually did not do that well in captivity. That was a year ago. This year he gave me twenty-eight plants back for the New York Botanical Garden, another twenty-eight plants to the Norcross Wildlife Sanctuary, and fourteen more to several individuals, still leaving a solid patch five feet across of this vigorous fern ally. A month later, the patch was ten feet across. So, if you have an open sunny place and want a scouring rush that has a fair chance of surviving, you can try growing this potent variety. Plant it and stand back!

An alternative use for this graceful plant is in a pot, where you can enjoy the scouring rush's slender form, moving it wherever you wish (it needs full sun), yet keeping it within bounds.

E. laevigatum

Smooth scouring rush

AERIAL STEMS: 18 to 24 inches tall, unbranched, erect, deciduous

RHIZOME HABIT: creeping

AVAILABILITY: rare

HARDINESS ZONES: 3 to 8

EASE OF CULTIVATION: easy

This is similar to *E. hyemale* except the stems are deciduous, the ridges smooth (not rough), and the leaf sheaths green and with a narrow black upper sheath margin. The cone tip is rounded rather than pointed. It occurs in midwestern North America.

E. scirpoides

Dwarf scouring rush

AERIAL STEMS: 4 to 8 inches tall, unbranched, twisted, evergreen

RHIZOME HABIT: short-creeping

AVAILABILITY: frequent

HARDINESS ZONES: 1 to 8

EASE OF CULTIVATION: easy

The characteristic small, twisted stems are three-sided with whorls of three teeth. The dwarf scouring rush prefers limy soils and occurs in northern North America, Europe, and Asia. It is easy to grow and does not spread rapidly.

Equisetum scirpoides.

E. sylvaticum

Woodland horsetail

AERIAL STEMS: 10 to 20 inches tall, branched, erect, deciduous

RHIZOME HABIT: long-creeping

AVAILABILITY: rare

HARDINESS ZONES: 1 to 5

EASE OF CULTIVATION: moderate to difficult

This distinctive horsetail of woodland habitats has very fine branches that are rebranched, giving the plant a lacy appearance. The branches are often drooping. The sheath teeth are reddish brown. The cones are borne at the stem tips, the branching and green color developing as the cone withers. It occurs in the moist woodlands of northern North America and Europe.

E. telmateia

Giant horsetail

AERIAL STEMS: 1 to 6 feet tall; sterile branched, fertile unbranched; erect, deciduous

RHIZOME HABIT: long-creeping

AVAILABILITY: frequent

HARDINESS ZONES: 7 to 9

EASE OF CULTIVATION: moderate to difficult

This large, bushy plant is similar to *E. arvense* but much larger. It is native to western North America, Europe, western Asia, and northern Africa.

E. variegatum

Variegated scouring rush

AERIAL STEMS: 10 to 16 inches tall, unbranched, erect, evergreen

RHIZOME HABIT: creeping

AVAILABILITY: frequent

HARDINESS ZONES: 1 to 8

EASE OF CULTIVATION: easy

This slender, erect *Equisetum* is not aggressive and stays small. The leaf sheath has bicolored teeth—white with a black central streak. It prefers limy soils in northern North America, Europe, and Asia. It grows well near water outdoors and can be used as a houseplant as well. I had it in a bonsai dish in my office for over a year before I forgot to have it watered while I was out of town.

Equisetum telmateia.
(PHOTO BY JUDITH
JONES)

*Equisetum
variegatum.*

GYMNOCARPIUM, Oak fern

The small, broadly triangular fronds of the oak fern are a delight in the cool, shady garden. The slender, long-creeping rhizomes result in a loose colony of delicate, apple green leaves. The fronds are pinnate-pinnatifid to tripinnate, thin-textured, and deciduous. The small, round sori are located on the lower surface of the blade and lack an indusium.

Gymnocarpium is a genus of five species of north temperate regions. In the wild it occurs in cool, rich, moist woods. Its creeping habit is not aggressive, and it makes a fine ground cover in northern gardens. It does not seem to tolerate hot summers.

G. dryopteris (syn. *Dryopteris disjuncta*)
Oak fern
FRONDS: 9 to 12 inches long, erect-arching, deciduous
RHIZOME HABIT: wide-creeping
AVAILABILITY: frequent
HARDINESS ZONES: 2 to 5; if cool, to 8
EASE OF CULTIVATION: easy

The delicate, three-parted fronds are scattered on slender, widely creeping rhizomes. The frond is bipinnate to tripinnate, the rachis and blade are glandless or nearly so, and only the basal pair of pinnae is stalked. It is found in wet, acidic woods in northern North America, Europe, and Asia. It makes a fine garden plant in northern gardens but must be kept cool and moist.

Gymnocarpium dryopteris.

Gymnocarpium robertianum. (Photo by Judith Jones)

G. d. 'Plumosum' has broader segments than the species, and they overlap.

G. oyamense
Fronds: 6 to 12 inches long, arching, deciduous
Rhizome habit: long-creeping
Availability: rare
Hardiness zones: 8 to 9
Ease of cultivation: easy

The blade is pinnate-pinnatifid or bipinnatifid, the pinnae contiguous, shallowly lobed, and slightly curved toward the frond tip. *Gymnocarpium oyamense* looks like a less-dissected oak fern and is just as attractive. It is native to China, Japan, and Taiwan.

G. robertianum
Limestone oak fern, Robert's oak fern
Fronds: 9 to 18 inches long, erect-arching, deciduous
Rhizome habit: long-creeping
Availability: infrequent
Hardiness zones: 2 to 5; if cool, to 8
Ease of cultivation: easy

This easily grown species has fronds that are not as widely triangular as in *G. dryopteris*. The rachis and blade are densely glandular, the lowest two pairs of pinnae are stalked, and the blade margins are curved downward slightly. *Gymnocarpium robertianum* occurs, but rarely, on shaded, wooded, limestone slopes and in calcareous swamps of northern North America, Europe, and Asia.

HYPOLEPIS

Closely related to *Dennstaedtia* and *Pteridium*, *Hypolepis* has a long creeping, much-branched rhizome that produces large stands of plants. The fronds are mostly large and two to four times divided. The round sori are located near the margin, and generally protected by a marginal flap or recurved tooth. *Hypolepis* is a tropical genus of about forty-five species, mostly native of Southeast Asia and the South Pacific.

Hypolepis is readily grown in mild climates in loose, well-drained soil, in which the long-creeping rhizome grows quickly. The species with large fronds and aggressive growth limit their usefulness in gardens, but the smaller species are quite adaptable.

H. millefolium
Thousand-leaved fern
FRONDS: 9 to 22 inches long, arching, deciduous
RHIZOME HABIT: long-creeping
AVAILABILITY: rare
HARDINESS ZONES: 7 to 10
EASE OF CULTIVATION: easy

As the name suggests, this species is a very finely divided fern, with the triangular fronds tripinnate-pinnatifid, hairy, and a lovely bright green color. It is the smallest and hardiest species of *Hypolepis* in cultivation and is quite easy to grow. It prefers acidic rocks but can tolerate some lime. It is very attractive, spreads well, and remains short, making a lacy ground cover. It is native to New Zealand.

Hypolepis millefolium.

H. punctata
Downy ground fern
FRONDS: 1½ to 4 feet long, arching, deciduous
RHIZOME HABIT: long-creeping
AVAILABILITY: rare
HARDINESS ZONES: 8 to 10
EASE OF CULTIVATION: easy

The blade is broadly oval, bipinnate-pinnatifid to tripinnate-pinnatifid, lacy, thin-textured, and densely clothed with sticky hairs. *Hypolepis punctata* can stand some sun and tends to spread rapidly, especially in damp situations. It is native to southern and eastern Asia, Australia, New Zealand, and Chile.

H. repens
Bramble fern
FRONDS: 3 to 8 feet long, arching, deciduous
RHIZOME HABIT: long-creeping
AVAILABILITY: infrequent
HARDINESS ZONES: 9 to 10
EASE OF CULTIVATION: easy

The large fronds are triangular and three to four times divided, and the stipe and rachis have small spines, the blade sparse hairs. *Hypolepis repens* occurs in moist, open woods and wet seepage meadows in much of tropical America. Since it is a large species with a long-creeping rhizome, it is best used in large, shady gardens.

H. rugulosa
Ruddy ground fern
FRONDS: 6 to 24 inches long, arching, deciduous
RHIZOME HABIT: long-creeping
AVAILABILITY: rare
HARDINESS ZONES: 8 to 10
EASE OF CULTIVATION: easy

This species forms colonies with dark red stipes and triangular, bipinnate, hairy fronds. It requires a shady to semishady situation but is easily grown and can spread rapidly under the right conditions. *Hypolepis rugulosa* is native to Australia and New Zealand.

Hypolepis tenuifolia.

H. tenuifolia
Giant hypolepis
FRONDS: 3 to 4 feet long, arching, deciduous
RHIZOME HABIT: long-creeping
AVAILABILITY: rare
HARDINESS ZONES: 8 to 10
EASE OF CULTIVATION: easy

The blade is broadly oval, bipinnate-pinnatifid to tripinnate-pinnatifid, and thin-textured with glandular hairs. The stipe is especially stout, about one half inch thick. *Hypolepis tenuifolia* is native to Asia and the South Pacific.

This delicate fern is a strong grower and easily grown in a damp situation. *Hypolepis dicksonoides* and *H. ambigua* have been divided from *H. tenuifolia*. True *H. tenuifolia* is thought to be confined to tropical regions. Plants in cultivation under that name are probably not that species but one of the other two.

LYCOPODIUM, Clubmoss, Firmoss

These mosslike fern allies have creeping stems and upright branches and many scalelike or needlelike leaves. The sporangia are borne at the bases of normal vegetative leaves or on specialized leaves that are clumped to form a terminal, club-shaped cone. Some gametophytes are green and formed on the soil surface; more commonly they are subterranean, nongreen, and fleshy or tuberous.

Lycopodium is a cosmopolitan genus of about 250 species, mostly natives of the wet tropics in middle to higher elevations and with several temperate species. They are rarely cultivated, and there is only limited potential for the clubmosses as ornamental plants. The presence of special fungi in the roots of most terrestrial species and the soil around them that is necessary for proper nutrition and growth of the plants makes them difficult to transplant successfully, so they are not recommended for cultivation. Some species do not require that fungus and are thus more adaptable to transplanting and cultivation. These include *L. lucidulum* and *L. obscurum*, but even with these species, the success rate is very low. They are interesting plants for a woodland or rock garden in rich, moist soil, mostly in shade, some in meadows.

Some botanists divide the genus into several genera (including *Diphasiastrum*, *Huperzia*, *Lycopodiella*, and *Lycopodium*), reflecting various lines of evidence that distinguish these groups. I prefer to take a conservative view of these genera here and treat them all in the genus *Lycopodium*.

Conditions needed are light, well-drained, highly acidic soil (pH 4.0 to 4.5—a growing mix might include three parts silica sand, two parts leaf mold and/or peat moss), constant moisture, preferably not alternate freezing and thawing during winter, and a cool place out of direct sunlight. Some potted plants of *L. lucidulum* and *L. selago* can be grown under artificial light. I had *L. lucidulum* in a bonsai dish for over a year in my office.

Some species of clubmosses are locally abundant, and small pieces might be removed without making a dent in the population. Spores are not a useful means of propagation as they require many months to germinate, and even then grow only with special conditions and nutrients.

For further information on clubmoss cultivation, see Michael Heim, "The Cultivation of our Native Clubmosses," *Minnesota Horticulturist* 116(1), (1988): 24–27.

In addition to divisions, *L. lucidulum* and *L. selago* can be propagated vegetatively by special little flaplike structures, called gemmae, that are produced near the growing tip and fall off to form new plants. These can be removed from the plant and planted in cool, moist sphagnum, but growth is slow.

L. alopecuroides (syn. *Lycopodiella alopecuroides*)
Foxtail clubmoss
STEMS: sterile creeping, evergreen; fertile erect, 8 to 12 inches tall, deciduous
AVAILABILITY: rare
HARDINESS ZONES: 6 to 9
EASE OF CULTIVATION: moderate to difficult
The vegetative stems are long-creeping, arching between the few rooted places. The strongly toothed leaves occur in many spiral rows and spread to give a bushy appearance. A one- to two-inch-long cone is borne at the tip

Lycopodium alopecuroides.

of each erect branch. *Lycopodium alopecuroides* occurs in acid bogs and wet meadows in eastern and southern coastal United States and Kentucky, and is found also in the West Indies and South America.

This unusual clubmoss can be grown in boggy conditions by a pond or stream but cannot tolerate competition from other plants.

L. dendroideum (syn. L. obscurum var. dendroideum)
Tree clubmoss, Princess pine
STEMS: 8 to 10 inches tall, erect, evergreen
AVAILABILITY: infrequent
HARDINESS ZONES: 2 to 6
EASE OF CULTIVATION: moderate to difficult
The subterranean rhizome sends up erect, treelike branches. The leaves are spreading, yellow-green, needlelike, one eighth to one quarter inch long, and borne in six rows. The cones are one to two inches long and without a stalk. *Lycopodium dendroideum* occurs in moist evergreen or deciduous woods and bogs in northern North America and northeastern Asia. It is similar to *L. obscurum* but the leaves are more yellowish and more arching.

L. lucidulum (syn. Huperzia lucidula)
Shining clubmoss, Shining firmoss
STEMS: 6 to 10 inches tall, erect, evergreen
AVAILABILITY: infrequent
HARDINESS ZONES: 2 to 7
EASE OF CULTIVATION: moderate to difficult

Lycopodium lucidulum.

Lycopodium obscurum.

The stems are all erect to form a clump, the older parts of the stems lying down and rooting. The leaves are one quarter to five eighths inch long, broadened and toothed above the middle, arching or rarely bent down. There are distinct zones of longer and shorter leaves along the stem. The sporangia are borne at the bases of vegetative leaves, so cones are absent. Gemmae are formed among the upper leaves. It occurs in rich, moist woods in eastern North America.

L. obscurum
Tree clubmoss, Princess pine
STEMS: 8 to 10 inches tall, erect, evergreen
AVAILABILITY: infrequent
HARDINESS ZONES: 2 to 6
EASE OF CULTIVATION: moderate to difficult
The rhizome is long-creeping, one to two inches below the ground, sending up erect, treelike branches. The leaves are dark green and needlelike, one eighth to one quarter inch long, mostly lying flat along the branches in six rows. The cones are one to two inches long and without a stalk. *Lycopodium obscurum* occurs in moist evergreen or deciduous woods and bogs in northern North America.

L. selago (syn. *Huperzia selago*)
Fir clubmoss, Northern firmoss
STEMS: 4 to 6 inches tall, erect, evergreen
AVAILABILITY: rare

EASE OF CULTIVATION: moderate to difficult

The stems are erect to form a clump and the older parts lie down slightly. The leaves are linear, more or less equally wide throughout their length and smooth-margined, one quarter to one half inch long, and spread or lie against the stem. There are no distinct zones of different-sized leaves along the stem. The sporangia are borne at the bases of vegetative leaves, so cones are absent. Gemmae are formed among the young leaves. *Lycopodium selago* occurs on rocky ledges or in acid bogs in northern North America, Europe, and Asia.

LYGODIUM, Climbing fern

These unusual plants are unique among ferns in their twining habit. The stem itself is a compact, horizontal rhizome just below the ground surface, but the fronds twine upward to a length of six to twenty feet if given a slender support. The stipe is wiry, as is the rachis, which gives off pinnae alternately along its length. The pinnules are usually hand-shaped, and the sporangia are borne on narrow, fingerlike projections from the pinnule margins, the sporangia in two rows on each projection.

Lygodium is a genus of about forty species, all but one of tropical or subtropical regions, three fourths of them of the Old World. They prefer forest margins and scrubby vegetation. Two species have escaped and become weeds in subtropical regions of Florida.

The climbing ferns are a curiosity in the garden, giving high vertical lines in contrast to the lower erect or arching forms of most ferns. It is important to have something for it to climb on, such as a small trellis. Although our single native species is difficult to grow well, the Japanese climbing fern does well as far north as New York.

L. japonicum
Japanese climbing fern
FRONDS: 5 to 20 feet long, erect-twining, deciduous
RHIZOME HABIT: short-creeping
AVAILABILITY: frequent
HARDINESS ZONES: 8 to 10
EASE OF CULTIVATION: moderate

*Lygodium
japonicum.*

*Lygodium
palmatum.*

The fronds are eight to twelve inches wide, and the pinnae have long-triangular segments. The fertile pinnae are similarly dissected with several fingerlike projections bearing the sporangia on each segment.

Lygodium japonicum likes open woods and exposed sites and is native to India, Australia, the Philippines, China, Taiwan, Japan, and Korea. It has become naturalized in the southeastern coastal United States and is hardy north to New York.

The Japanese climbing fern is easier to grow than our native species. A rich, loose, well-drained soil in open shade is best, and some sort of support for the fronds to twine on is needed. A slender post, lattice, strings, or a shrub, such as a lilac, will do nicely. The compact rhizome does not creep widely. Be sure to cut down the old fronds before new ones come up in the spring to avoid an unsightly tangle. In northern gardens it is wise to cover the plants with a mulch of dry leaves before winter as insurance against severe cold in case there is no snow cover. I had plants for ten years and mulched every winter, but one year I got overconfident, did not add the leaves, and lost my climbing ferns.

L. palmatum
Hartford fern, Climbing fern
FRONDS: 4 to 15 feet long, erect-twining, evergreen
RHIZOME HABIT: short-creeping
AVAILABILITY: infrequent
HARDINESS ZONES: 3 to 10
EASE OF CULTIVATION: difficult
The fronds are only three to six inches wide. The sterile pinnae have hand-

shaped segments with six narrow lobes, and the fertile segments are divided into several small, slender, fingerlike segments. *Lygodium palmatum* occurs in sandy bogs and swamps in the eastern and southern United States. The evergreen fronds used to be collected in winter and used for Christmas decorating in homes, but this caused such wide destruction of the plants that it led to an 1869 protective law in Connecticut, the first plant-conservation law in the United States.

Lygodium palmatum is touchier and more difficult to grow than *L. japonicum*, and the overall success rate is not good. It needs strictly acid conditions, and not all tap water is suitable for this species. It is quite fussy and needs rainwater for its survival. A downspout diverted to a rain barrel will give you a supply.

Planting the Hartford fern in sandy soil under a pine tree or in peaty soil under blueberry bushes or rhododendrons will help improve its chances for survival.

Plants can be grown from spores, but here again there are obstacles. The spores mature in late November or December and seem to lose their viability quickly. The spores germinate easily and the sporelings grow to two inches or so, but it is hard to get the plants to grow to maturity.

MARSILEA, Water clover, Pepperwort

The common name of the water clover refers to the four characteristic wedge-shaped leaflets that occur at the end of the long stipe. The slender rhizome creeps widely in the mud at pond margins or in wet ditches. The fronds are small, glabrous or hairy, and very thin-textured. Nutlike sporocarps at the stipe base enclose two kinds of spores, microspores and megaspores, in a gelatinous matrix.

Marsilea is a genus of about seventy species, with most species native to Africa and Australia. The New World species have been recently monographed by Johnson (1986).

Water clovers can be grown along quiet bodies of water, either at the margin or in shallow water, in full sun or light shade. They can also be kept as potted plants with the pot sitting in a pan of water to keep the soil very wet.

M. macropoda

Golden water clover

FRONDS: 6 to 10 inches long, erect, deciduous

RHIZOME HABIT: long-creeping

AVAILABILITY: infrequent

HARDINESS ZONES: 8 to 9

EASE OF CULTIVATION: easy

The pinnae are three eighths to three quarters inch long and wide, and densely hairy with two to six sporocarps per stalk. The golden water clover is native to Alabama, Louisiana, and southern Texas.

This species is used as a ground cover at the San Antonio Botanic Garden in a shaded area that is not especially wet.

M. quadrifolia

European water clover

FRONDS: 6 to 8 inches long, erect, deciduous

RHIZOME HABIT: long-creeping

AVAILABILITY: infrequent

HARDINESS ZONES: 5 to 6

EASE OF CULTIVATION: easy

The pinnae are one half to one inch long and wide, and glabrous. Normally two sporocarps are borne at the base of the stipe.

The European water clover normally is found in ponds and slow-moving streams. It is widespread in its native Europe, but has become widely naturalized in the northeastern United States.

Marsilea macropoda.

Marsilea quadrifolia. (PHOTO BY F. GORDON FOSTER)

M. vestita (syn. M. oligospora, M. mucronata)

Hairy water clover

FRONDS: 6 to 8 inches long, erect, deciduous

RHIZOME HABIT: long-creeping

AVAILABILITY: rare

HARDINESS ZONES: 3 to 10

EASE OF CULTIVATION: easy

The pinnae are one quarter to one half inch long and wide, and lightly hairy. The sporocarps are borne one per stipe.

Marsilea vestita is found along the edges of ponds and rivers, in ditches, and wet meadows in southern and western North America.

MATTEUCCIA, Ostrich fern, Shuttlecock fern

Unsurpassed for its perfect, vase-shaped form, the ostrich fern is one of the most widely used ferns in temperate gardens. Plumelike, deciduous vegetative fronds are borne on an erect rhizome. Spores are produced on shorter, compact, erect fronds that emerge in midsummer and remain erect and woody, releasing the spores in late winter. It does best in shaded locations with rich, moist soil, but can tolerate some sun.

M. orientalis (syn. Onoclea orientalis)

Oriental ostrich fern

FRONDS: 1 to 2½ feet long, erect-arching, deciduous

RHIZOME HABIT: erect crown

AVAILABILITY: rare

HARDINESS ZONES: 6 to 8

EASE OF CULTIVATION: moderate

This is a beautiful fern but rare and may be difficult to cultivate because of slugs. The fronds have a long stipe (about one third the frond length), and the blade stops abruptly at the base, not tapering as in *M. struthiopteris*. Rather, the basal pinnae are long and downward-pointing. There are eight to twenty pairs of shallowly lobed pinnae. The rhizome is creeping with a crown at its apex. This species is native to eastern and southern Asia.

M. struthiopteris (syn. *M. pensylvanica, Pteretis nodulosa, Struthiopteris filicastrum*)

Ostrich fern, Shuttlecock fern

FRONDS: 2 to 6 feet (to 9 feet), erect, deciduous

RHIZOME HABIT: erect crown

AVAILABILITY: common

HARDINESS ZONES: 2 to 6

EASE OF CULTIVATION: easy

The rhizome is stout and erect, producing a vase-shaped clump of fronds. Each plant sends out two or three slender underground runners (stolons) that form new plants nearby. The vegetative fronds are large and plumelike, broadest above the middle and tapering gradually to the base of the frond. There are thirty to fifty pairs of pinnatifid pinnae, and the stipe is very short. The fertile fronds arise in midsummer, are six to twelve inches tall, and tough, becoming woody and brown in fall. The segments are tightly rolled to protect the sori within, and the spores are released during the winter or early the following spring. *Matteuccia struthiopteris* occurs in wooded river bottomlands and swamps in neutral or alkaline muck, and is abundant in northeastern North America, extending across Canada and Alaska, northern Asia, and Europe.

The European ostrich fern is sometimes listed as a separate variety but there seem to be no consistent differences between European and American plants. On the other hand, plants purported to be oriental in origin have extremely large, stout stems, resembling those of *Dicksonia* with their many thick leaf bases. The trunk is four to five inches in diameter and reaches twelve inches in height as opposed to one to two inches in diameter and two to four inches tall for typical plants of the ostrich fern. Also, the fertile fronds

Matteuccia struthiopteris.

Matteuccia struthiopteris, its fertile fronds arising in the center.

are much larger, a full two feet tall, in contrast to only one to one and one half feet for those of the typical ostrich fern.

Matteuccia struthiopteris is a vigorous fern and one of the easiest ferns to cultivate in the northern states. (It does not do well in the hot summers of the South.) It spreads readily by the underground runners from the base of the stem. These send up new plants one to three feet from the parent plant. I was given six plants, and fifteen years later these have given rise to more than seven hundred; and I give away one to two hundred each year! This is the sorcerer's apprentice of the fern world; the more of them you give away, the more are produced. To divide, dig up the new plants and cut the stolon connecting them to the parent plant. The young plants will have enough roots to establish themselves.

Although in the wild ostrich ferns are normally found in the heavy, rich soils of river floodplains, in cultivation they do quite well in rich, light soil. They appreciate constant moisture but do not require a swampy condition. Some of my plants reach nearly six feet in height in summers with no drought periods.

The fiddleheads can be collected in the spring for eating. With a sharp knife cut the fiddleheads when they are two to three inches tall and still tightly coiled. Generally, the smaller plants send up their crosiers first and the larger plants emerge as much as one or two weeks later. Once they start, they unroll quickly, and it is easy to miss them. Store them in a plastic bag in the refrigerator until you're ready to use them.

Under a steady stream of water, wash off (perhaps with gentle rubbing) the loose coating of large tan scales, and boil the fiddleheads for three to four minutes. Drain, and they are ready for eating. They may be used immediately as a hot vegetable with butter and salt, or cold in a mixed salad,

Matteuccia struthiopteris crosiers.

Matteuccia struthiopteris stolons.

or by themselves. Ostrich fern fiddleheads taste something like asparagus. My favorite way of eating them is to have them hot and dipped in hollandaise sauce as an hors d'oeuvre. I have had them cold on a slice of hard-boiled egg on a cracker. They are also good in soup, quiche, or even on a pizza. They go well with about anything involving lemon, egg, or cheese.

Cutting fiddleheads does not seem to harm the plant seriously. New fronds arise to replace the cut ones, even if you remove them all, but that is not recommended since it greatly cuts into the food supply stored in the rhizome and makes the plants more susceptible to damage or weakness. One year, as an experiment, I cut all the fronds from a few plants (sixteen from one plant), and within three weeks new fronds had fully replaced them. Later the same summer we had a serious drought and all the fronds died, but when the rains resumed in August, a third set of fronds emerged. This is drastic for the plants as it greatly weakens them, but it does show that the plants have fronds already started for the coming year or perhaps two, which can be quickly developed in case of emergency. Moderate cutting of fiddleheads is recommended, taking only three or four from each crown.

The brown, woody fertile fronds that remain erect during the winter are attractive in winter bouquets.

ONOCLEA SENSIBILIS, Sensitive fern, Bead fern

FRONDS: 1 to 3 feet long, erect, deciduous
RHIZOME HABIT: short-creeping
AVAILABILITY: common
HARDINESS ZONES: 2 to 10
EASE OF CULTIVATION: easy

Closely related to the ostrich fern, the sensitive fern is one of three ferns most often omitted from lists of protected ferns, the other two being *Dennstaedtia punctilobula* and *Pteridium aquilinum*. *Onoclea* spreads readily by both spores and creeping rhizomes, and because of its familiarity is generally undeservedly shunned in cultivation. The fronds are long-stiped (one half to two thirds the frond length), net-veined, and dimorphic. The sterile fronds are deeply pinnatifid to bipinnatifid and thin-textured whereas the fertile fronds, which emerge in late summer (growing ten to sixteen inches tall), are woody with beadlike segments, brown at maturity, and persistent through the winter. The green spores are released during the winter or early the

*Onoclea
sensibilis.*

The fertile and
sterile fronds of
Onoclea sensibilis
(the netted veins
are visible).

following spring. *Onoclea sensibilis* occurs in marshes, ditches, and swamps, both shaded or exposed. It is the only species in the genus and abundant in eastern North America.

Commonly found in spreading colonies, this medium-sized fern is a good garden plant in the right situation but becomes tired late in the season and is sensitive to frost and drought, going limp or brown. It can take wet or moist conditions. The sensitive fern tends to spread, so it needs some control (but it is not so aggressive that it can't be left a year or two). It grows well in the shade, where it may reach three feet in height, or in the sun with adequate soil moisture. The sterile fronds closely resemble those of the netted chain fern (*Woodwardia areolata*) in size, dissection, and netted veins. *Onoclea sensibilis* is different from that species in that it has a smooth rather than minutely toothed blade margin, and fertile fronds that are woody, beaded, and persistent rather than with fragile, slender pinnae that die down in the winter. Both are assertive, with strong-growing, creeping rhizomes.

Onoclea can be used around water or in the garden, either as an individual, creeping plant or in quantity. One of my neighbors has a fine patch growing quite effectively in her pachysandra. It gives some elevational and color variety to an otherwise uniform sea of dark green ground cover. Choose the location carefully so this fast grower does not overwhelm more delicate plants.

Richard Rush (1984) notes that a colorful and distinct red-stalked form is also in cultivation.

O. s. var. *interrupta*, Asian sensitive fern. This is similar to the species but the fertile segments are more widely separated. This variety is native to Japan, Korea, Manchuria, and eastern Russia.

Onychium japonicum.

ONYCHIUM JAPONICUM, Japanese claw fern, Carrot fern

FRONDS: 1 to 2½ feet long, arching, deciduous
RHIZOME HABIT: short-creeping
AVAILABILITY: rare
HARDINESS ZONES: 9 to 10
EASE OF CULTIVATION: moderate

This attractive fern is sometimes called a weed because although it is delicate, it is fast-growing once it gets started. The blade is oval-triangular and three to five times divided, the segments small and narrow. The sori are continuous along the segment margin and protected by an indusium. *Onychium japonicum* is native to southern and eastern Asia. "Claw fern" refers to the segments, which are narrow and pointed.

The Japanese claw fern is clump-forming and very attractive. The light, airy texture is so reminiscent of carrot foliage that it is called carrot fern in the nursery trade. It commonly naturalizes, though it is difficult to keep the plants in good condition. The soil should be well-drained but consistently moist. It requires bright light and high humidity. It is evergreen in zones 9 to 10 but is really at its best in the spring and summer.

OPHIOGLOSSUM, Adder's-tongue fern

The adder's-tongues are easy to miss in the moist meadows, ditches, and other disturbed grassy habitats where they grow. The best place to find them in the southeastern United States is in cemeteries. Imagine thirty botanists on their hands and knees in a Lousiana cemetery on a Sunday morning in a special kind of prayer meeting. The rhizome is subterranean, fleshy, short, and upright. The roots are also fleshy and commonly give rise to new plants from root buds. The fronds are small and undivided, the sterile blade oval or lance-shaped and of a thin texture. A fertile spike arises from the base of the blade with two vertical rows of large sporangia, each opening by a horizontal slit.

The genus consists of about twenty-five species which are found over most of the world but are more abundant in warmer regions.

Ophioglossums are largely of botanical interest and a curiosity, and not a likely prospect for the garden. Most of the species are difficult to establish due to special fungi that need to be present in the roots and the soil. They occur mostly in disturbed grassy places in the open or in light shade.

O. petiolatum
Stalked adder's-tongue
FRONDS: 2 to 8 inches long, erect, deciduous
RHIZOME HABIT: erect, fleshy, underground
AVAILABILITY: rare
HARDINESS ZONES: 7 to 10
EASE OF CULTIVATION: moderate
The blade is lance-shaped and one to two and one half inches long, and the fertile stalk is one to three and one half inches long. *Ophioglossum petiolatum* occurs in moist meadows in Florida and Arkansas, and is widespread in tropical areas of the world. Judging from its Arkansas distribution, the species is probably hardy further up the Atlantic coast than its current localities suggest. It is more readily grown in the greenhouse than most other adder's-tongues since there apparently is no fungus in the roots.

O. pusillum (syn. O. vulgatum var. pseudopodum)
Northern adder's-tongue
FRONDS: 4 to 12 inches long, erect, deciduous
RHIZOME HABIT: erect, fleshy, underground
AVAILABILITY: rare
HARDINESS ZONES: 2 to 7
EASE OF CULTIVATION: difficult
The blade is oblong and one to four inches long, and the fertile stalk is

Ophioglossum pusillum. (Photo by Joseph Beitel)

one to seven inches long. It is found in moist pastures, grassy ditches, and open woods in northern North America. It is frequent but commonly overlooked in the wild.

O. vulgatum (syn. *O. pycnostichum*)

Common adder's-tongue
Fronds: 4 to 16 inches long, erect, deciduous
Rhizome habit: erect, fleshy, underground
Availability: rare
Hardiness zones: 7 to 9
Ease of cultivation: difficult

This resembles the northern adder's-tongue, with only subtle differences. In *O. vulgatum* the sterile blade is oval (broader in the lower half) and it occurs largely in the southern and western parts of the United States, but as far north as Michigan. It is also widely distributed in temperate areas of Europe and Asia.

OSMUNDA, Flowering fern

The members of this majestic group are all quite large if grown in moist or wet situations, but they are also excellent in the average garden in both sun and shade. The stout, slow-growing, horizontal rhizome bears a dense, wiry mass of roots. The deciduous fronds form a tall crown and all species have the spores on specialized fronds or parts of fronds. The sterile blade is pinnate-pinnatifid to bipinnate and glabrous, but the stipe is densely hairy, at least when young. Hummingbirds collect this soft down to line their nests. These hairs are seen as a silvery clothing on the fiddleheads, which are among the first of all ferns up in the spring. The fertile areas (fronds or pinnae) lack leafy tissue entirely, and the masses of sporangia look like huge bunches of tiny green grapes until the green spores are shed. The empty sporangia are tan. The green spores rapidly lose their viability and must be sown in the first month or two after they are ripe, but they can be kept up to a year under refrigeration.

Osmunda is a genus of ten species native to temperate and subtropical regions, occurring in marshes, swamps, and moist forests, or in the open further north. All the species make a mass of fibrous roots on slow-growing rhizomes. This root fiber is used extensively in horticultural soil preparations, and thus wild stocks will soon be decimated.

O. cinnamomea
Cinnamon fern
FRONDS: 2½ to 5 feet long, erect, deciduous
RHIZOME HABIT: compact, horizontal
AVAILABILITY: common
HARDINESS ZONES: 2 to 10
EASE OF CULTIVATION: easy

This fern is named for its bright cinnamon-colored fertile fronds (occurring after the green spores are shed), which die down early in the summer. The sterile fronds are pinnate-pinnatifid, with a dense tuft of small rusty hairs beneath the base of each pinna. The fertile fronds totally lack any leafy tissue,

Osmunda cinnamomea.

Osmunda cinnamomea crosiers.

arising in late spring and collapsing by midsummer. *Osmunda cinnamomea* is a robust fern of swamps and other wet, generally lime-free areas in North America, Mexico, and the West Indies. It can tolerate some sun and some lime but plants do not reach maximum size under these conditions.

O. c. var. *fokiensis*. This native of eastern Asia has long black hairs as well as brown ones mixed with the sporangia, but is not readily distinguished from typical *O. cinnamomea*.

O. claytoniana
Interrupted fern
FRONDS: 2 to 4 feet long, erect, deciduous
RHIZOME HABIT: compact, horizontal
AVAILABILITY: common
HARDINESS ZONES: 2 to 8
EASE OF CULTIVATION: easy

Another majestic fern, this resembles the cinnamon fern in the pinnate-pinnatifid frond but is distinct in having the sporangia borne on several pairs of pinnae in the middle of the frond with vegetative pinnae above and below, giving an "interrupted" effect to the frond. There is no dense tuft of hairs at the base of each pinna. It occurs in moist woods rather than swamps, or in open areas in the northern part of its range, in eastern North America and eastern Asia.

The fertile pinnae of *Osmunda claytoniana* with ripe sporangia.
(PHOTO BY F. GORDON FOSTER)

The fertile pinnae of *Osmunda claytoniana* (beginning to release their spores), with vegetative pinnae above and below.

Osmunda claytoniana sporangia.
(PHOTO BY F. GORDON FOSTER)

It is abundant in Vermont and Maine where it is commonly used in landscaping along fences, walls, and foundations. It is easily grown in moist, acid soil.

O. japonica

FRONDS: 1½ to 3 feet long, erect, deciduous
RHIZOME HABIT: compact, horizontal
AVAILABILITY: rare
HARDINESS ZONES: 6 to 9
EASE OF CULTIVATION: easy

This resembles *O. regalis* in frond and segment form but the fronds are less than three feet in height and fully dimorphic; that is, each frond is entirely vegetative or entirely fertile. The fertile fronds are shorter than the sterile (one to one and one half feet tall), and segments of the sterile frond are lance-shaped, rounded at their base, and more pointed than in *O. regalis*. *Osmunda japonica* is widespread in southern and eastern Asia.

O. lancea

FRONDS: 1½ to 3 feet long, erect, deciduous
RHIZOME HABIT: compact, horizontal
AVAILABILITY: rare
HARDINESS ZONES: 8 to 9
EASE OF CULTIVATION: easy

This distinctive Japanese species closely resembles *O. regalis* but is slightly smaller and less hairy, and its pinnules are more leathery and narrowed at the segment base rather than rounded as in *O. japonica*.

O. regalis
Royal fern, Flowering fern

FRONDS: 2 to 5 feet (though sometimes to 10 feet) long, erect, deciduous
RHIZOME HABIT: compact
AVAILABILITY: frequent
HARDINESS ZONES: 2 to 10
EASE OF CULTIVATION: easy

This extremely attractive species has a bipinnate blade with oblong segments spaced apart on the pinna rachises, naked except for a few scattered hairs on the rachises. The fertile pinnae comprise the terminal one quarter to one third of the frond.

It occurs in swamps and other wet sites in eastern North America, tropical America, and Europe. Forms with green and purple stipes and rachises are found in each variety, the latter often called 'Purpurascens'.

O. r. var. *regalis*. The fronds of this European variety are stouter, fleshier, and often much larger than those of var. *spectabilis*, reaching ten feet in height. Plants of this variety remain green until hard freezing weather, whereas var. *spectabilis* and the other two native North American osmundas (*O. cinnamomea* and *O. claytoniana*) turn a delightful golden color.

O. r. var. *r.* 'Crispa' (syn. 'Undulatifolia') has crisped margins.

O. r. var. *r.* 'Cristata' has crested segment tips.

O. r. var. *r.* 'Gracilis' has more slender fertile parts than other European material, resembling somewhat the American var. *spectabilis* and may be the same.

O. r. var. *r.* 'Purpurascens'. The stipe and rachis are purplish rather than green.

O. r. var. *spectabilis*. The segments are thinner and more widely spaced than in var. *regalis*. It usually grows in acidic swamps and marshes across much of the Americas.

Osmunda regalis 'Crispa'.   *Osmunda regalis* 'Cristata'.   *Osmunda regalis* var. *spectabilis*.

Osmunda regalis var. *spectabilis* crosiers. (PHOTO BY F. GORDON FOSTER)

A physiological form of var. *spectabilis* from Brazil (sometimes called var. *brasiliensis*) puts out new fertile fronds all through the growing season rather than only at the beginning. Growing plants in a common garden from different parts of the Americas would help clarify the variations of growth and development.

O. r. var. *s.* 'Purpurascens'. As in var. *regalis*, the stipe and rachis can be purplish rather than green.

O. × *ruggi* (O. *claytoniana* × *regalis* var. *spectabilis*)
Rugg's hybrid royal fern
FRONDS: 2 to 4 feet long, erect, deciduous
RHIZOME HABIT: compact, horizontal
AVAILABILITY: rare
HARDINESS ZONES: 2 to 8
EASE OF CULTIVATION: easy

Hybrids are very rare in *Osmunda*, this one being found only twice in the wild. It is sterile (abortive spores) and does not make offsets, branching only uncommonly, so it is very rare in cultivation. It is outstanding of form, though, and hopefully some way will be found to propagate it, such as by tissue culture.

PAESIA SCABERULA, Lace fern

FRONDS: 1 to 3 feet long, erect, deciduous
RHIZOME HABIT: long-creeping
AVAILABILITY: rare
HARDINESS ZONES: 8 to 10
EASE OF CULTIVATION: moderate

The fronds are stiff and three to four times divided with a zigzag rachis. Abundant glandular hairs are found on the undersurface of the blade, and the sori are located along the margin, protected by the recurved margin. The genus is closely related to *Pteridium* and *Hypolepis*, as is shown by the long-creeping, much-branched rhizome. *Paesia scaberula* is native to New Zealand, where it can be weedy in disturbed habitats. In the Seattle area it is hardy in lightly shaded gardens with acidic soil.

PARACETERACH REYNOLDSII (syn. *Gymnopteris vestita*), Mouse-ear fern

FRONDS: 6 to 12 inches long, erect-arching, deciduous
RHIZOME HABIT: short-creeping
AVAILABILITY: rare
HARDINESS ZONES: 8 to 10
EASE OF CULTIVATION: moderate

This beautiful species with its small silver leaves has pinnae shaped like

The upper surface of a frond of *Paraceterach reynoldsii*.

The lower surface of *Paraceterach reynoldsii*, showing the sporangia among the scales.

little woolly ears. The clumped fronds are once-pinnate, the pinnae oval to oblong and one inch long. They are densely white-scaly beneath and pale green above. The sori run along the veins and lack an indusium but are hidden among the scales. *Paraceterach reynoldsii* is native to southern and western China, the Himalayas, Pakistan, and Taiwan. It is grown outdoors at Kew Gardens near London, England, so it ought to be hardy in the milder parts of North America. The mouse-ear fern grows well in a loamy, acid soil in light shade or partial sun.

PELLAEA, Cliff brake

The cliff brakes are largely native to America and are well adapted to use in rock gardens. The rhizome is short- to long-creeping. The fronds are small to medium-sized, one to three times divided, and naked or with only a few scattered hairs. The sori are marginal with the leaf margin recurved to protect the sporangia. Many have bluish green or bluish gray fronds contrasting with the dark stipes.

This is a genus of about eighty species of temperate and subtropical dry regions, found in rock crevices and ledges, often on calcareous rocks.

Pellaea requires good drainage, and can often grow in full sun. It is important to have the soil packed around the roots and to keep it moist. Once they are established, cliff brakes can tolerate sun and dry periods, but if they are not well established, drought will kill them.

P. andromedifolia
Coffee fern
FRONDS: 6 to 24 inches long, erect, deciduous
RHIZOME HABIT: long-creeping

Pellaea andromedifolia, purple form.

AVAILABILITY: infrequent
HARDINESS ZONES: 8 to 9
EASE OF CULTIVATION: moderate

The triangular blade is tripinnate, with smooth-margined, oval pinnules. It occurs on noncalcareous rocks in California and Baja California.

There is a form of *P. andromedifolia* with purple frond segments which is very attractive. It is grown side by side with the green form in the Tilden Park Botanic Gardens in Berkeley, California.

P. atropurpurea
Purple cliff brake
FRONDS: 8 to 20 inches long, erect-arching, evergreen
RHIZOME HABIT: short-creeping
AVAILABILITY: frequent
HARDINESS ZONES: 4 to 9
EASE OF CULTIVATION: moderate

The dark purple to black stipe gives the name to this species. The lance-shaped to triangular blade is bipinnate to nearly tripinnate, and each pinna has two to five pairs of narrowly oblong, bluish gray pinnules. *Pellaea atropurpurea* occurs on calcareous rocks over much of North America and Mexico. It is easy to grow from spores and does well in a rock garden among limestone rocks, or at least with lime in the soil.

P. brachyptera
Sierra cliff brake
FRONDS: 4 to 15 inches long, erect, evergreen

Pellaea atropurpurea.

RHIZOME HABIT: short-creeping
AVAILABILITY: rare
HARDINESS ZONES: 7 to 8
EASE OF CULTIVATION: difficult

This small cliff brake has a narrowly oblong blade that is bipinnate. The pinnae are very short, with two to six pairs of linear, bluish gray pinnules crowded on the pinna rachis. Each pinnule is about one half inch long with a strongly inrolled margin and a sharp-pointed tip. *Pellaea brachyptera* occurs on basalt or serpentine rocks from Washington to northern California.

P. bridgesii
Bridges' cliff brake
FRONDS: 8 to 14 inches long, erect, deciduous
RHIZOME HABIT: short-creeping
AVAILABILITY: rare
HARDINESS ZONES: 6 to 8
EASE OF CULTIVATION: difficult

The linear-oblong blade is once-pinnate with a chestnut brown stipe and rachis. The round to oblong pinnae are leathery and a dusty bluish green. The fertile pinnae are often folded in half along the midvein, and the sori are slightly elongate along the veins with no indusium. Bridges' cliff brake occurs on rocky slopes at high elevations in the western United States.

P. cordifolia
FRONDS: 10 to 16 inches long, erect, deciduous
RHIZOME HABIT: compact, horizontal
AVAILABILITY: rare
HARDINESS ZONES: 9 to 10
EASE OF CULTIVATION: easy

The bipinnate fronds have round to heart-shaped, light green to gray-green segments. It occurs in dry, rocky regions of the southwestern United States and Mexico.

P. glabella
Smooth cliff brake
FRONDS: 5 to 14 inches long, erect-arching, evergreen
RHIZOME HABIT: short-creeping or ascending

AVAILABILITY: frequent
HARDINESS ZONES: 3 to 7
EASE OF CULTIVATION: moderate

This species closely resembles *P. atropurpurea* but has a smooth, chestnut brown stipe (rather than hairy and purplish black). The blade is narrowly oblong and once-pinnate to bipinnate, with one to three pairs of lobes or pinnules on each pinna. It generally occurs on calcareous rocks, often in the mortar of old bridges, throughout much of North America. It can be grown from spores, but is not as easy to establish as *P. atropurpurea*.

P. intermedia
Intermediate cliff brake
FRONDS: 6 to 24 inches long, erect, deciduous
RHIZOME HABIT: long-creeping
AVAILABILITY: rare
HARDINESS ZONES: 8 to 9
EASE OF CULTIVATION: moderate

The triangular blade is mostly bipinnate with a yellow to brown stipe and rachis. The pinnules are oval or oblong and are held on short stalks. *Pellaea intermedia* occurs on calcareous or noncalcareous rocks and slopes in the southwestern United States and northern Mexico.

P. mucronata
Bird's-foot fern
FRONDS: 3 to 16 inches long, erect, deciduous
RHIZOME HABIT: short-creeping
AVAILABILITY: rare

Pellaea mucronata.
(PHOTO BY F. GORDON FOSTER)

Pellaea ovata.
(PHOTO BY JUDITH JONES)

HARDINESS ZONES: 7 to 9

EASE OF CULTIVATION: difficult

This species is distinguished by its small blade segments that are set in groups of three, resembling little bird's feet. The oval blade is bipinnate to tripinnate and the stipe and rachis are chestnut brown. The segments are often folded in half lengthwise. *Pellaea mucronata* occurs on noncalcareous rocks in California and Baja California.

P. ovata

Flexuous cliff brake

FRONDS: 10 to 30 inches long, arching or scrambling, deciduous

RHIZOME HABIT: short-creeping

AVAILABILITY: infrequent

HARDINESS ZONES: 8 to 10

EASE OF CULTIVATION: moderate

Pellaea ovata is remarkable in having a zigzag rachis, which forces the pinnae to point downward. This pinna orientation allows the flexuous cliff brake to scramble over nearby plants. The narrowly oblong blade is tripinnate, and the stipe and rachis are yellow, woody, and usually short-hairy. The pinnules are oval and yellow-green, their bases rounded or slightly heart-shaped. *Pellaea ovata* occurs on noncalcareous or sometimes calcareous soil or rocks in Texas and is widespread in tropical America.

This species is at least marginally hardy in the Seattle area, tolerating deep freezing as a pot plant, and should be tried more often in cultivation. The fronds clamber onto nearby vegetation or are pendent.

PENTAGRAMMA TRIANGULARIS
(syn. *Pityrogramma triangularis*)

Goldback fern

FRONDS: 4 to 8 inches long, erect, deciduous

RHIZOME HABIT: compact, ascending

AVAILABILITY: infrequent

HARDINESS ZONES: 6 to 9

EASE OF CULTIVATION: moderate

Usually listed under *Pityrogramma*, the goldback fern has a yellow wax covering the lower surface of its triangular to pentagonal fronds, contrasting

Pentagramma triangularis, a closeup of the lower surface, showing the wax and sporangia. (PHOTO BY F. GORDON FOSTER)

Pentagramma triangularis. (PHOTO BY ALAN SMITH)

dramatically with the smooth dark green of the upper surface. The blade is pinnate-pinnatifid (bipinnate at the very base), the lowest pair of pinnae strongly elongated on the basiscopic side. The stipe makes up two thirds of the frond length. The fronds often curl up when dry but recover with moisture. The sporangia run along the veins and lack an indusium. *Pentagramma triangularis* occurs on or among rocks from British Columbia to Baja California. It is well suited for the sunny rock garden if it has good drainage and the plants are well established.

Pentagramma triangularis and two silver-backed species with glands on their upper blade surfaces form a small, closely related group in western North America. *Pentagramma pallida* has a purplish black stipe and occurs in central California whereas *P. viscosa* has a reddish brown stipe and less divided blade, and occurs in southern California. The latter two species are less hardy than *P. triangularis*.

PHANEROPHLEBIA

The genus *Phanerophlebia* is closely related to *Polystichum* and *Cyrtomium*, as shown by the round, umbrella-shaped indusium and leathery blade. The rhizome is ascending with tan scales, and the fronds are once-pinnate. The eight species are native largely to rich, wet forests of Mexico, with species extending into southern Texas and south to Venezuela.

P. auriculata
Eared holly fern
FRONDS: 6 to 27 inches long, arching, evergreen

RHIZOME HABIT: ascending
AVAILABILITY: rare
HARDINESS ZONES: 8 to 10
EASE OF CULTIVATION: moderate

The fronds have three to twelve pairs of pinnae, each broadly wedge-shaped and usually with an auricle on the upper side of the base. The margins are finely toothed with bristle tips or sometimes with incisions. The indusium is delicate and often soon disintegrates. The species occurs on damp canyon walls and cliffs in the southwestern United States and northern Mexico.

P. macrosora

FRONDS: 12 to 30 inches long, arching, evergreen
RHIZOME HABIT: ascending
AVAILABILITY: rare
HARDINESS ZONES: 8 to 10
EASE OF CULTIVATION: moderate

This species has the largest fronds in the genus, with the many tan stipe scales up to one half inch long. The blade has six to seventeen pairs of pinnae and the juvenile foliage has the distinctive smell of a skunk. *Phanerophlebia macrosora* is found in high-elevation wet forests from southern Mexico to Costa Rica.

P. pumila

FRONDS: 3 to 12 inches long, arching, evergreen
RHIZOME HABIT: ascending
AVAILABILITY: rare

Phanerophlebia macrosora.

HARDINESS ZONES: 8 to 10

EASE OF CULTIVATION: moderate

Phanerophlebia pumila is the most variable species in the genus, at least in the wild. Plants found in the wild at the original collection locality are only three inches long and have only three pinnae (one pair and the apical one), but when transplanted to the greenhouse, new fronds had five pairs. The stipe base scales are brown, lance-shaped, and about one quarter inch long. This is a native on limestone cliffs in cloud forests of southern Mexico and Guatemala.

PHYLLITIS, Hart's-tongue fern

The hart's-tongue fern is one of the most readily recognized ferns, its leathery, strap- or tongue-shaped fronds arising from an ascending rhizome. What look like individual, linear sori are really pairs of sori on adjacent veins facing each other, each with its own indusium, but at maturity the pair appears to coalesce. The fronds are clumped, erect-arching, with a very short, scaly stipe, and the blade base is heart-shaped.

Phyllitis is a genus of five similar species, largely of north temperate regions, occurring in Europe, Asia, North America, and southern Mexico and Hispaniola. The genus is closely allied to *Asplenium* (some botanists include *Phyllitis* within *Asplenium*), and there are several intergeneric hybrids.

Hart's-tongue ferns are limestone-loving plants but occasionally they are found on slightly acidic soil or rocks. They are fairly easy to grow, but do appreciate a topdressing of humus. Be careful not to overwater; the plants must have good drainage to avoid root rot. If your rocks are acid, you can make the soil basic by incorporating concrete rubble, limestone chips, or oyster shells around the plants. *Phyllitis* can be propagated by spores, but in the case of sterile varieties or varieties that do not come true from spores, vegetative propagation is necessary. Rhizome divisions are rare, but the hart's-tongue can be grown from pieces of the stipe base. See Chapter 3: Propagation.

P. scolopendrium (syn. *Asplenium scolopendrium, Scolopendrium vulgare*)

Hart's-tongue fern

FRONDS: 8 to 16 inches long, erect-arching, evergreen

Phyllitis scolopendrium.

Phyllitis scolopendrium from below, showing the sori.

RHIZOME HABIT: ascending

AVAILABILITY: common

HARDINESS ZONES: 5 to 9

EASE OF CULTIVATION: easy to difficult

Scolopendra is Greek for "centipede," alluding to the resemblance of the two rows of regularly arranged linear sori on the lower surface of the frond to the many legs of a centipede. The species and its varieties in cultivation are affectionately known as "scollies."

The two varieties are virtually impossible to distinguish. All cultivated material is of the European variety. The American variety does poorly in cultivation and not much better in the wild. It must not be collected.

P. s. var. *americana.* This variety occurs on cool, moist, shaded, dolomitic limestone as a rarity from northern Michigan, across southern Ontario, to western New York, with distant populations in Tennessee and Alabama.

Wherry (1961, p. 170) says that conservationists have rescued clumps from quarries and set them out in seemingly favorable spots, but without much success.

P. s. var. *scolopendrium.* In extreme cases the fronds can reach three feet in length and four inches in width. It occurs on both acid and calcareous rocks, on old walls, and in hedgerows in Europe and Asia.

At the fern glen of the New York Botanical Garden's Cary Arboretum at Millbrook, New York, we developed a limestone cobble and planted it heavily with var. *scolopendrium* in 1979. Less than half the plants made it through the first winter, and the remaining plants died in the following winter. In the summer of 1981, however, we noticed that numerous hart's-tongue sporelings had established themselves at the bases of rocks. They survived the winter of 1981–1982, which had a low temperature of − 24 degrees Fahrenheit. Thus, it seems that it is not so much a problem of being hardy in this area but rather one of ecology. The spores in the right niche survive and do better than do the full-grown transplanted parent plants, at least in this situation. Another factor may be the amount of moisture available as the plants enter winter. Dry conditions may have weakened the plants, making them less able to withstand the low temperatures.

Unfortunately, the original plants were from several documented sources, and we have no way of knowing the origins of the volunteer plants—whether the babies are from certain more vigorous parents or whether they came from all of the original plants.

This difference in success rate between young plants or sporelings as opposed to mature plants helps us understand hardiness problems in other species. Further testing of plants from different regions and of different ages would prove very interesting.

The European hart's-tongue crosses with species of *Asplenium* to form *Asplenophyllitis*, and with *Ceterach* to form *Phyllitoceterach*. Remarkably, it also crosses with *Asplenosorus ebenoides* (the hybrid of *Asplenium platyneuron* and *Camptosorus rhizophyllus*) to form the only known trigeneric cross among the ferns.

Phyllitis scolopendrium var. *scolopendrium* is one of the handful of ferns displaying unbelievable variation in the British Isles. Lowe (*British Ferns and Where Found*, 1890) listed 445 varieties. In his enthusiasm he was doubtless naming every slight variation, but even so, there is a tremendous display of variants. A visit to just a few British fern gardens gives a dramatic glimpse of these marvelous ferns, and although relatively few are available in North America, more are entering the market each year. Unfortunately, these cultivars are not reliable from spores.

I have listed and illustrated here just a sampling of the many forms. Not all of these are available in North America but these samples show the amazing diversity within the species. Some varieties will combine the characters of more than one character group, such as 'Cristata Muricata' or 'Sagittata Cristata' (see British Varieties on page 26). For a more detailed discussion of the variation in this remarkable species, see Dyce, "British Fern Varieties— The Scolopendriums," *British Pteridological Society Newsletter* 10 (1972): 20–22.

Crested forms: This is the most common type of variation. The frond apex is divided, ranging from once-forked to flat crests (multiple forkings in one plane) to bunched tassels or corymbs (tight, three-dimensional crests).

Phyllitis scolopendrium 'Cristata'.

P. s. 'Cristata'. This name is used loosely for any crested form but more particularly for a form with the forkings in one plane. Other names applying to this sort of cresting include 'Digitata', 'Flabellata', and 'Multifida'. At one time these names designated very specific forms, but that has not proved practical, and today the names are used rather indiscriminately for crested forms in general. Names used for three-dimensional cresting include 'Capitata' and 'Corymbifera'.

P. s. 'Glomerata' is a dazzling dwarf crested form, with fronds only three to six inches tall and generally lacking any strap-shaped portion of the blade. The blade forks several times in three dimensions to form a round ball, somewhat resembling a head of broccoli.

P. s. 'Keratoides' is six to nine inches long, forked near the base two to three times, with a roughened finish (muricate—see below) on the upper surface. The blades branch several times, making it look like a staghorn, the name meaning "hornlike."

P. s. 'Ramosa' indicates forking but lower on the frond than normal cresting,

Phyllitis scolopendrium 'Glomerata'.

Phyllitis scolopendrium 'Keratoides'.

Phyllitis scolopendrium 'Ramosa
Cristata'.

branching three to four times, with each division ending in a crest. It is
called "crested" if the forking is in the terminal third of the blade, or "ramose"
if it is in the lower two thirds of the blade or even on the stipe. Obviously,
there is every transition, so there is no sharp distinction between the two.
Blades can be broad to very narrow. The plant can also be crisped ('Ramosa
Crispa'), marginate ('Ramosa Marginata'—see below), or any other combination of characteristics. 'Ramosa Cristata' has fronds branching from the
stipe to form five crested blades, looking like pinnae of a compound leaf.

There are some forms of cresting that are so dense at the end of a very
long stipe that the weight of water caught in the tassels will cause the fronds
to topple and break.

Crisped, or undulate, margin: The frond remains undivided but the margin
is undulate, from slightly wavy to so deeply wavy as to resemble ribbon candy
or lasagna.

P. s. 'Crispa'. The frond margin is deeply frilled like a Elizabethan ruff.
Usually it is barren, and propagation must be done vegetatively.

P. s. 'Crispa Bolton's Nobile'. Kaye (1968) says this is the best of the crispas.
The dark green fronds can attain two feet in length and four inches in width,
and the frond is deeply frilled.

P. s. 'Crispa Cristata' has the frond both frilled and crested, displaying
varying degrees of forking.

P. s. 'Crispa Fimbriata'. The ruffling is finely broken into delicate fringes
and may be very heavily tasseled.

P. s. 'Crispa Golden Moly' has the frond tip tapering off quickly to a sharp

Phyllitis scolopendrium 'Crispa'.

Phyllitis scolopendrium 'Crispa Bolton's Nobile'.

point. The frond is narrow with a yellowish tinge, and the pleats are especially deep.

P. s. 'Undulata'. The blade margins are wavy and not as deeply frilled as those of 'Crispa'. The fronds are fertile, which tends to interfere with the depth of the margin's waviness.

Dissected margin: The margin may be finely and evenly cut (fimbriate) or deeply and irregularly dissected (lacerated) and is often combined with other characters such as 'Crispa Fimbriata'.

P. s. 'Dwarf Fimbriate'. It is difficult to recognize this even as a fern with its tiny fronds and delicately dissected margin.

P. s. 'Fimbriata' has a finely dissected margin, the incisions cut one quarter of the way to the midvein. This is thought to be one of the marginate group

Phyllitis scolopendrium 'Crispa Golden Moly'.

Phyllitis scolopendrium 'Dwarf Fimbriate'.

Phyllitis scolopendrium 'Kaye's Lacerate'.

(see below) with a raised ridge on the undersurface running the length of the blade more or less midway between the midvein and the margin, with the sori, when present, external to the ridge. However, the cut margin is easier to distinguish than the ridge, so I have placed it in the dissected group.

P. s. 'Kaye's Lacerate'. The blade is broadly oval, the margins deeply and irregularly cut and somewhat ruffled like lettuce. Fronds reach twelve inches in length and four inches in width, and it tends to form miniature crests.

Other variations:

P. s. 'Marginata' has a raised ridge the length of the frond, usually on the underside, about halfway between the midvein and margin. The frond is narrow, and the margin deeply and closely lobed.

P. s. 'Marginata Irregulare'. Fronds are eight to twelve inches long and only about one inch wide. The margin is irregularly wavy and the raised ridge is not as evident in this form.

P. s. 'Muricata' has a roughened surface and lacks the shiny green of other forms. The upper surface is a mass of raised, sharply ridged wrinkles. This condition is sometimes combined with the marginate and crested characteristics ('Muricata Marginata' and 'Muricata Cristata').

P. s. 'Sagittata'. The base of the blade is extended laterally into long lobes, giving the frond an arrowhead shape. These projections are very short to quite long.

P. s. 'Sagittata Cristata' is crested at the blade apex and on the extended basal lobes as well.

P. s. 'Vivipara' is a rare form with plantlets developing on the upper surface of the blade.

PILULARIA, Pillwort

These small aquatic ferns are closely related to *Marsilea*. The rhizome is slender and widely creeping, forming colonies. Most peculiarly, the fronds consist only of the leaf stalk and totally lack any leaf blade, appearing much like grass but bely their fern nature by their unrolling stipes. The sporangia are borne in round, leathery or stony sporocarps formed at the base of the leaf stalks. *Pilularia* has six species occurring in warm temperate regions.

Plants are easily cultivated from divisions. It is wise to keep dividing them since they tend to fade, perhaps from being too crowded. If you are starting the pillwort in a pot, plant it in potting soil and set the pot in a dish of water to keep the soil wet at all times. Strong light is required for good growth. This novelty might be planted outside in a muddy area by a small pool.

P. americana
American pillwort
FRONDS: 1½ to 5 inches long, erect, deciduous
RHIZOME HABIT: creeping
AVAILABILITY: rare
HARDINESS ZONES: 6 to 9
EASE OF CULTIVATION: moderate

This aquatic fern has uncurling stalks without any blades; the sporocarps are located at the base of the fronds and are one sixteenth to one eighth inch long. The American pillwort is found on wet soil by ponds or in seasonal pools in Georgia, Arkansas, Texas, Oklahoma, Kansas, California, and Oregon.

P. globulifera
European pillwort
FRONDS: 1 to 3 inches long (to 10 inches in the wild), erect, deciduous

RHIZOME HABIT: creeping

AVAILABILITY: rare

HARDINESS ZONES: 6 to 9

EASE OF CULTIVATION: moderate

The European pillwort is similar to the American species, differing only in the number of sori in the sporocarp.

POLYPODIUM, Polypody

The polypodies are generally rock-loving plants found in temperate parts of the world. *Polypodium* means "many feet," alluding to the creeping, much-branched rhizome. The fronds are small and the blade pinnatifid, leathery, and evergreen. Unusual among ferns, the fronds fall off cleanly from the rhizome rather than just lying down. The large, round, moundlike sori lack an indusium, and the spores (and mature sori) are a bright golden yellow. *Polypodium* is a genus of about 150 species, largely of the New World tropics. Most species are epiphytes, whereas the temperate species occur on the ground and rocks.

Some of the North American species are cultivated, but most cultivated material is of the European *P. vulgare* complex (*P. cambricum*, *P. interjectum*, *P. vulgare*), which is abundant in Europe on walls, roofs, rocks, and on trees. They are readily cultivated in rock gardens but do not do as well in deep garden soil, preferring a rocky area or stony soil. High humidity is needed for best development. They tend to be slow to grow from spores and slow-growing in general.

P. amorphum (syn. *P. montense*)
Mountain polypody

FRONDS: 4 to 12 inches long, erect, evergreen

RHIZOME HABIT: creeping

AVAILABILITY: rare

HARDINESS ZONES: 6 to 8

EASE OF CULTIVATION: moderate

The mountain polypody is only about one inch wide, occurring on igneous rocks, cliffs, and ledges on the Pacific Coast and Cascade Range from British Columbia to California. It has crossed with *P. sibiricum* to form the fertile hybrid *P. hesperium* (page 254).

Polypodium californicum.
(PHOTO BY JUDITH JONES)

P. californicum
California polypody
FRONDS: 7 to 15 inches long, arching, deciduous
RHIZOME HABIT: creeping
AVAILABILITY: infrequent
HARDINESS ZONES: 8 to 9
EASE OF CULTIVATION: moderate

The fronds are two to three and one half inches wide. There are nine to thirteen pairs of pinnae with rounded to slightly pointed tips and sharply toothed margins. It occurs mostly on rocks in California and northern Mexico.

P. cambricum (syn. P. australe)
Southern polypody
FRONDS: 6 to 12 inches long (to 18 inches in the wild), erect, evergreen
RHIZOME HABIT: short- to long-creeping
AVAILABILITY: frequent
HARDINESS ZONES: 8 to 9
EASE OF CULTIVATION: moderate

The blades are triangular-oval, yellow-green, often with a long, narrow apical segment. The pinnae often taper to a pointed tip with a conspicuously toothed margin. Unlike those of most other polypodies, the fronds are produced in late summer, remaining green through the winter, releasing their spores in the spring, and dying down early the next summer. It occurs on limestone and mortared walls in the warmer parts of Britain and across southern Europe.

This species has been known most commonly as *P. australe*, meaning, appropriately, the southern polypody. Linnaeus gave the name *P. cambricum* to a dissected plant that turned out to be a dissected form of *P. australe*. Unfortunately for the familiar *australe*, *cambricum* is the earliest name for the species and therefore, by the rules of nomenclature, must be used as the species name, even though it is not typical of the species. The varietal name 'Cambricum', though, is still used for the dissected form itself.

There are several cultivars of this species, but unfortunately *P. cambricum* is very difficult to distinguish from *P. vulgare* and *P. interjectum*. Most of the varieties were originally described under *P. vulgare* and only in recent years have botanists found that it is a complex of three species, in which *vulgare* crossed with *cambricum* to form the fertile *interjectum*. Ironically, hardly any of the varieties actually belong to the true *vulgare*. From a practical standpoint, it makes little difference which species they really belong to, since it is very difficult to distinguish the three species. Thus, I will treat all the varieties under *P. vulgare*.

As a brief summary of the characteristics of the three species:

Polypodium vulgare has very narrowly lance-shaped fronds; the pinnae are smooth-margined; the mature yellow sporangia have a reddish annulus; the rhizome scales have a pointed but not long tip, about three times as long as wide; the fronds are green and appear in early summer; there are no special hairs (paraphyses) in the sori; it has many sori, over most of the blade.

Polypodium cambricum has broadly oval-triangular fronds; the pinnae are often toothed; the annulus of the mature sporangia is indistinct, and special hairs (paraphyses) are present in the sorus; the rhizome scales are long, over three times as long as they are wide, the tip is attenuated; the fronds are yellowish green and appear in late summer and early fall; and it has few sori, on the upper third of the blade.

Polypodium interjectum, the hybrid between the other two, is intermediate in its characteristics: The fronds are narrowly oval; the annulus is indistinct; the rhizome scales are long-pointed, over three times as long as they are wide, and the tip long; the fronds are light green and appear in late summer; there are no paraphyses; the sori are many, occurring over the upper one to two thirds of the blade.

More technical characteristics of sporangium, spores, and chromosome number are used by botanists for definite identification.

P. formosanum
Green serpent
FRONDS: 8 to 16 inches long, erect-arching, deciduous

Polypodium formosanum.   Rhizome of *Polypodium formosanum.*

RHIZOME HABIT: creeping
AVAILABILITY: infrequent
HARDINESS ZONES: 9 to 10
EASE OF CULTIVATION: moderate

The rhizome is most distinct and attractive in being nearly smooth, whitish green, with only minute, scattered, black scales that are deciduous with age. The pinnae are very slender, long, pointed, and pale green, and the blade is glabrous except for minute hairs on the top of the rachis and along the blade margin. It is native to Japan, China, and Taiwan.

P. glycyrrhiza

Licorice fern

FRONDS: 5 to 24 inches long, erect-arching, summer-deciduous, winter-green
RHIZOME HABIT: creeping
AVAILABILITY: frequent
HARDINESS ZONES: 6 to 8
EASE OF CULTIVATION: moderate

The blade is broadly oblong and two to four inches wide. The ten to twenty-five pairs of pinnae are sharp-pointed and finely toothed. It occurs on trees and rocks in western North America.

The licorice fern is ideal for rock gardens, especially in milder, humid regions. The common name comes from a licorice flavor in the rhizome.

P. g. 'Longicaudatum'. The apex of the frond is greatly elongated, like a tail.

Polypodium glycyrrhiza 'Longicaudatum'.

P. g. 'Malahatense' resembles 'Cambricum' of England but the lobes are not as long (not overlapping those of adjacent pinnae), and the pinna tips are all slender and barren although there is a fertile form that is not as finely divided.

P. hesperium
Western polypody
FRONDS: 4 to 15 inches long, erect, evergreen
RHIZOME HABIT: creeping
AVAILABILITY: rare
HARDINESS ZONES: 5 to 8
EASE OF CULTIVATION: moderate
The blade is narrowly oblong, one to one and three quarters inches wide. The pinnae occur in four to fourteen pairs, with rounded tips. It occurs in rock crevices in western North America. It is the fertile cross between *P. amorphum* and *P. glycyrrhiza*.

P. interjectum
FRONDS: 6 to 18 inches (to 24 inches) long, erect, deciduous
RHIZOME HABIT: creeping
AVAILABILITY: infrequent
HARDINESS ZONES: 6 to 8
EASE OF CULTIVATION: moderate
The blade is narrowly oval-lance-shaped, two and one half to three inches wide, medium green, the new leaves produced in late summer and autumn. It is evergreen in England. It occurs on rocky banks and cliffs, and mortared

walls in Europe. *Polypodium interjectum* is a wonderful garden plant, needing limestone and wetter conditions than other polypodiums.

P. polypodioides
Resurrection fern, Gray polypody
FRONDS: 4 to 8 inches long, erect, evergreen
RHIZOME HABIT: long-creeping
AVAILABILITY: infrequent
HARDINESS ZONES: 6 to 10
EASE OF CULTIVATION: moderate

The blade is lance-shaped. The eight to fourteen pairs of pinnae are about one eighth inch wide, densely scaly on the lower surface, with few or no scales on the upper surface. *Polypodium polypodioides* is common on trees and rocks in the southeastern United States north to Maryland and southern Ohio, west to Missouri, and widespread in tropical America.

This might be used in rock gardens in the southern states, either in the ground between rocks or attached to a branch or log.

P. scouleri
Leathery polypody
FRONDS: 4 to 18 inches long, erect-arching, evergreen
RHIZOME HABIT: creeping
AVAILABILITY: infrequent
HARDINESS ZONES: 8 to 9
EASE OF CULTIVATION: moderate

This is an especially attractive species with only two to six broad, rounded

Polypodium polypodioides. (PHOTO BY SUE OLSEN)

Polypodium polypodioides sori. (PHOTO BY F. GORDON FOSTER)

Polypodium scouleri. (Photo by Pamela J. Harper)

pinnae of a leathery texture and very dark green color to the fronds. Scales are scattered on the rachis and the lower surface of the pinna midveins. The pinnae are usually in two to six pairs. The sori are large (one eighth inch or more wide), and crowded against the pinna midveins. It occurs on rocks and trees, usually within a mile of the Pacific Ocean, in western North America.

Polypodium scouleri can be cultivated in the western United States, but does not do well in the East, due probably to the hot summers, colder winters, and lower humidity.

P. thyssanolepis
FRONDS: 4 to 16 inches long, erect, evergreen
RHIZOME HABIT: creeping
AVAILABILITY: rare
HARDINESS ZONES: 8 to 10
EASE OF CULTIVATION: easy

This robust polypody has a dense covering of scales on the undersurface of the blade and three to fifteen pairs of pinnae about one half inch wide. It occurs on rocky slopes in open woods and clearings from southwestern United States to Bolivia.

P. virginianum (P. vulgare in some catalogs; syn P. vulgare var. virginianam)
Virginia polypody, Rockcap fern
FRONDS: 4 to 14 inches long, erect, evergreen
RHIZOME HABIT: creeping
AVAILABILITY: frequent
HARDINESS ZONES: 2 to 8
EASE OF CULTIVATION: moderate

Polypodium virginianum.

Polypodium virginianum sori. (Photo by Barbara Hallowell)

This delightful little rock fern has eleven to eighteen pairs of pinnae, each about three sixteenths inch wide and the tips narrowly rounded to pointed. It is found on or among moist, shaded rocks in eastern and central North America. It often forms large clumps by way of its much-branched, creeping rhizome. Wherry (1961) stated: "It can be grown in a shaded rock garden, though it is difficult to get started as the soil must be rich in humus but poor in nutrients, and kept both moist and well drained."

It has been shown that *P. virginianum* is composed of three elements: *P. appalachianum* (eastern North America) and *P. sibiricum* (northern Canada, Alaska, and eastern Asia), which crossed sometime in the past to form the fertile hybrid *P. virginianum* in a restricted sense (eastern North America).

P. vulgare
Common polypody
FRONDS: 3 to 10 inches long, erect, evergreen
RHIZOME HABIT: creeping
AVAILABILITY: frequent
HARDINESS ZONES: 5 to 8
EASE OF CULTIVATION: moderate

This is similar to *P. interjectum* but produces new leaves in early summer rather than late summer and fall. The fronds are medium green and the blades are narrowly lance-shaped (juvenile or stunted fronds are triangular). Dense colonies of fronds are produced at intervals from the stout, scaly, branched, creeping rhizome. Sori are abundant on the upper one quarter to three quarters of the blade. It occurs on both acidic and limestone rocks on steep slopes and rocky outcrops in Europe and Asia.

An old poem goes, "*Polypodium vulgare*, how remarkably you vary." And

Polypodium vulgare.

Polypodium vulgare 'Bifidum Cristatum'.

Polypodium vulgare 'Grandiceps' (with 'Cornubiense').

no wonder, since *P. vulgare* turns out to be really three species (*P. cambricum*, *P. interjectum*, and *P. vulgare*) along with their many forms. The following examples include varieties of all three (mostly of *P. cambricum*, some of *P. interjectum*, and perhaps none at all of *P. vulgare* itself), but since it is difficult to distinguish the three species with certainty, we will still consider them as varieties of *P. vulgare*. The varieties are generally not reliable from spore. For more detailed analysis of this group, see Rickard, "Survey of Variation in British Polypodiums," *British Pteridological Society Bulletin* 1(3)(1981): 138–140.

Crested forms: Fertile forms with frond or pinnae branched, forked once to several times.

   P. v. 'Bifidum' has the pinnae once-forked (bifid) and the blade lacking a terminal crest.

   P. v. 'Bifidum Cristatum'. The pinnae are once-forked and the frond apex crest is narrower than the blade.

   P. v. 'Bifidum Grandiceps'. The crest on the blade tip is broader than the frond and may be the same as 'Cristatum' or 'Multifidum'.

   P. v. 'Bifidum Multifidum'. The pinna tips are forked and sometimes the blade tip is opened out into a flat crest. A vigorous grower, the fronds are long (over twelve inches) and narrow.

P. v. 'Cristatum'. The crest on the blade tip is narrower than the frond.

P. v. 'Glomeratum' is a compact, variable, branched (ramose) variety, with some of the pinnae once-forked.

P. v. 'Ramosum'. The frond is branched several times, forking far down the rachis.

Dissected forms: Many forms have fronds that are more divided than the typical pinnatifid architecture, ranging from bipinnatifid to quadripinnatifid. Although there have been literally hundreds of forms named, they fall into a few groups that have been called sections by some authors.

'Cambricum'. This is the original *P. cambricum* described by Linnaeus and would of course fall under the species *P. cambricum* described above. This dissected form is regularly divided, bipinnatifid, and barren. The yellowish green fronds die down in summer, with new ones arising in late summer and early fall. The blade is nearly as wide as it is long. The pinnae are narrow at the base, then deeply cut (pinnatifid), with the segments of adjacent pinnae overlapping to make a very attractive frond. Several variations of this are known, such as those with wavy margins or more finely divided fronds.

P. v. 'Cornubiense'. The fronds are long and broad, usually nearly tripinnatifid with linear segments, and fertile, much like 'Pulcherrimum' but often

Polypodium vulgare 'Ramosum'.

Polypodium vulgare 'Cambricum' pictured on the facade of the Museum of North Devon, Barnstaple, England.

Polypodium vulgare 'Cornubiense'.

with one or more fronds reverting to the normal type of fronds. Thus, a plant will have fronds that are finely cut or the normal wild-type or intermediate, all on the same plant, and occasionally all three conditions may appear on the same frond.

P. v. 'Omnilacerum' has pinnae that are deeply and irregularly cut. 'Semilacerum' is similar in the type of cutting but only the lower pinnae are divided, the upper ones being normal for the species.

P. v. 'Pulcherrimum' resembles 'Cambricum' but is fertile and regularly tripinnatifid, with thicker-textured fronds and less pointed segments than in 'Cambricum'. The barren dissected fronds are beautifully plumose.

P. v. 'Trichomanoides' is a smaller, tripinnate to quadripinnate form with fine segments and an occasional normal frond. Often the basal pinnae are directed forward toward you as you face the upper surface of the frond. 'Trichomanoides', and to lesser extent 'Cornubiense', may have bulbils in the sori instead of sporangia on the more dissected fronds. This is reminiscent of the situation in the plumose forms of *Athyrium filix-femina*.

Other sorts of variation:
'Acutum', 'Attenuatum', and 'Longipinnatum' all have lengthened, pointed pinnae.
 'Crenatum' has the margin wavy in one plane.
 'Crispum' has pinnae twisted and wavy in more than one plane.
 'Macrostachym' is a robust grower with the upper third of the frond undivided, extending like a tail (caudate).

Polypodium vulgare 'Pulcherrimum'.

Polypodium vulgare 'Trichomanoides'.

Polypodium vulgare 'Macrostachyum'.

POLYSTICHUM, Holly fern, Shield fern, Sword fern

The species of *Polystichum* are marked by their leathery, once- to twice-pinnate fronds, with bristle-tipped teeth, and round sori covered by umbrellalike or shield-shaped indusia. In most species the spores and sporangia are dark brown, almost black, but a few species have yellow spores. The rhizome is generally erect and stout; it and the stipe bases are densely scaly. Some species reproduce vegetatively by buds on the rachis produced near the frond tip or at the bases of several pinnae.

Polystichum is a largely temperate genus of nearly two hundred species, with most of the tropical species occurring in regions of higher elevation. It is especially diverse in North America, Europe, and eastern Asia, where it occurs in moist, rocky woods.

This is one of the most valuable genera for use in temperate gardens. There are several popular species in cultivation with an unusual number of variations and many other distinctive species that make excellent garden plants. Most of the species of *Polystichum* are evergreen, and their dark, lustrous fronds are a welcome sight in both summer and winter. Hybridization is frequent in the genus, but not many of the hybrids are cultivated. The holly ferns do well in shaded, rich, well-drained soil, both in a general garden and among rocks.

Polystichums sometimes suffer from crown rot, especially in the winter, and appreciate good drainage. Planting the rhizome at a slight angle and locating it by a rock often helps.

P. acrostichoides
Christmas fern
FRONDS: 1 to 2 feet long, arching, evergreen
RHIZOME HABIT: slender, much-branched with multiple crowns (see below)
AVAILABILITY: common
HARDINESS ZONES: 3 to 9
EASE OF CULTIVATION: easy

The Christmas fern is a robust evergreen plant, easily grown in diverse habitats. It gets its common name from the fact that the early settlers of North America used it for Christmas decoration. Some people think it got its name from the boot- or stocking-shaped pinnae, and although this seems to be more fanciful, it may help in remembering this species. In the spring the silvery-scaled crosiers contrast dramatically against the dark green of the the old fronds. The blade is once-pinnate, linear, and broadest at the base, the stipe and rachis are scaly, and the pinnae auricled, with marginal bristle teeth, occasionally deeply toothed. The yellow-spored sori are found only in the terminal one third of the frond, with the fertile pinnae distinctly contracted. This part of the frond often falls off after the spores are shed. The Christmas fern is native and common in the moist woods of eastern North America, making beautiful patches of green all winter.

What appears as a crown of the Christmas fern is really several. This species is highly unusual in the genus in that nearly all the species have compact crowns that rarely branch. The Christmas fern, on the other hand, usually has a slender, branched rhizome with several growing tips. This is good for the garden; you can dig it up and carefully separate the branches to multiply this species.

Polystichum acrostichoides.

Polystichum acrostichoides 'Cristatum'.

In cultivation *P. acrostichoides* is not at all fussy. Although it likes the moist woodland, it does very well not only in a rich, moist woodland garden but also among rocks or on dryish slopes. It is excellent for planting on slopes to prevent erosion. For some reason, it does not do well in the Northwest and similarly, the abundant northwestern species, *P. munitum*, does not do well in the Northeast.

P. a. 'Crispum'. The pinna margins are ruffled.

P. a. 'Cristatum'. The tip of the blade is crested.

P. a. 'Incisum'. The pinnae are coarsely and deeply toothed, with all the pinnae fertile rather than just the terminal third of the blade.

P. a. 'Multifidum'. The blades are pinnate-pinnatifid, cut nearly to the pinna midveins.

P. aculeatum
Hard shield fern
FRONDS: 1 to 3 feet long, arching, evergreen
RHIZOME HABIT: erect crown
AVAILABILITY: infrequent
HARDINESS ZONES: 4 to 8
EASE OF CULTIVATION: easy
This hardy fern's dramatic fronds are bipinnate, glossy, dark green, leathery,

Polystichum acrostichoides 'Multifidum'.

Polystichum aculeatum.

Polystichum aculeatum sori.

and generally stiff and bristly, with reddish brown scales. It closely resembles and is often confused with *P. setiferum*. That species can be distinguished by its stipe being more than one sixth of the frond length. Also, its lowest pinnae are nearly equal to the middle pinnae in length, it is soft to the touch, and the spores are light brown, whereas in *P. aculeatum* the stipe is less than one sixth the frond length, the lowest pinnae are about half the middle pinna length, it is stiff to the touch, and the spores are dark brown. It is an upland species favoring steep, damp, lime-rich outcroppings in river-valley woodlands, hedgerows, and ravines throughout Europe but more frequently in northern Europe.

Polystichum aculeatum is impressive as a single specimen plant and, in fact, in the wild usually occurs individually or in small numbers only. There are essentially no extant cultivars of this species. Several varieties were described under this name, but virtually all have now been found to belong to *P. setiferum*, though many of the old names still exist in the horticultural trade.

P. andersonii
Anderson's holly fern
FRONDS: 2 to 4 feet long, erect-arching, evergreen
RHIZOME HABIT: erect crown
AVAILABILITY: infrequent
HARDINESS ZONES: 6 to 8
EASE OF CULTIVATION: easy
The magnificent crown of fronds makes this a fine accent plant in the

Polystichum andersonii.

Polystichum andersonii bearing a bud on the rachis at the base of a pinna.

Polystichum braunii.

garden in the Northwest, but unfortunately it does not grow as well in the East. The fronds are lance-shaped, pinnate-pinnatifid to bipinnate, tapering somewhat at the base, with the stipe only about one sixth the frond length. The pinnules are glossy dark green and have bristle teeth on the margin. Like a few other species in the genus, the rachis has one to three buds near the tip on the underside, which enlarge as the frond matures. Finally, as the frond touches the ground, they take root and develop into new plants. *Polystichum andersonii* occurs on cool, moist, rocky slopes in northwestern North America.

P. braunii
Braun's holly fern
FRONDS: 10 to 28 inches long, erect-arching, evergreen
RHIZOME HABIT: erect crown
AVAILABILITY: frequent
HARDINESS ZONES: 3 to 5 (to 8)
EASE OF CULTIVATION: easy

This popular holly fern makes a beautiful crown of lustrous, bipinnate fronds and does very well in northern gardens. The fiddleheads, and subsequently the stipe and rachis, are spectacular with their dense covering of silvery scales, the scales becoming tan with age. The blade tapers to the base, with the stipe only about one quarter of the frond length. The bristle-toothed leathery pinnules are a lustrous dark green. In early summer the back of the frond is a mass of blackish sporangia. *Polystichum braunii* occurs uncommonly in moist woods in northeastern and northwestern North America, Europe, China, and Japan. North American plants are sometimes named var. *purshii*, which differs only in chromosome number from the Eurasian material.

P. californicum
California holly fern
FRONDS: 1 to 3 feet long, arching, evergreen
RHIZOME HABIT: erect crown
AVAILABILITY: rare
HARDINESS ZONES: 8 to 9
EASE OF CULTIVATION: moderate

The fronds are pinnate-pinnatifid to barely bipinnate, having originated as a hybrid between the bipinnate *P. dudleyi* and the once-pinnate *P. munitum* or *P. imbricans*. Some forms are sterile, others fertile. It is uncommon in the western coastal states, but is a wonderful, smaller holly fern for milder regions.

P. craspedosorum

FRONDS: 5 to 16 inches long, arching, rooting at tip, evergreen
RHIZOME HABIT: erect crown
AVAILABILITY: rare
HARDINESS ZONES: 5 to 9
EASE OF CULTIVATION: moderate

This remarkable species is one of the smallest of the holly ferns. The small, narrow, once-pinnate fronds are widely arching to nearly flat on the ground with the rachis extending beyond the blade tip and rooting in the soil to form new plantlets. We saw the attractive little rosettes of *P. craspedosorum* on moist, shaded limestone cliffs in western China. It also occurs in Japan, Korea, and Manchuria, and we hope to see it more in cultivation in American rock gardens.

P. cystostegia
Alpine shield fern

FRONDS: 6 to 16 inches long, erect-arching, deciduous
RHIZOME HABIT: erect crown
AVAILABILITY: rare
HARDINESS ZONES: 6 to 9
EASE OF CULTIVATION: moderate

On first glance you would think this little alpine fern was a *Cystopteris* with its small, pale green, thin-textured, finely dissected fronds. The stipe and rachis have loose, pale brown scales, the blade is linear-lance-shaped, bipinnate to bipinnate-pinnatifid. The sori have a dome-shaped, convex-dented round indusium. Since *P. cystostegia* naturally occurs in alpine regions of New Zealand, it should make a good plant for northern rock gardens.

It needs plenty of light, but must be kept damp and cool in stony soil with good drainage. It is difficult to grow in milder regions.

P. dudleyi
Dudley's holly fern

FRONDS: 16 to 40 inches long, erect-arching, evergreen
RHIZOME HABIT: erect crown
AVAILABILITY: infrequent
HARDINESS ZONES: 8 to 9
EASE OF CULTIVATION: moderate

This tall western holly fern has a bipinnate blade that does not taper strongly at the base. The stipe and rachis are scaly, with the stipe one third the frond length. The pinnules have a basal lobe, or auricle. *Polystichum dudleyi* is limited to moist woods in California and is happy in cool gardens of the West.

P. × illyricum (= P. aculeatum × lonchitis)
FRONDS: 1 to 2 feet long, erect, evergreen
RHIZOME HABIT: erect crown
AVAILABILITY: rare
HARDINESS ZONES: 4 to 8
EASE OF CULTIVATION: moderate

The very narrow, evergreen fronds of this sterile hybrid are intermediate in dissection between its once-pinnate and bipinnate parents. This especially handsome plant from Europe has a firm, leathery texture, lustrous surface, and the pinnae curve upward at their tips toward the frond apex.

P. imbricans (syn. P. munitum var. imbricans)
Dwarf western sword fern
FRONDS: 1 to 2½ feet long, erect-arching, evergreen
RHIZOME HABIT: erect crown
AVAILABILITY: infrequent
HARDINESS ZONES: 6 to 9
EASE OF CULTIVATION: moderate

Polystichum × *illyricum.*

Polystichum imbricans. (PHOTO BY JUDITH JONES)

This interesting species is similar to *P. munitum* but smaller and with overlapping pinnae. The rhizome and stipe base scales are long and red-orange, but the rest of the stipe is naked. The stipe is one third to one half the overall frond length, and the rachis is only sparsely scaly. *Polystichum imbricans* occurs from California to British Columbia and does well in western gardens.

P. × kruckebergii (= P. lemmonii × lonchitis)
Kruckeberg's holly fern
FRONDS: 6 to 12 inches long, erect, evergreen
RHIZOME HABIT: erect crown
AVAILABILITY: rare
HARDINESS ZONES: 6 to 8
EASE OF CULTIVATION: moderate to difficult

Kruckeberg's holly fern is rare but a real prize. The stiffly erect evergreen fronds are but six to twelve inches long, narrow, dark green, and glossy and have short, somewhat triangular pinnae, each with only one to two pairs of lobe teeth. This hybrid is found rarely in rock crevices at high elevations in the northwestern United States. The experienced grower will find this to be a good fern for the cool rock garden.

P. lemmonii
Shasta holly fern
FRONDS: 4 to 12 inches long, erect, semievergreen
RHIZOME HABIT: erect crown
AVAILABILITY: rare
HARDINESS ZONES: 6 to 8
EASE OF CULTIVATION: moderate

Polystichum × kruckebergii.

This small, dissected holly fern is not commonly grown but is very attractive. The blade is narrowly lance-shaped, bipinnate-pinnatifid, and only one to one and one half inches wide; the segments are not bristle-tipped. The stipe and rachis are clothed with tan scales. It is found among rocks from Washington to coastal California. It is similar to *P. mohrioides* of South America and confused with it in cultivation.

P. lentum
Himalayan holly fern
FRONDS: 1 to 2 feet long, arching, semievergreen
RHIZOME HABIT: erect crown
AVAILABILITY: rare
HARDINESS ZONES: 7 to 9
EASE OF CULTIVATION: moderate

The fronds are linear and once-pinnate, the pinnae deeply toothed, some of the lower pinnae having a distinct basal pinnule. A bud near the end of the rachis develops into a plantlet that roots itself when it touches the ground. *Polystichum lentum* is common in the Himalaya Mountains. It has not been tested in American gardens, but should make a handsome addition to southern and far western gardens.

P. lepidocaulon
FRONDS: 1 to 2 feet long, arching, evergreen
RHIZOME HABIT: erect crown
AVAILABILITY: rare
HARDINESS ZONES: 7 to 9
EASE OF CULTIVATION: moderate

This distinctive species has glossy, once-pinnate, arching fronds, with the

Polystichum lentum.

Polystichum lepidocaulon.

rachis extending beyond the blade and rooting when it touches the ground. When growing well in humid conditions, it can make an extensive bed of plants in this way. The stipe and rachis are densely scaly, hence the specific epithet, *lepidocaulon*, which means "scaly stem." The pinnae are dark green, slender, and leathery. *Polystichum lepidocaulon* is widespread in eastern Asia. We tried it outdoors without success at the New York Botanical Garden, but judging from its natural range, it should be hardy in some of the milder parts of the United States.

P. × lonchitiforme (= P. lonchitis × setiferum)

FRONDS: 1 to 2 feet long, erect-arching, evergreen
RHIZOME HABIT: erect crown
AVAILABILITY: rare
HARDINESS ZONES: 4 to 8
EASE OF CULTIVATION: moderate

This beautiful sterile hybrid has a very narrow blade that is broadest above the middle and tapers to the base. The stipe is short and the blade once-pinnate with the pinnae shallowly lobed.

Polystichum × lonchitiforme resembles another hybrid holly fern, *P. × illyricum* (syn. *P. aculeatum × lonchitis*), which is more deeply lobed and lustrous, the pinnae more curved. Unfortunately, they are hard to tell apart without technical confirmation (chromosome number) because of the wide variation in both *P. aculeatum* and *P. setiferum*. *Polystichum × lonchitiforme* occurs in Europe where its parents grow together.

P. lonchitis

Northern holly fern

FRONDS: 6 to 18 inches long, erect, evergreen
RHIZOME HABIT: erect crown
AVAILABILITY: infrequent
HARDINESS ZONES: 3 to 8
EASE OF CULTIVATION: moderate

This uncommon alpine plant is a striking candidate for the rock garden. The once-pinnate blade with its many pairs of closely set, glossy, dark green pinnae is linear, tapering at the base, with a very short stipe (less than one tenth the frond length). The stipe and rachis are sparsely scaly, and the pinnae are short, with bristle teeth. It occurs on moist, shaded calcareous rocks in

Polystichum × lonchitiforme.   *Polystichum lonchitis.*   *Polystichum makinoi.*

woods or alpine conditions of northern and western North America, Europe, and Asia.

Moore (1859) commented that this species was "a plant of shy growth and very tardy increase," which is confirmed by present-day growers. It is difficult to cultivate, needing light soil with a large amount of fine gravel in raised beds or a rockery. It likes to be wedged between limestone rocks and enjoys light shade or partial sun, fair humidity, and, most of all, coolness.

In Britain there were said to be a few varieties in the past—'Confertum' with more numerous, narrower, overlapping pinnae; 'Gemmiferum' with bulblets in the axils of the lowest pinnae, and 'Multifidum' with the frond apex divided. These do not now seem to exist in cultivation.

P. makinoi
Makino's holly fern

FRONDS: 20 to 30 inches long, arching, evergreen

RHIZOME HABIT: erect crown

AVAILABILITY: frequent

HARDINESS ZONES: 5 to 9

EASE OF CULTIVATION: easy

This is one of my favorite holly ferns. The fronds are bipinnate and lustrous, with numerous tan scales on the stipe and rachis, which contrast beautifully with the brilliant green segments. It is native to China and Japan.

Polystichum makinoi is one of the stronger-growing, attractive holly ferns in cultivation. It is adaptable and happy in both northern and southern gardens.

P. mohrioides

FRONDS: 6 to 18 inches long, erect, semievergreen
RHIZOME HABIT: erect crown
AVAILABILITY: rare
HARDINESS ZONES: 5 to 8
EASE OF CULTIVATION: moderate

Polystichum mohrioides is similar to *P. lemmonii* and very attractive with small bipinnate-pinnatifid fronds. It is a real gem from southernmost Chile, Argentina, and the Falkland Islands, and should be used more often in the rock garden.

P. munitum

Western sword fern
FRONDS: 1½ to 5 feet long, arching, evergreen
RHIZOME HABIT: erect crown
AVAILABILITY: common
HARDINESS ZONES: 6 to 9
EASE OF CULTIVATION: easy

The western sword fern is among the largest of the cultivated polystichums. The fronds are long and narrow, the blade once-pinnate and only slightly reduced at the base. The stipe is less than one fourth the frond length and densely scaly with both large and small scales. The slender, dagger- or sword-like pinnae have bristle teeth. *Polystichum munitum* is one of the most common ferns found in the moist woods of western North America, especially among the coastal redwoods.

This large, handsome fern is adaptable and easy to use in northwestern gardens, but does not do well in the East, where it remains very small if it

Polystichum mohrioides.

Polystichum munitum.

survives at all. I would recommend instead using *P. acrostichoides* (page 262) for eastern gardens.

P. m. 'Crested' has a narrow and repeatedly forking frond tip.

P. m. 'Crisped Form' is a common variation with the pinnae twisted out of the flat plane.

P. neolobatum
Long-eared holly fern
FRONDS: 1 to 2 feet long, erect, evergreen
RHIZOME HABIT: erect crown
AVAILABILITY: frequent
HARDINESS ZONES: 5 to 8
EASE OF CULTIVATION: easy

The glossy, very hard-textured blade is bipinnate and sparsely scaly on the underside, with the first pinnule on each pinna being the largest, like an ear. The stipe and rachis are scaly, almost shaggy. This fern occurs in the moist woods of China, Taiwan, India, and Japan.

Polystichum neolobatum is slower growing, more upright, and narrower than *P. makinoi*.

P. nepalense
Nepal holly fern
FRONDS: 1½ to 2 feet long, arching, evergreen
RHIZOME HABIT: erect crown

Polystichum munitum 'Crested'.

Polystichum neolobatum.

AVAILABILITY: rare
HARDINESS ZONES: 5 to 8
EASE OF CULTIVATION: moderate

The fronds are narrowly lance-shaped and only once-pinnate, the pinnae leathery, slightly curving toward the frond tip, auricled, and finely toothed, with minute scales on the veins of the lower surface. It is native to India, western China, and Taiwan, and prefers a rocky, well-drained position.

P. polyblepharum (P. setosum of hort.)

Bristle fern, Japanese tassel fern
FRONDS: 1 to 2 feet long, arching, evergreen
RHIZOME HABIT: erect crown
AVAILABILITY: common
HARDINESS ZONES: 5 to 8
EASE OF CULTIVATION: easy

This popular fern has bipinnate fronds that are markedly lustrous and dark green, and the stipe and rachis are heavily scaly. The species name means "many eyelashes," alluding to the bristlelike scales of the stipe and leaflets. This native of Japan and southern Korea is very handsome, does well in rich garden soil, and appreciates consistent moisture.

P. × potteri (= P. acrostichoides × braunii)

Potter's holly fern
FRONDS: 1 to 2 feet long, arching, evergreen
RHIZOME HABIT: erect crown
AVAILABILITY: rare
HARDINESS ZONES: 3 to 6
EASE OF CULTIVATION: moderate

This sterile hybrid develops where the parents occur together in north-eastern forests. It looks much like *P. braunii* (page 265) in the dissected blade but has a longer stipe and is not quite as distinctly bipinnate.

P. prescottianum

Prescott's holly fern
FRONDS: 8 to 14 inches long, erect-arching, evergreen
RHIZOME HABIT: erect crown
AVAILABILITY: rare

*Polystichum
polyblepharum.*

*Polystichum
proliferum.*

HARDINESS ZONES: 5 to 9

EASE OF CULTIVATION: moderate

This species comes to us from high elevations of the Himalayas and Taiwan and is distinguished by its relatively small, narrow, upright fronds. The blade is pinnate-pinnatifid to nearly bipinnate, tapering to the base with a very short stipe. Its soft texture is unusual in the genus. This fern needs to be tried in American gardens to determine its true potential.

P. proliferum

Mother shield fern

FRONDS: 1½ to 3 feet long, arching, semievergreen

RHIZOME HABIT: erect crown

AVAILABILITY: infrequent

HARDINESS ZONES: 5 to 9

EASE OF CULTIVATION: easy

The blade in *P. proliferum* is broadly lance-shaped, bipinnate or sometimes tripinnate, and dark green. The plant gets its common name from the proliferous bud near the tip of the rachis. The pinnules are toothed and leathery. The species grows at high elevations in Australia and New Zealand.

Polystichum proliferum is easily propagated by the buds. Peg the frond tips down on moist soil or a sand-peat mixture until a new plant roots itself.

P. retrosopaleaceum

FRONDS: 1½ to 3½ feet long, arching, evergreen

RHIZOME HABIT: erect crown

AVAILABILITY: rare

The lower pinnae of *Polystichum retrosopaleaceum*.

HARDINESS ZONES: 5 to 9

EASE OF CULTIVATION: easy

The lustrous, bipinnate blade is especially distinct in its downward-pointing basal pinnae and heavily scaly stipe. *Polystichum retrosopaleaceum* is native to Japan.

P. richardii
Richard's holly fern

FRONDS: 8 to 24 inches long, erect, evergreen

RHIZOME HABIT: erect crown

AVAILABILITY: rare

HARDINESS ZONES: 6 to 8

EASE OF CULTIVATION: moderate

The stipe and rachis are densely covered with blackish brown scales. The blade is bipinnate to tripinnate, dark bluish green, and leathery. It is a common, beautiful species of New Zealand.

P. rigens

FRONDS: 1 to 2½ feet long, erect-arching, evergreen

RHIZOME HABIT: erect crown

AVAILABILITY: frequent

HARDINESS ZONES: 5 to 8

EASE OF CULTIVATION: moderate

This native of Japan has rigid, glossy, leathery fronds, which are narrowly triangular and bipinnate. The pinnules are curved toward the pinna apex, and each pinnule has a spinelike tip.

The tender young fronds have a faint smell of skunk, but this does not pervade the garden or detract in any way from this handsome fern.

P. scopulinum
Western holly fern
FRONDS: 6 to 16 inches long, erect, semievergreen
RHIZOME HABIT: erect crown
AVAILABILITY: rare
HARDINESS ZONES: 4 to 8
EASE OF CULTIVATION: moderate

The western holly fern is a distinct, small, alpine plant with narrow, pinnate-pinnatifid fronds. It likes dry, noncalcareous rock crevices in sun or shade. Like most alpine plants, it needs cool soil. It is frequent in western North America and rare in the Gaspé Peninsula of eastern Canada and is the fertile hybrid of *P. imbricans* × *lemmonii*.

P. setiferum (syn. P. angulare, Aspidium angulare)
Soft shield fern
FRONDS: 1½ to 4 feet long, erect-arching, semievergreen
RHIZOME HABIT: erect crown
AVAILABILITY: common
HARDINESS ZONES: 5 to 8
EASE OF CULTIVATION: easy

Polystichum rigens.

Polystichum setiferum.

Polystichum setiferum is one of the more common lowland species of fern in southern Europe. Its lance-shaped, bipinnate fronds are glossy and grass green when mature, with pale, golden brown scales. The fronds are soft when young and tend to eventually spread and droop. The segments are stalked and have bristlelike teeth along the margins. This species closely resembles *P. aculeatum* in its size and form, but it can be distinguished from the latter by several characteristics. *Polystichum setiferum* has a longer stipe, over one sixth the frond length, the lowest pinnae are nearly as long as the middle pinnae, and the spores are light brown, in contrast to *P. aculeatum*, which has a stipe less than one sixth the frond length, its lowest pinnae are only about half as long as the middle pinnae, and the spores are dark brown. However, there is so much variation in both species that it is difficult to distinguish them with complete confidence without technical confirmation (chromosome number).

This species does best in permanently slightly moist soil that is slightly acid to slightly basic (pH 6.5 to 8.0) and with consistently high humidity. It needs more warmth, shelter, and drier conditions than *P. aculeatum*, and is not as strong a grower as that species. Often it is the dominant plant in sheltered lanes in southern England. Its habit is more or less arched with drooping fronds which are soft and pale green, in marked contrast to the dark leathery glossiness of *P. aculeatum*. The pinnules are bristly and broad at the base with a distinct slender stalk. The fronds die down more quickly too. It is easy to grow in cool, shady gardens, and extremely variable in shape and habit. At one time 366 named varieties were published (1890, Lowe, *British Ferns and Where Found*).

The list below includes the varieties that are most commonly available and a few that illustrate some of the broad diversity in this species. I have arranged these varieties into several groups based on what I think are the most conspicuous forms. For more detailed analysis of the variation in this remarkably diverse species, see Dyce, "Variation in *Polystichum* in the British Isles," *British Fern Gazette* 9(4)(1963): 97–109 and "Classification of Fern Variation in Britain," *Pteridologist* 1(4)(1987): 154–155.

Crested forms:

P. s. 'Capitatum'. Crested at the apex only.

P. s. 'Cristatum'. Crested apex and/or pinnae.

P. s. 'Cristulatum'. Has small crests on frond tip and/or pinnae.

Polystichum setiferum
'Cristatum
Pumilum'.

Polystichum setiferum
'Percristatum'.

P. s. 'Grandiceps Fox'. Has large head of broad crests at the frond tip.

P. s. 'Percristatum'. Crested at the tips of frond, pinnae, and pinnules.

P. s. 'Polydactylum'. A few slender forkings on each pinna, resembling fingers.

P. s. 'Ramosum'. The rachis is branched.

More finely divided forms: Most of the presently grown forms belong to this group. At one time all plants bearing bulbils (buds) along the rachis were placed in a variety called 'Proliferum', but now the proliferous forms are classified according to their types of dissection and are found in several major varieties, such as 'Divisilobum' and 'Rotundatum'.

Polystichum setiferum
'Ramulosum'.

Polystichum setiferum
'Divisilobum'.

P. s. 'Divisilobum'. The fronds are fully tripinnate or even slightly more divided, giving a very lacy appearance. The pinnules are divided into spine-tipped lobes that are narrowed, the basiscopic pinnules being distinctly larger than the acroscopic ones. Some forms combine cresting and longer pinnules. 'Herrenhausen' and 'Dahlem' are forms of 'Divisilobum' but are not especially distinct.

P. s. 'Divisilobum Plumosum'. The fronds are two to three feet long, four times divided, and plumelike with overlapping pinnae.

P. s. 'Multilobum' resembles 'Divisilobum' but the pinnules are divided into segments that are not narrowed. This is often difficult to distinguish though.

P. s. 'Plumosum Bevis' (syn. *P. aculeatum* 'Pulcherrimum Bevis'). This is the real prize. The fronds are a very dark green, tall, and extremely graceful. Unfortunately, it is nearly always barren and does not divide generously, so we await tissue culture to provide a good supply of this marvelous variety. It was thought to be a form of *P. aculeatum* because of its glossy frond, but recently it has been found to be a *P. setiferum*.

P. s. 'Plumosum Gracillimum' has a distinctly feathery appearance. The linear pinnules have such finely crested tips as to appear as tufts of filamentous algae.

P. s. 'Plumosum Grande' has fronds over four feet tall that are tripinnate, barren, and semievergreen, with the pinnae overlapping.

Polystichum setiferum 'Plumosum Green'.

Polystichum setiferum 'Plumosum Multilobum'.

P. s. 'Pulcherrimum'. The fronds are bipinnate, with narrow, widely spaced pinnules.

P. s. 'Pulcherrimum Moly's Green'. This vigorous grower has the basiscopic pinnules and sometimes the acroscopic ones sickle-shaped, deeply cut, and drawn out into threadlike tips.

P. s. 'Rotundatum' has nearly round pinnules.

P. s. 'Rotundatum Cristatum' has rounded segments and a forking frond tip. Bulbils are scattered on the rachis.

Dwarf forms:
P. s. 'Barfod's Dwarf' has evergreen fronds six to ten inches long, with the pinnae condensed (congested). It is a small version of 'Rotundatum Cristatum', with rounded pinnules, a forked frond tip, and buds along the rachis.

P. s. 'Congestum'. The axes are shortened, causing all the pinnae and pinnules to be very close together and overlapping. This condition is often temporary due to adverse conditions.

P. s. 'Congestum Cristatum' has dense, overlapping pinnae and a crested frond tip. The stipe and rachis have tan, chaffy scales.

P. s. 'Imbricatum' is less condensed than 'Congestum', slightly taller, and less brittle.

Polystichum setiferum 'Rotundatum'.

Polystichum setiferum 'Rotundatum Cristatum'.

Cruciate form:

P. s. 'Wakeleyanum'. This resembles *Athyrium filix-femina* 'Victoriae' in the crisscross pattern of the overlapping forked pinnae.

P. setigerum (syn. *P. alaskense*)

Alaska holly fern (not to be confused with *P. setiferum*, which is sometimes mistakenly labeled Alaska fern)

FRONDS: 20 to 40 inches long, arching, evergreen

RHIZOME HABIT: erect crown

AVAILABILITY: rare

HARDINESS ZONES: 6 to 8

EASE OF CULTIVATION: moderate

The narrowly lance-shaped blade is pinnate-pinnatifid to nearly bipinnate, and only slightly reduced at the base. The stipe is about one fourth the frond length. *Polystichum setigerum* may have arisen as a fertile hybrid between *P. braunii* (bipinnate) and *P. munitum* (once-pinnate). Its pinnules are broadly attached and have bristle teeth. It is rare in the cool, moist woods of British Columbia and southeast Alaska.

The Alaska holly fern is slow-growing and prefers cool soil and high humidity.

P. stenophyllum

FRONDS: 5 to 18 inches long, arching, evergreen

RHIZOME HABIT: erect crown

AVAILABILITY: rare

HARDINESS ZONES: 6 to 8

EASE OF CULTIVATION: moderate

This small, leathery holly fern has fronds only one half to one inch wide, with many pairs of oval, auricled pinnae. The lower pinnae are smaller and pointed downward, and the stipe is very short. It comes from high elevations in northern India, Tibet, China, and Taiwan. *Polystichum stenophyllum* makes a fine, slender specimen in the rock garden.

P. stimulans (syn. *P. ilicifolium*)

FRONDS: 5 to 12 inches long, arching, evergreen

RHIZOME HABIT: erect crown

AVAILABILITY: rare

HARDINESS ZONES: 6 to 8

EASE OF CULTIVATION: moderate

Polystichum stimulans is once-pinnate with very short pinnae, making the frond only about an inch wide. The pinnae are deeply bristle-toothed, like a holly. It occurs in the Himalayas, China, and Taiwan.

P. sylvaticum

FRONDS: 10 to 18 inches long, erect-arching, evergreen

RHIZOME HABIT: erect crown

AVAILABILITY: rare

HARDINESS ZONES: 8 to 9

EASE OF CULTIVATION: moderate

The fronds are lance-shaped and bipinnate-pinnatifid with long, slender tips to the pinnae and the frond. This species is similar to *P. vestitum* but with more delicate, feathery fronds. *Polystichum sylvaticum* is confined to the cool, damp forests of New Zealand.

P. tagawanum

Tagawa's holly fern

FRONDS: 1 to 2 feet long, arching, evergreen

RHIZOME HABIT: erect crown

AVAILABILITY: frequent

HARDINESS ZONES: 4 to 8

EASE OF CULTIVATION: easy

Polystichum tagawanum.

This Japanese native is a sturdy plant for the fern garden. The bipinnate fronds are lustrous, the pinnae slightly shorter at the blade base, and the basal pinnae are pointed downward. The stipe and rachis have reddish brown scales.

P. tripteron
Trifid holly fern
FRONDS: 1 to 2 feet long, erect, deciduous
RHIZOME HABIT: short-creeping
AVAILABILITY: infrequent
HARDINESS ZONES: 5 to 8
EASE OF CULTIVATION: easy to moderate

Polystichum tripteron is one of the most unusual species of the genus in that the fronds are thin-textured, deciduous, and without bristle teeth on the segments. Furthermore, the rhizome is short-creeping and rather fleshy. Most of the frond is once-pinnate but the basal pair of pinnae is itself pinnate and much longer, about half the length of the rest of the frond, making the blade look like an upside-down T. The segments are narrowly triangular with coarse teeth and are dull, not bristle-tipped. The stipe has a dense covering of small, pale scales. *Polystichum tripteron* occurs in moist woods in the mountains of Japan, Korea, China, and eastern Siberia.

Tripteron means "three wings or fronds," alluding to its remarkable frond architecture.

P. tsus-simense
Tsus-sima holly fern, Korean rock fern
FRONDS: 8 to 18 inches long, erect, deciduous or semievergreen
RHIZOME HABIT: erect crown
AVAILABILITY: common
HARDINESS ZONES: 6 to 8
EASE OF CULTIVATION: easy

This dainty holly fern is small and glossy, usually grown as a greenhouse plant, but it does well outdoors to zone 6. The blade is lance-shaped and bipinnate, with black veins. The basal acroscopic pinnules of the pinna are conspicuously separate and the largest. *Polystichum tsus-simense* is native to the warm, temperate regions of Japan, Korea, China, and Taiwan.

This little species likes a shady bed or rock garden with good drainage

Polystichum tripteron.

*Polystichum tsus-
simense.*

and rich soil. It is marginal in its hardiness around New York City, but works much better in Virginia.

P. vestitum
Prickly shield fern
FRONDS: 1 to 3 feet long, arching, semideciduous
RHIZOME HABIT: erect crown
AVAILABILITY: rare
HARDINESS ZONES: 6 to 8
EASE OF CULTIVATION: easy

This strong-growing import from New Zealand and Australia brings an interesting "feel" to the fern garden. The stipes and rachises are densely covered with broad, shiny scales. The blade is lustrous and dark green in color, narrowly oblong and bipinnate. The segments have a basal acroscopic lobe, ending in sharply pointed tips, which give the blade a harsh, prickly feel.

It prefers cold, in the shade or open, and is frost-hardy on many soil types.

PTERIDIUM, Bracken

Bracken is distinctive in its medium-sized to large, triangular, leathery leaves and very long-creeping, hairy, subterranean rhizomes. It is one of the few ferns with rhizomes deep in the soil, usually two to four inches down. There are dark nectaries at the base of the first and sometimes upper pairs of pinnae that are often visited by ants. The blade is two to four times pinnate, and the basal pinnae are often strongly enlarged basiscopically, each basal pinna nearly equal to the upper part of the frond in size. It is sometimes called "eagle fern" because the unrolling fiddleheads have three curled parts, resembling an eagle's talons. The fronds are sparsely to densely hairy beneath, and the sori are marginal and protected by the recurved frond margin.

Pteridium has about ten species and several varieties; in the past all were treated as varieties of a single worldwide species. Some tropical species reach sixteen feet in height, whereas the northeastern North American varieties, var. *latiusculum* and var. *pseudocaudatum*, are two to four feet long. The plants are generally aggressive, invading disturbed areas in pastures, cultivated fields, and roadsides. Bracken does best in sandy, well-drained, acid soil and can survive fire by virtue of its deeply buried rhizome. The genus is closely allied to *Hypolepis* and *Dennstaedtia*, sharing with those genera the wide-creeping, hairy rhizomes.

Bracken is generally not cultivated due to its very widely creeping rhizome and invasive nature, but where there is room enough or barriers for its control, it can make a handsome planting. It is useful as a fern that can survive full sun and is suitable for large areas.

The fiddleheads are often eaten in the Orient and by some Oriental persons in the United States, but this practice should be strongly discouraged since bracken is known to be strongly carcinogenic.

P. aquilinum

FRONDS: 1½ to 12 feet long, erect-arching, deciduous
RHIZOME HABIT: very long-creeping
AVAILABILITY: frequent
HARDINESS ZONES: 3 to 10
EASE OF CULTIVATION: easy

This is the most widespread species and contains several recognized varieties.

P. a. var. *aquilinum* is native to Europe and is taller and its fronds more lance-shaped than the eastern North American varieties.

P. a. var. *a.* 'Cristatum'. All the terminal segments are crested.

P. a. var. *a.* 'Polydactylum'. The segments end in many-fingered crests.

Pteridium aquilinum var. *aquilinum* 'Cristatum'.

Pteridium aquilinum var. *aquilinum* 'Polydactylum'.

P. a. var. *latiusculum*. This variety has fronds that are one and one half to five feet tall and sparsely hairy beneath. The pinnule tips are less than four times as long as they are wide (mostly about one quarter inch wide). It is native to northeastern North America as a common fern of old fields, pine barrens, conifer woods, and oak forests.

P. a. var. *pseudocaudatum* has fronds that are naked beneath and have pinnule tips more than six times as long as they are wide (mostly about one eighth inch wide). The fronds reach five feet in height. In nature it occurs in the Southeast, north to New York City.

Pteridium aquilinum var. *latiusculum*.

Pteridium aquilinum var. *latiusculum* sori. (PHOTO BY BARBARA HALLOWELL)

Pteridium aquilinum var. *pseudocaudatum.*

P. a. var. *pubescens* is widespread in the West, with its fronds reaching nine feet in height. The blade is densely hairy beneath, and has the pinnules perpendicular to the midveins in contrast to the eastern varieties that have the pinnules at an angle to the midveins. It was the first plant growing on the slopes of Washington State's Mount Saint Helens after its eruption in May 1980.

PTERIS, Brake

Pteris is a diverse and widely distributed genus of largely tropical ferns, but has several popular species that can be grown in the milder regions of the United States. The common name "brake" comes from "bracken," and botanists used to consider *Pteris* and *Pteridium* the same genus. *Pteris* has a short-creeping to compact rhizome. The fronds are medium-sized and occur in clumps with short to long stipes. The blade is leathery, one to three times divided, and often the basal pinnae are basiscopically enlarged. The marginal sori are protected by a recurved margin, or false indusium.

The nearly three hundred species are found primarily in wet tropical forests. *Pteris* is adaptable to a wide range of soils but some species favor limestone rocks in the sun. They generally do not like to be kept too moist. Most are easy to grow from spores. *Pteris* is an important crop commercially and species of brake are among our more common indoor ferns, though some can survive light to heavy frost.

P. cretica
Cretan brake, Ribbon fern
FRONDS: 8 to 24 inches long, erect, deciduous
RHIZOME HABIT: compact

AVAILABILITY: common
HARDINESS ZONES: 8 to 10
EASE OF CULTIVATION: easy

The fronds of this species are dimorphic and thin-textured. The fertile ones are held stiffly erect. The stipe is more than half the frond length. The blade is once-pinnate and broadly triangular, with one to three pairs of pinnae, each lowest pinna having a large basiscopic pinnule. The sterile fronds have finely toothed margins. *Pteris cretica* has escaped and become naturalized from Florida to Louisiana, and in southern California. It occurs naturally on limestone ledges, shaded slopes, and rocky meadows in tropical and subtropical regions of the world.

Pteris cretica is easily grown from spores. Being apogamous, the new plantlets arise quickly. It also volunteers readily in the greenhouse.

P. c. var. *albolineata*. The sterile leaves are broader than the fertile ones and have a distinctive, broad white band along the midvein. This striking fern is well worth a try in sheltered zone 8 and southward. It has strong roots and is not fussy about soil but does need lime.

P. ensiformis
Slender brake
FRONDS: 10 to 15 inches long, erect, deciduous
RHIZOME HABIT: compact
AVAILABILITY: frequent
HARDINESS ZONES: 9 to 10
EASE OF CULTIVATION: easy

Pteris cretica var. *albolineata*. (PHOTO BY PAMELA J. HARPER)

Pteris ensiformis 'Victoriae'.

The fronds of this lovely brake are narrowly lance-shaped, and bipinnate to tripinnate. *Pteris ensiformis* is widespread from southeastern Asia to northeastern Australia in disturbed areas or on walls.

P. e. 'Victoriae' has variegated fronds with a white band along the midvein. It has become naturalized in peninsular Florida. It resembles *P. cretica* but has more pinnae that are narrower and have white streaks. This variety looks beautiful among rocks.

P. multifida (syn. Pteris serrulata)
Chinese brake, Spider brake
FRONDS: 10 to 24 inches long, erect, deciduous
RHIZOME HABIT: compact
AVAILABILITY: frequent
HARDINESS ZONES: 6 to 10
EASE OF CULTIVATION: easy

This popular fern has fronds with asymmetrical narrow pinnae with erratic branching near the rachis. The stipe is about one third the frond length. The bright green blade is once-pinnate and oblong, with three to seven pairs of pinnae. The fronds have long, narrow, pointed segments, mostly undivided, but the lowest one to three pairs have one to two pairs of large pinnules. (The sterile fronds are more leafy than the fertile ones.) The margins of the sterile fronds are finely toothed. A native of Japan, Korea, China, and Indochina, *Pteris multifida* has escaped and become naturalized on limestone and mortar of walls from North Carolina to Texas. It is often cultivated in greenhouses. This species is not hardy north of New York City; it survived only one winter in my garden. More information is needed about its hardiness.

P. tremula
Trembling brake, Australian brake
FRONDS: 10 to 24 inches long (much larger in wild), erect-arching, deciduous
RHIZOME HABIT: erect
AVAILABILITY: frequent
HARDINESS ZONES: 8 to 10
EASE OF CULTIVATION: easy

This large, delicate fern with pale green fronds is fast-growing. The blade

Pteris tremula.
(Photo by F.
Gordon Foster)

Pteris multifida. (Photo by F.
Gordon Foster)

Pteris vittata. (Photo by F.
Gordon Foster)

is narrowly oblong and tripinnate to tripinnate-pinnatifid. It is another *Pteris* which grows easily. It is widespread in its native Australia, New Zealand, and Fiji.

P. vittata
Ladder brake
FRONDS: 1 to 3 feet long, erect, deciduous
RHIZOME HABIT: compact
AVAILABILITY: frequent
HARDINESS ZONES: 8 to 10
Ease of cultivation: easy

Widely found in sunny areas of the Old World tropics and subtropics, *P. vittata* has narrow, dark green fronds. The blade is once-pinnate, broadest above the middle, with a long apical pinna. There are fifteen to thirty pairs of linear pinnae. This species has escaped in the Gulf states and north to the District of Columbia, and in southern California. It also volunteers in greenhouses and outdoors in the southern states on the mortar of old walls, on the ground, or on limestone. It is easily grown in southern gardens.

PYRROSIA, Felt fern

Felt ferns are so-named for their dense covering of minute, white to brown star-shaped hairs, especially on the lower surface of the blade. The rhizome is short- to long-creeping and scaly. The fronds are mostly undivided, linear to lance-shaped, and occasionally deeply lobed. The blade is leathery and dark green. The numerous round sori lack indusia and are close to one another toward the tip of the blade.

There are about fifty species of *Pyrrosia* distributed throughout Africa and southern and eastern Asia to New Zealand, usually occurring on trees or rocks.

The felt ferns are rarely grown out-of-doors in frosted areas of the United States. However, several species are remarkably tough and adaptable and can survive dry conditions well. As pot plants, they have survived freezing in Seattle, so these are plants that should be tried in shaded gardens in other areas.

P. hastata (syn. *P. tricuspis*)
FRONDS: 6 to 14 inches long, erect, evergreen
RHIZOME HABIT: short-creeping
AVAILABILITY: rare
HARDINESS ZONES: 8 to 10
EASE OF CULTIVATION: moderate

This very attractive, small, trilobed species from Japan and Korea has a stipe half to three quarters the frond length, with a dense mat of persistent brown stellate hairs on the lower blade surface. In nature it grows mostly on rocks, sometimes on trees. In the garden it can be grown among rocks and it is beautiful in a hanging basket. It needs well-drained soil.

P. linearifolia
FRONDS: 1 to 5 inches long, erect, evergreen
RHIZOME HABIT: long-creeping
AVAILABILITY: infrequent
HARDINESS ZONES: 8 to 9
EASE OF CULTIVATION: moderate

The small linear fronds have no stipe. The underside of the blade is densely covered with a loose mat of persistent brownish stellate hairs. It is found on rocks and tree trunks in the mountains of eastern Asia in sheltered or exposed situations. A crested variety is recorded in Britain.

P. lingua
Tongue fern, Felt fern
FRONDS: 8 to 12 inches long, erect, evergreen
RHIZOME HABIT: long-creeping
AVAILABILITY: frequent
HARDINESS ZONES: 6 to 10
EASE OF CULTIVATION: moderate

Widely cultivated and popular in hanging baskets in greenhouses or frost-free climates, the tongue fern has sterile fronds that are only slightly wider and shorter than the fertile ones. The stipe comprises one fifth to one half the frond length, and the leathery, lance-shaped blade tapers to a long-pointed tip. The lower blade surface is densely clothed with persistent white to grayish

Pyrrosia lingua.

Pyrrosia lingua sori.
(PHOTO BY F. GORDON FOSTER)

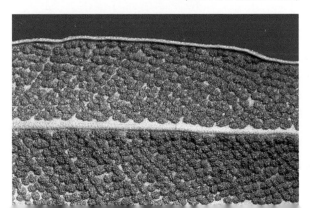

Pyrrosia lingua. (PHOTO BY F. GORDON FOSTER)

293

brown stellate hairs. *Pyrrosia lingua* is found mostly on rocks, less often on trees, usually in exposed places, in Japan, Taiwan, and China to Indochina.

The tongue fern needs bright light and is tolerant of dryness once it is established. It also makes an interesting houseplant with its long rhizome and tonguelike fronds, especially in a hanging basket. There are several beautiful cultivars in the trade, including 'Cristata' and 'Nankin-shishi' (both crested) and 'Monstrifera' (lacerated).

P. polydactyla

FRONDS: 2 to 8 inches long, erect, evergreen
RHIZOME HABIT: short-creeping
AVAILABILITY: infrequent
HARDINESS ZONES: 8 to 10
EASE OF CULTIVATION: moderate

This *Pyrrosia* is similar to *P. hastata*, both looking like a hand with fingerlike lobes. The stipe is half to two thirds the frond length, and the blade is covered with a dense mat of grayish brown stellate hairs on the underside. *Pyrrosia polydactyla* occurs on rocks, trees, and earth banks in Taiwan. It differs from *P. hastata* in having a more finely dissected blade with narrower divisions.

P. porosa (syn. *P. davidii*)

FRONDS: 6 to 10 inches long, erect-arching, evergreen
RHIZOME HABIT: creeping
AVAILABILITY: infrequent
HARDINESS ZONES: 8 to 10
EASE OF CULTIVATION: moderate

Pyrrosia polydactyla.

Pyrrosia porosa. (PHOTO BY JUDITH JONES)

This variable and widespread species is distinctive in the absence of any stipe. The undivided blade is narrowly oblong and is covered with a dense brown mat of stellate hairs. It is found on rocks, frequently limestone, and on trees, and even on the forest floor in northern China, Japan, the Philippines, and Madagascar.

P. sheareri

FRONDS: 1 to 2 feet long, erect-arching, evergreen
RHIZOME HABIT: short-creeping
AVAILABILITY: rare
HARDINESS ZONES: 8 to 10
EASE OF CULTIVATION: moderate

This native of China, Taiwan, and Vietnam has a stipe one quarter to half the frond length. The relatively large blade is lance-shaped with the typical dense mat of brown to grayish brown stellate hairs on the lower blade surface. It is found on rocks and cliffs and, less often, on trees.

RUMOHRA ADIANTIFORMIS, Leather fern

FRONDS: 1½ to 3 feet long, erect-arching, evergreen
RHIZOME HABIT: short- to long-creeping
AVAILABILITY: common
HARDINESS ZONES: 8 to 10
EASE OF CULTIVATION: easy

The rhizome of *Rumohra* is short- to long-creeping, fleshy, and scaly. The fronds are two to three times pinnate at the frond base, triangular, leathery, lustrous, and dark green. The sori are round, with an umbrella-shaped indusium.

Rumohra adiantiformis.

Botanical study has shown there is only one species in *Rumohra*, and all species other than *R. adiantiformis* are now classified under *Arachniodes*. *Rumohra adiantiformis* is native to South Africa, South America, New Zealand, and Australia.

Because of the attractive thick-textured fronds, this species is grown extensively in central Florida for the cut foliage trade and can be found in nearly every centerpiece and corsage in America. Fronds without sori are generally chosen for this purpose, because the dark fruiting dots might be construed as insects or disease by people not familiar with ferns. When temperatures go below 32 degrees Fahrenheit, *Rumohra* fronds are not as attractive; for commercial purposes special sprinkling systems are set up on cold nights to encase the fronds with ice for insulation, but for the home gardener, *Rumohra* is fully hardy and can be planted outdoors in central Alabama, Texas, and other regions in zones 8 to 10.

This beautiful, shiny fern likes rich, well-drained soil. It resents disturbance, but once established grows well in light shade. It can also be used in a hanging basket with an epiphyte soil mixture.

SALVINIA, Water spangles, Floating fern

Salvinia is a most unusual fern that floats on the water with paired, round or oblong leaves and trailing rootlike structures (actually dissected leaves). The upper surface of the leaves has four-pronged hairs, the tips of which are free or fused to form a cagelike structure. The spores are of two types, megaspores and microspores, borne in round sporocarps on the rootlike organs.

Salvinia is a genus of about eleven species native to tropical regions of the world. They are plants of ponds and slow-moving rivers. One species, *S. molesta*, has been a troublesome weed in Africa, Australia, and Borneo, clogging waterways and killing plant and animal life alike by cutting off light and oxygen. Other species are readily cultivated in small ponds in warmer regions, as well as in aquaria. Salvinias are frequently available in stores dealing in tropical fish.

S. auriculata
PLANTS: floating, deciduous
AVAILABILITY: frequent

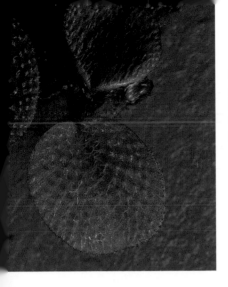

Salvinia auriculata,
close-up to show
hairs with 4 free tips.
(Photo by F.
Gordon Foster)

Salvinia minima. (Photo by
Barbara Hallowell)

HARDINESS ZONES: 8 to 10

EASE OF CULTIVATION: easy

The leaves are oval and about one inch long. The hairs on the upper leaf surface have their four prongs uniting to form a small cage. It is native to Central and South America.

S. minima (syn. *S. rotundifolia*)

PLANTS: floating, deciduous

AVAILABILITY: frequent

HARDINESS ZONES: 6 to 10

EASE OF CULTIVATION: easy

The leaves are round or oval, about one quarter to one half inch long, their upper surface hairs each having four arching branches. *Salvinia minima* is found floating on the quiet water of ditches, ponds, and slow-moving streams in the southeastern United States and tropical America, but it has also been reported in Minnesota.

SELAGINELLA, Spikemoss

The spikemosses are an amazingly diverse group of fern allies. The plants vary from small, creeping, and mosslike, to fully erect and frondlike. The very small leaves are abundant, round to linear, with a single vein, and often end in a hairlike tip called a seta. The sporangia are borne at the bases of special leaves that form four-sided cones at the ends of the branches. The spores are of two types and are borne in different sporangia but in the same cone. Megasporangia each contain four megaspores, and each microsporangium contains one to two thousand microspores.

Selaginella has about seven hundred species, mostly of tropical regions. Two major groups are recognized: one, about fifty mosslike species with leaves that are long, slender, and all alike, occurring mostly in dry regions of Mexico and western United States; and two, 650 species, mostly natives of wet tropical forests, with scalelike leaves of two sizes, two rows of arching lateral leaves and two rows of smaller leaves on the top side of the stem (median leaves).

Although most species of *Selaginella* are tropical, some are hardy in North America and are worth planting in the garden. Spikemosses are not commonly cultivated but they are interesting plants for those wanting something different. Some are novelty plants, whereas others can make a respectable ground cover. Spikemosses are propagated almost entirely by division. Rhizomes can be divided or, in some species, branchlets can be broken off and rooted. Plant the divisions in soil or moist sand and keep them humid until established. The mat-forming species with leaves all alike generally can take full sun; those with two kinds of leaves are by and large shade-loving. Both can do well in light shade.

Spore culture is not a practical method of propagation in the spikemosses since it takes two kinds of spores whose germination and development have to be coordinated. This is done only in research laboratories.

S. apoda

Meadow spikemoss
PLANTS: creeping, evergreen
AVAILABILITY: infrequent
HARDINESS ZONES: 5 to 10
EASE OF CULTIVATION: moderate

This is a creeping species of mosslike stature that frequently appears in lawns. The leaves are finely toothed and of two kinds; the lateral leaves are oval, the median leaves narrower with a pointed tip. The cones are inconspicuous. *Selaginella apoda* is found in wet woods, swamps, and meadows in the eastern United States. The only known locality for this species in Europe is in the lawn of a park in southern Berlin. How it got there is a real mystery.

Although the meadow spikemoss normally grows in association with grass, it can be cultivated as a small ground cover in the garden.

S. braunii (occasionally S. pallescens in hort.)

Braun's spikemoss, Arborvitae fern, Chinese lace-fern spikemoss
PLANTS: erect, 6 to 20 inches tall, semievergreen
AVAILABILITY: infrequent
HARDINESS ZONES: 5 to 10
EASE OF CULTIVATION: easy

This lacy spikemoss is most attractive. The creeping rhizome sends up erect, woody, frondlike stems to twenty inches tall with many short hairs. New "fronds" come up in late spring or early summer (June in New York), and at the end of the growing season turn brown in hard winters or stay green in milder ones, and do not fall until the following spring. The minute leaves are scalelike and of two kinds—oval lateral leaves with rounded tips and narrower, pointed median leaves. Leaves are sparse on the main erect stem, and the cones are about one half inch long. *Selaginella braunii* is native to western China and has become naturalized in parts of the southeastern United States.

S. douglasii

Douglas's spikemoss
PLANTS: creeping, evergreen
AVAILABILITY: infrequent
HARDINESS ZONES: 6 to 8
EASE OF CULTIVATION: moderate

The stems are creeping, prostrate on the ground. The leaves are of two kinds, the lateral leaves smooth-margined with rounded tips and the median leaves smooth-margined with slender pointed tips and a few hairs at the base.

Selaginella braunii.

Selaginella douglasii.

Selaginella douglasii occurs on moist shaded rocks in the northwestern United States.

S. eremophila
Desert spikemoss
PLANTS: creeping, evergreen
AVAILABILITY: rare
HARDINESS ZONES: 8 to 9
EASE OF CULTIVATION: moderate
Selaginella eremophila forms a dense mat. The leaves are all alike, with marginal hairs and an apical, twisted, often deciduous seta. *Selaginella eremophila* is found in rock crevices in southwestern Arizona and southern California.

S. hansenii
Hansen's spikemoss
PLANTS: creeping, evergreen
AVAILABILITY: rare
HARDINESS ZONES: 5 to 9
EASE OF CULTIVATION: moderate
The leaves are all alike, with hairlike teeth and straight setae that do not fall off easily. *Selaginella hansenii* occurs normally in central California, but Thomas Morgan has found it to be hardy in his garden near Carmel, New York, about fifty miles north of New York City.

S. involvens (syn. S. caulescens)
Tree spikemoss
PLANTS: erect, 6 to 14 inches tall, evergreen
AVAILABILITY: frequent
HARDINESS ZONES: 6 to 9
EASE OF CULTIVATION: easy
The rhizome is creeping, with upright plumose branches about two inches apart. The leaves are of two kinds, overlapping at the stem base and are minutely toothed. The lateral leaves are broadly oval, the median ones narrowly oblong with two longitudinal grooves. *Selaginella involvens* is native to China, Korea, and Japan.

The many overlapping leaves give this plant a denser appearance than the lacier *S. braunii*.

S. kraussiana

Krauss's spikemoss

PLANTS: creeping, semievergreen

AVAILABILITY: frequent

HARDINESS ZONES: 6 to 10

EASE OF CULTIVATION: easy

The wide-creeping stems form extensive loose, low mats on the ground. The leaves are of two kinds—oval lateral leaves and linear median leaves. *Selaginella kraussiana* is found in Africa and the Azores and is the most commonly grown spikemoss in greenhouses and has escaped in the southeastern United States. We grew this species for several years at the New York Botanical Garden's Cary Arboretum seventy-five miles north of New York City, where it was only marginally hardy. It and *S. uncinata* were planted in a swampy area, where it grew during the summer, and died down in the winter with the terminal half inch of the branches remaining alive over the winter.

S. k. 'Aurea' has a yellowish green color, which is an intermediate genetic condition between greenness and albinism. Among the offspring, roughly one quarter are green, half are golden, and one quarter are white, which cannot make food and die.

S. k. 'Brownii'. The branches are very short, compact, and erect, resulting in a delightful mound form.

S. k. 'Gold Tips' has yellowish tips on the branches.

Selaginella kraussiana.

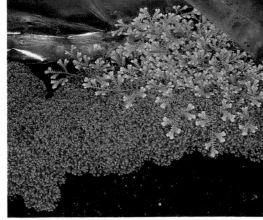

Selaginella kraussiana 'Brownii' and 'Gold Tips'.

S. moellendorffii
Gemmiferous spikemoss
PLANTS: erect, 5 to 18 inches tall, deciduous
AVAILABILITY: rare
HARDINESS ZONES: 6 to 10
EASE OF CULTIVATION: easy

The creeping rhizome bears upright, plumose stems that have ciliate leaves of two kinds. The leaves near the base of the stem are distant from one another and all alike. Higher on the plant the lateral leaves are broadly oval, the median ones small, oval, with a long slender tip, and the white margins. The plants at maturity bear four-sided cones as do other species of *Selaginella*, but this species is unique in also producing small leafy structures on the branchlets that look very much like small cones—stubby, leafy—but not square like the cones, and falling off readily, acting as vegetative propagules. In the greenhouse they drop on the bench gravel and into other pots, sprout, and quickly make new plants, often overgrowing the pots' intended inhabitants. Outside, depending on the climate, *S. moellendorffii* may not get large enough in a growing season to produce cones or gemmae. In New York this species remains green in the winter if protected by a leaf mulch, but otherwise the aerial branches die down after a hard freeze. It is native to eastern Asia.

S. nipponica
PLANTS: creeping-erect, evergreen
AVAILABILITY: rare
HARDINESS ZONES: 5 to 8
EASE OF CULTIVATION: moderate

Among the hardy cultivated spikemosses, this species is unique in having creeping vegetative stems that form a loose mat and erect, sparsely branched fertile stems. The leaves are more or less all alike, oval, ciliate-margined, and spirally arranged on the stem. The two- to four-inch-high fertile stems consist of a long, open cone with the sporangia visible at the base of the loosely arranged leaves. This trailing species occurs naturally in Japan, Korea, and China.

S. oregana
Oregon spikemoss
PLANTS: creeping, evergreen
AVAILABILITY: infrequent

HARDINESS ZONES: 5 to 8

EASE OF CULTIVATION: moderate

This species is most unusual in being epiphytic. It hangs from mossy trunks, rarely growing on rocks or in shaded soil in the northwestern United States. The stems are twelve inches or more long and trailing, and the branches are long and distant from each other. The leaves have short hairlike teeth on the leaf bases and a short seta at the leaf tip. *Selaginella oregana* can be grown among rocks or on soil in the garden and is hardy in Connecticut.

S. rupestris

Rock spikemoss

PLANTS: short-creeping, mound-forming, evergreen

AVAILABILITY: rare

HARDINESS ZONES: 2 to 7

EASE OF CULTIVATION: moderate

Selaginella rupestris forms a loose to compact mat of creeping to erect branches one half to two inches high. The leaves are all alike and have hairlike teeth and long setae. It occurs on or among exposed acidic rocks and cliffs in central and eastern North America.

S. stauntoniana

PLANTS: erect, 3 to 8 inches tall, evergreen

AVAILABILITY: infrequent

HARDINESS ZONES: 7 to 8

EASE OF CULTIVATION: easy

The rhizomes send up erect stems about one inch apart. The erect, frondlike stems are three to eight inches tall and bear two kinds of leaves. The median leaves are slender, somewhat fleshy, and lack a distinct midvein, whereas the lateral leaves are broadly oval. The cones are one half to one inch long. *Selaginella stauntoniana* is found on dry rocky cliffs in eastern Asia.

One form called golden spikemoss, 'Eco Mt. Emei', is plumose with short broad "fronds" to six inches tall and four and one half inches wide. It resembles *S. involvens* but is more golden.

Apparently this has been confused with *S. moellendorffii*. Reports of growing this from spores by laying the cones in soil are mistaken. The "cones" were actually the vegetative buds of *S. moellendorffii* which resemble cones. It is possible that there is no true *S. stauntoniana* in cultivation in America.

Selaginella uncinata. (PHOTO BY PAMELA J. HARPER)

Selaginella wallacei.

S. uncinata
Peacock spikemoss, Rainbow moss
PLANTS: wide-creeping, semievergreen
AVAILABILITY: infrequent
HARDINESS ZONES: (5) 6 to 10
EASE OF CULTIVATION: moderate

Selaginella uncinata is one of the most distinctive of all the spikemosses in having iridescent bluish green leaves and flat, frondlike branches. The leaves are of two kinds, with a pale, shiny margin without teeth. The lateral leaves are oval, the median ones narrowly oblong with a long slender tip. The peacock spikemoss grows in moist woods in China, has become naturalized in Florida and Louisiana, and is at least marginally hardy north to New York and Connecticut. Unfortunately, slugs are strongly attracted to this plant.

S. wallacei
Wallace's spikemoss
PLANTS: short-creeping, evergreen
AVAILABILITY: rare
HARDINESS ZONES: 6 to 9
EASE OF CULTIVATION: easy to moderate

This spikemoss forms a loose or compact mat one half to three inches high. The leaves are all alike, with or without hairlike teeth and with long white setae. It is found on cliffs and rocky slopes in the northwestern United States and, once established, is quite drought-tolerant.

S. watsonii

Watson's spikemoss

PLANTS: short-creeping, evergreen

AVAILABILITY: rare

HARDINESS ZONES: 6 to 9

EASE OF CULTIVATION: easy to moderate

Watson's spikemoss forms loose, low mats less than one inch high. The leaves are all alike, with virtually no teeth and a long greenish seta. *Selaginella watsonii* occurs on or among igneous rocks in moist or shaded localities in the southwestern United States.

THELYPTERIS, Maiden fern

Thelypterises are small to large deciduous ferns with pinnate-pinnatifid blades (rarely more divided) that bear minute, needle-shaped hairs. The rhizomes are long- to short-creeping or erect, and the round sori are located on the lower surface, usually with kidney-shaped indusia.

Thelypteris is one of the largest genera of ferns, comprising nearly a thousand species native to tropical wet forests. A few species are found in temperate areas. The genus has been subdivided by some botanists into natural groups that have been variously treated as genera, subgenera, or sections, including *Amauropelta*, *Cyclosorus*, *Macrothelypteris Oreopteris*, *Parathelypteris*, and *Phegopteris*. At one time species now considered under *Thelypteris* were treated as species of *Dryopteris*, but *Thelypteris* is distinct in having needlelike hairs, thin texture, two conducting bundles in the stipe rather than five to nine, and different spores and chromosome numbers.

The few hardy species occur mostly in moist woods or swamps, and are strong growers in the shady fern garden with rich, moist, slightly acid soil.

T. decursive-pinnata (syn. *Phegopteris decursive-pinnata*)

Japanese beech fern

FRONDS: 1 to 2 feet tall, erect, deciduous

RHIZOME HABIT: erect, having runners

AVAILABILITY: frequent

HARDINESS ZONES: 4 to 10

EASE OF CULTIVATION: easy

Thelypteris decursive-pinnata sori.

Thelypteris decursive-
pinnata.

Thelypteris hexagonoptera.

This vigorous grower is closely related to the two native North American beech ferns (*T. hexagonoptera* and *T. phegopteris*) as seen by the winged rachis. In contrast to those species, the rhizome of *T. decursive-pinnata* is erect, and new plants are produced on short runners, so it does not spread widely. Furthermore, the hairy, pinnatifid blade is narrow, erect, and tapers at both ends. The sori lack an indusium. The species is associated with walls and rocks in the lowlands and low mountains of eastern and southern Asia.

Plants are easily divided by digging them from the ground, pulling the small plants from the parent, and replanting them all separately. *Thelypteris decursive-pinnata* is a constant bright green throughout the growing season and through the first frosts of autumn until a hard freeze finally puts it to rest for the winter.

T. hexagonoptera (syn. *Dryopteris hexagonoptera, Phegopteris hexagonoptera*)

Broad beech fern, Southern beech fern
FRONDS: 15 to 24 inches long, arching, deciduous
RHIZOME HABIT: long-creeping
AVAILABILITY: frequent
HARDINESS ZONES: 5 to 9
EASE OF CULTIVATION: easy

The broadly triangular, bipinnatifid blade with a winged rachis readily identifies this species. The lower surface of the blade has fine hairs, and the small, round sori lack an indusium. The broad beech fern grows in moist woods and swamp margins of eastern North America. It is more common in the southern states, though native north to New York and Ohio. Plants need light shade and moist, humusy soil. *Thelypteris hexagonoptera* is an attractive plant, but the rhizome is a little too far-ranging for a tidy garden, and it tends to be chewed by slugs early in the summer.

T. kunthii (syn. *T. normalis, Cyclosorus kunthii*)

River fern, Southern maiden fern

FRONDS: 2 to 4 feet long, arching, deciduous

RHIZOME HABIT: short- to long-creeping

AVAILABILITY: common

HARDINESS ZONES: 8 to 10

EASE OF CULTIVATION: easy

The pinnate-pinnatifid blade is very hairy on both the upper and lower surfaces, and the hairs are all nearly equal in length and longer than the sporangia. It is found on wooded rocky slopes in the southeastern United States, West Indies, and Middle America.

Thelypteris kunthii is easily grown in the southern states. It spreads quickly to form extensive colonies with large fronds.

T. limbosperma (syn. *T. oreopteris, Dryopteris montana, Lastrea montana, Oreopteris limbosperma*)

Mountain fern, Lemon-scented fern, Sweet mountain fern

FRONDS: 1½ to 3 feet (to 5 feet) tall, erect, deciduous

RHIZOME HABIT: short-creeping

AVAILABILITY: infrequent

Thelypteris kunthii.

Thelypteris limbosperma.

Pinnae of *Thelypteris limbosperma.*

Hardiness zones: 5 to 9

Ease of cultivation: easy to moderate

This strong-growing fern has pinnate-pinnatifid fronds that are narrowly lance-shaped, broadest about the middle, and with a short stipe. The yellow-green blade is of firm texture, bears pale hairs and slender scales, and the lower surface has yellow glands and smells of lemon or balsam when crushed. The sori are round and located near the margin; the indusium drops off early.

The mountain fern is found in woods and on strictly acidic rocky banks, often near water, in mountains, as one of its common names indicates, in northwestern North America and Newfoundland, and Europe. The European material is called var. *limbosperma* and the American plants var. *americana*, but the differences between them are very slight.

Lowe (1891) recognized seventy-seven kinds but today there are no significant variations in cultivation.

T. nevadensis (syn. *Parathelypteris nevadensis*)

Nevada wood fern, Sierra water fern

Fronds: 1½ to 2½ feet long, erect, deciduous

Rhizome habit: short- to long-creeping

Availability: rare

Hardiness zones: 4 to 6

Ease of cultivation: easy

The pinnate-pinnatifid blade tapers at both ends and is very thin-textured. It closely resembles *T. noveboracensis* in the tapering frond base, but *T. nevadensis* has a more compact rhizome and orange glands on the lower frond surface. The sori are located halfway between the pinnule midvein and the margin. *Thelypteris nevadensis* occurs on wooded slopes and wet meadows in northwestern North America.

T. noveboracensis (syn. *Parathelypteris noveboracensis*)

New York fern, Tapering fern

Fronds: 1 to 2 feet long, erect, deciduous

Rhizome habit: long-creeping

Availability: frequent

Hardiness zones: 4 to 8

Ease of cultivation: easy

This common fern of eastern North America has a delicate, yellow-green, pinnate-pinnatifid blade that tapers gradually at both ends. The sori are positioned closer to the margin than to the pinnule midvein.

The New York fern is a very strong grower and very aggressive with its long-creeping rhizomes. It is excellent for filling in spaces in lightly shaded woodlands or gardens where space is not a problem. A small patch must be pruned regularly to keep it within bounds.

T. ovata (syn. *Cyclosorus ovatus*)
Oval maiden fern
FRONDS: 2 to 4 feet long, arching, deciduous
RHIZOME HABIT: short- to long-creeping
AVAILABILITY: frequent
HARDINESS ZONES: 9 to 10
EASE OF CULTIVATION: easy

The oval blade is pinnate-pinnatifid, the pinnae about one half inch wide and cut three quarters of the way to the pinna midvein, hairy below and naked above. *Thelypteris ovata* is found in moist woods in the southeastern United States and Mexico.

T. palustris (syn. *T. thelypteroides, Dryopteris thelypteris, Lastrea thelypteris*)
Marsh fern
FRONDS: 1½ to 2½ feet long, erect, deciduous
RHIZOME HABIT: wide-creeping
AVAILABILITY: common
HARDINESS ZONES: 2 to 10

Thelypteris noveboracensis.

Thelypteris palustris. (PHOTO BY BARBARA HALLOWELL)

EASE OF CULTIVATION: easy

The delicate, bluish green fronds are scattered individually on widely creeping rhizomes. The narrowly oval blade is pinnate-pinnatifid, and the pinnae do not taper toward the base of the blade but stop abruptly, the lowest pinnae more than half as long as the longest pinnae. The fertile fronds have inrolled segments, appearing more contracted than the sterile ones. The sori are located halfway between the pinnule midvein and the blade margin but appear closer to the margin because of the curled margin. The marsh fern occurs in wet meadows and swamps in eastern North America and many other temperate portions of the world.

Thelypteris palustris is unimpressive in its natural habitat, mixed with grasses and other plants of a marsh, but it can be an attractive plant in cultivation, either in sun (with moist to very wet soil) or in shade. The long-creeping rhizome signals that it may be more aggressive than you may wish in some gardens, but kept as a pure stand or mixed with a flowering plant species, it can be a graceful and effective fern. I have seen it cultivated in a thick, pure stand around an old stump, and in another garden mixed among iris, both in full sun.

T. p. f. *pufferae*. The pinnae have forking tips.

T. phegopteris (syn. *Dryopteris phegopteris*, *Phegopteris connectilis*)
Narrow beech fern, Northern beech fern
FRONDS: 8 to 18 inches long, arching, deciduous
RHIZOME HABIT: long-creeping
AVAILABILITY: frequent
HARDINESS ZONES: 2 to 5
EASE OF CULTIVATION: easy

The triangular blade is pinnate-pinnatifid to bipinnatifid, thin-textured, and covered below with hairs and narrow scales that look like coarse hairs. The upper pinnae are connected by a rachis wing, but the wing is lacking between the lowest two pairs of pinnae. The basal pair of pinnae is usually strongly turned downward. The sori are small and located near the margin, and there is no indusium. The narrow beech fern grows in moist woods in northern North America, Europe, and Asia.

Thelypteris phegopteris is an easy grower in shady, lime-free northern gardens, but does not like the hot weather farther south. Although the much-branched rhizome creeps, *T. phegopteris* is not nearly as far-ranging as *T. hexagonoptera*

Thelypteris phegopteris.

and its fronds are not as large, so this more compact low-grower is extremely useful as a ground cover or to fill in rock crevices or a space in a rock garden, or as a low edging plant. Like *T. hexagonoptera*, though, it is often damaged by slugs early in the summer.

T. simulata
Massachusetts fern, Bog fern
FRONDS: 1½ to 2½ feet long, erect, deciduous
RHIZOME HABIT: long-creeping
AVAILABILITY: rare
HARDINESS ZONES: 4 to 6
EASE OF CULTIVATION: moderate

This denizen of very acidic conifer and blueberry swamps is very similar to the more common *T. palustris* and often grows with it. Like that species, the pinnate-pinnatifid, lance-shaped blade does not taper at the base, the lowest pinnae being more than one half as long as the longest pinnae, but *T. simulata* can be distinguished by having all the veins undivided from the midveins to the margin (forked in *T. palustris*), the base of each pinna reduced next to the rachis, and the fertile pinnae not strongly inrolled. *Thelypteris simulata* is rare across much of northeastern North America but fairly common in New England.

The Massachusetts fern is not as vigorous a grower in cultivation as the other species of the genus, but it will grow if you give it acidic, swampy ground. Apparently it does not require the garden soil to be as strongly acidic as the soil it occupies in the wild, but it should be planted near water.

Thelypteris torresiana. (PHOTO BY PAMELA J. HARPER)

T. *torresiana* (syn. *Dryopteris setigera, D. uliginosa, Macrothelypteris torresiana*)

Marianna maiden fern, Mariannas fern

FRONDS: 2 to 3½ feet long, erect-arching, deciduous

RHIZOME HABIT: short-creeping

AVAILABILITY: infrequent

HARDINESS ZONES: 8 to 10

EASE OF CULTIVATION: easy

Named for the Marianna Islands, this large, handsome fern is common in the tropics and hardy in the southern United States. The vast majority of *Thelypteris* species are pinnate-pinnatifid, but the broadly triangular blades of *T. torresiana* are bipinnate to tripinnate. It can be identified as a *Thelypteris*, however, by the presence of needle-shaped hairs on the blade. The stipe has a distinctive whitish bloom, the sori are small and round, and the indusia minute. *Thelypteris torresiana* is native to the Old World tropics but is arching rapidly, and is now one of the more common fern species in tropical America. It was first found in Florida in 1904 and since then has become naturalized north to South Carolina and west to Texas and Arkansas. It grows in moist woods and does not seem particular as to whether the soil is acidic or calcareous.

In the greenhouse this fern reproduces quickly by spores and turns up in many pots and under benches. It should be used more outdoors in the southern United States because it is very attractive with its large, lacy triangular fronds and whitish stipes.

WOODSIA

The woodsias boast a number of low-growing species suitable for rock gardens. They are small, compact plants that normally grow on or among rocks in the wild. The rhizome is short and compact, horizontal to ascending. The fronds are generally small and clumped, and the blade is once-pinnate to bipinnate-pinnatifid, thin-textured, and deciduous. The indusium, consisting of scale- or hairlike lobes, surrounds the round young sorus like a napkin drawn up around a bunch of grapes.

Woodsia is a widely distributed genus of about twenty-five species, mostly of temperate North America and Asia. They are all associated with rocks, some acidic, some calcareous, and are ideal for growing in light shade or full sun. Like the *Cystopteris* species, the woodsias appear very early in the spring, unrolling their delicate crooks when little else is stirring in the garden.

W. gracilis

FRONDS: 8 to 16 inches long, arching, deciduous
RHIZOME HABIT: compact, ascending
AVAILABILITY: rare
HARDINESS ZONES: 6 to 8
EASE OF CULTIVATION: moderate

This handsome rock garden plant displays its slender fronds in a broadly arching manner, almost as a rosette. The blade is pinnate-pinnatifid and the pinnae are most graceful with long-attenuate tips.

Woodsia gracilis.

Woodsia ilvensis.

W. ilvensis
Rusty woodsia
FRONDS: 3 to 8 inches long, erect-arching, deciduous
RHIZOME HABIT: compact, ascending
AVAILABILITY: infrequent
HARDINESS ZONES: 2 to 6
EASE OF CULTIVATION: moderate

A small tufted species, the dull green fronds are narrowly oblong and pinnate-pinnatifid to bipinnate. The lower surface of the blade is covered with hairs and scales that are silvery when young, turning to a rusty shade as the frond matures. The sorus is adorned with an indusium of hairs. Rusty woodsia is found on dry cliffs and acidic rocky slopes in northern North America, Europe, and Asia.

This little gem is not difficult to grow and is a dainty addition among rocks or in gravelly soil.

W. intermedia
FRONDS: 3 to 6 inches long, arching, deciduous
RHIZOME HABIT: compact, ascending
AVAILABILITY: infrequent
HARDINESS ZONES: 5 to 8
EASE OF CULTIVATION: moderate

The narrowly oblong blade is once-pinnate, the five to twelve pairs of pinnae are shallowly round-lobed and have auricles. The blade is lightly hairy all over, with narrow scales on the lower surface. This species is native to Japan, Korea, and China.

W. manchuriensis

Manchurian woodsia

FRONDS: 4 to 14 inches long, arching, deciduous
RHIZOME HABIT: compact
AVAILABILITY: rare
HARDINESS ZONES: 5 to 8
EASE OF CULTIVATION: moderate

This charming woodsia has a narrowly oblong, pinnate-pinnatifid blade that tapers to the base leaving almost no stipe. The pinna lobes are held obliquely and are devoid of any hairs or scales. This species grows on shaded rocks in China, Manchuria, Korea, and Japan.

W. obtusa

Blunt-lobed woodsia

FRONDS: 5 to 16 inches long, erect, deciduous
RHIZOME HABIT: compact
AVAILABILITY: infrequent
HARDINESS ZONES: 3 to 10
EASE OF CULTIVATION: easy

The rhizome is compact with tan scales that have conspicuous dark streaks. The narrowly oblong blade is bipinnate-pinnatifid. The fronds are gray-green due to the many small white glands and hairs on both surfaces. The indusium is composed of about four broad lobes and is nearly cuplike. *Woodsia obtusa* is found on shaded acidic or calcareous cliffs and rock ledges in eastern North America.

It is easily grown in a mixed garden or a rock garden. Its fronds are erect whereas most other species of *Woodsia* have arching fronds.

Woodsia obtusa.
(PHOTO BY BARBARA
HALLOWELL)

Woodsia obtusa sori.
(PHOTO BY F.
GORDON FOSTER)

W. plummerae
Plummer's woodsia
FRONDS: 4 to 14 inches long, erect-arching, deciduous
RHIZOME HABIT: compact
AVAILABILITY: infrequent
HARDINESS ZONES: 7 to 9
EASE OF CULTIVATION: moderate

The blade is bipinnate, with ten to sixteen pairs of pinnae, whose segments have sparse broad teeth. On the blade surface there are scattered short glandular hairs, and the indusium is composed of broad lobes around the sorus. *Woodsia plummerae* occurs on ledges and in rock crevices in the southwestern United States and Mexico. It makes a fine small plant for the rock garden.

W. polystichoides
Holly-fern woodsia
FRONDS: 6 to 12 inches long, arching, deciduous
RHIZOME HABIT: compact, ascending
AVAILABILITY: infrequent
HARDINESS ZONES: 5 to 8
EASE OF CULTIVATION: easy

Woodsia polystichoides is the only cultivated woodsia that is once-pinnate. The fronds have fifteen to twenty-four pairs of undivided pinnae, which are slightly auricled, thin-textured, and have small hairs on both surfaces. The indusium is composed of threads surrounding the sorus. *Woodsia polystichoides* is found among sunny rocks in eastern Asia.

It resembles a small, once-divided holly fern (*Polystichum*) in form but has a softer texture. It is a superb plant in rock gardens, with its rosette of widely

Woodsia polystichoides

Woodsia scopulina. (PHOTO BY JOSEPH BEITEL)

arching fronds that may lie nearly flat on the ground, but sometimes stand more erect. As the plant increases in size, the crowns can be divided by gently pulling them apart. *Woodsia polystichoides* prefers full sun or only light shade. When I obtained a plant of this cutie, I put it in the shady corner I reserve for plants needing careful watching. Very quickly the plant declined in vigor until I moved it to a sunny location, where it has thrived ever since.

W. scopulina
Rocky Mountain woodsia
FRONDS: 4 to 12 inches long, erect, deciduous
RHIZOME HABIT: compact, ascending
AVAILABILITY: infrequent
HARDINESS ZONES: 2 to 8
EASE OF CULTIVATION: moderate

The blade is bipinnate to bipinnate-pinnatifid and narrowly oblong. The stipe and blade have white hairs and short-stalked glands, and the indusium is composed of narrow, straplike lobes. *Woodsia scopulina* occurs on cliffs and rocks over much of western North America.

WOODWARDIA (syn. *Lorinseria*), Chain fern

The common name of "chain fern" refers to the characteristic elongate sori with indusia arranged in a broken line along the pinnule midveins like the links of a chain. Most of the species have a massive, woody, ascending rhizome and leathery, evergreen fronds three to six feet long. These species are limited to hardiness zones 8 to 10. On the other hand, the two species occurring in eastern North America have fleshy, creeping rhizomes and thin-textured, deciduous fronds only one to two feet tall. The blades of all species are pinnatifid to pinnate-pinnatifid, and at least some of the veins unite to form a network. Another distinctive feature of this genus and the closely related *Blechnum* is the pink to bronze color of the unrolling fronds. Species with distinctly different sterile and fertile fronds are often segregated as the genus *Lorinseria*.

Woodwardia is a largely north temperate genus of about twelve species, mostly found in eastern Asia and North and Central America, plus one in the Atlantic islands. The species in tropical areas occur at high elevations.

The larger species, such as *W. fimbriata* and *W. radicans*, are unsurpassed for their strong sculptural effects in the mild-climate fern garden. *Woodwardia areolata* is among the easiest of all ferns to cultivate. All species appreciate shaded, moist conditions.

W. areolata (syn. *Lorinseria areolata*)

Netted chain fern

FRONDS: 1 to 2 feet long, erect, deciduous

RHIZOME HABIT: long-creeping

AVAILABILITY: frequent

HARDINESS ZONES: 3 to 9

EASE OF CULTIVATION: easy

The sterile and fertile fronds are quite distinct, the sterile ones oval-triangular and pinnatifid, and all the veins are netted. They are reddish green in early spring, becoming a glossy dark green as they mature. The fertile fronds develop in midsummer and are as tall as the sterile; the pinnae are linear, the chains of sori filling the underside when ripe. This species is found in acidic bogs and swamps of eastern North America.

Netted chain fern can be confused with the more common sensitive fern (*Onoclea sensibilis*), but the latter has a smooth blade margin and woody, beadlike fertile segments whereas *W. areolata* has minute teeth along the margin and linear, more ephemeral fertile pinnae.

Although *W. areolata* is native to swampy conditions, it does very well in the average garden. The rhizome branches and grows quickly, so be sure there is room for its perigrinations.

W. fimbriata (syn. *W. chamissoi*)

Giant chain fern

FRONDS: 3 to 5 feet (to 10 feet) long, arching, evergreen

RHIZOME HABIT: compact, ascending

AVAILABILITY: infrequent

HARDINESS ZONES: 8 to 10

EASE OF CULTIVATION: moderate

The rhizome is stout, woody, ascending, and densely clothed with large, brown scales. The large, lance-shaped fronds are pinnate-pinnatifid, the lobes long and sharp-pointed with finely toothed margins. *Woodwardia fimbriata* grows in moist forests of far western North America.

This dramatic chain fern makes a fountain of large, arching fronds and is

Woodwardia fimbriata.

Woodwardia areolata.

one of several lush native ferns of the Northwest. It is a strong grower and deserves a place in all but the smallest of western gardens.

W. orientalis
Oriental chain fern
FRONDS: 3 to 5 feet long, arching, evergreen
RHIZOME HABIT: compact, ascending
AVAILABILITY: infrequent
HARDINESS ZONES: 8 to 10
EASE OF CULTIVATION: easy

The lustrous surface of this large fern bears many very small plantlets that are easily dislodged. They have no roots, appearing only as a small wedge-shaped leaf and tiny growing point at the plantlet's base. These can be planted in damp soil or sand and kept humid until roots are formed. The blade is

Woodwardia orientalis, frond with plantlets.

Woodwardia orientalis, close-up of plantlets.

pinnate-pinnatifid with long pinna lobes, the acroscopic ones longer than the basiscopic ones. *Woodwardia orientalis* is native to Japan, China, and the Himalayas.

W. o. var. *formosana* (syn. *W. formosana*). This variety differs from the species in having fronds that are somewhat larger (to six feet long), and pinnae that are more pointed and cut nearly to the midvein. Var. *formosana* comes from Japan, China, Taiwan, and the Philippines.

W. radicans
European chain fern
FRONDS: 3 to 5 feet long, arching, evergreen
RHIZOME HABIT: compact, ascending
AVAILABILITY: infrequent
HARDINESS ZONES: 9 to 10
EASE OF CULTIVATION: easy
Woodwardia radicans closely resembles *W. fimbriata* but bears a large bud near the tip of the rachis on the underside. As the frond arches over and touches the ground, this bud takes root and develops into a new plant. The species is a native of southern Europe and is a rare escape in Florida and southern California.

W. unigemmata
FRONDS: 3 to 4 feet long, arching, deciduous
RHIZOME HABIT: compact, ascending
AVAILABILITY: rare
HARDINESS ZONES: 8 to 10
EASE OF CULTIVATION: easy
The fronds are large and the blade is pinnate-pinnatifid with a single large bud on the rachis near the tip on the lower surface. It is native to eastern Asia.

W. virginica (syn. *Anchistea virginica*)
Virginia chain fern
FRONDS: 1½ to 2 feet long, erect, deciduous
RHIZOME HABIT: long-creeping

Woodwardia virginica. (PHOTO BY F. GORDON FOSTER)

Woodwardia radicans.

The young fronds of *Woodwardia unigemmata* display an attractive burgundy color.

AVAILABILITY: infrequent
HARDINESS ZONES: 3 to 10
EASE OF CULTIVATION: moderate

The stipe is blackish and the blade is pinnate-pinnatifid with short and blunt lobes. It occurs in acidic bogs and swamps, often with the rhizome submerged in the water, in eastern North America and Bermuda.

Woodwardia virginica does best in moist areas, as near a stream or pond; it can be tried in an average garden, but it is not nearly as dependable as *W. areolata.*

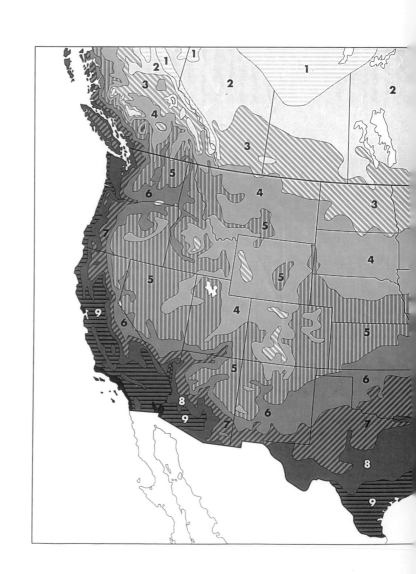

USDA Map of Hardiness Zones

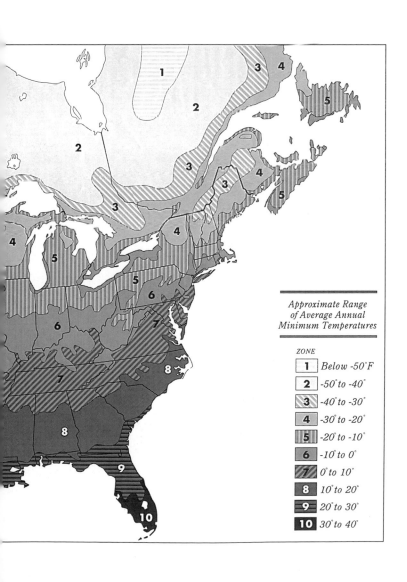

*Approximate Range
of Average Annual
Minimum Temperatures*

ZONE

1	*Below -50°F*
2	*-50° to -40°*
3	*-40° to -30°*
4	*-30° to -20°*
5	*-20° to -10°*
6	*-10° to 0°*
7	*0° to 10°*
8	*10° to 20°*
9	*20° to 30°*
10	*30° to 40°*

List of Ferns for Special Conditions

These are not the only possibilities for the special conditions mentioned but are more readily available and more broadly useful.

Foundation Plantings
(PLANTS MOSTLY OVER 24 INCHES TALL)

Athyrium angustum
A. cyclosorum
A. filix-femina
A. thelypteroides
Dennstaedtia punctilobula
Diplazium pycnocarpon
Dryopteris affinis
D. × australis
D. clintoniana
D. crassirhizoma
D. dilatata
D. erythrosora
D. filix-mas
D. f.-m. 'Barnesii'
D. goldiana
D. intermedia

D. marginalis
D. × mickelii
Matteuccia struthiopteris
Onoclea sensibilis
Osmunda cinnamomea
O. claytoniana
O. regalis
Polystichum aculeatum
P. andersonii
P. munitum
P. setiferum
Thelypteris kunthii
T. ovata
T. torresiana
Woodwardia fimbriata

Rock Gardens
(PLANTS MOSTLY UNDER 12 INCHES TALL)

Adiantum aleuticum 'Sub-pumilum'

A. venustum

Asplenium platyneuron

*A. resiliens**

*A. ruta-muraria**

*A. trichomanes**

*Asplenosorus ebenoides**

Athyrium filix-femina, dwarf forms

Blechnum penna-marina

B. spicant

*Camptosorus rhizophyllus**

*Ceterach officinarum**

Cheilanthes species

Cryptogramma acrostichoides

*C. stelleri**

*Cystopteris bulbifera**

C. protrusa

Doodia media

Dryopteris affinis 'Crispa Gracilis'

Equisetum scirpoides

E. variegatum

Gymnocarpium dryopteris

*G. robertianum**

*Pellaea atropurpurea**

*P. glabella**

*Phyllitis scolopendrium**

Polypodium species

Polystichum lonchitis

P. setiferum, dwarf forms

P. tsus-simense

Selaginella species

Thelypteris phegopteris

Woodsia ilvensis

*W. obtusa**

W. polystichoides

* Limestone lovers

For Filling Large Spaces
(THESE SPECIES HAVE WIDELY CREEPING RHIZOMES AND SPREAD QUICKLY)

Dennstaedtia punctilobula

Matteuccia struthiopteris

Onoclea sensibilis

Pteridium aquilinum

Thelypteris noveboracensis

T. palustris

Ferns for Sunny Spots

(THESE SPECIES CAN TOLERATE SUN MOST OF THE DAY; INCREASED SOIL MOISTURE ALLOWS EVEN MORE POSSIBILITIES)

Asplenium adiantum-nigrum

A. ruta-muraria

A. trichomanes

Athyrium filix-femina

Blechnum penna-marina

Ceterach officinarum

Cheilanthes species

Cryptogramma acrostichoides

Dennstaedtia punctilobula

Dryopteris affinis

D. filix-mas

Hypolepis millefolium

Matteuccia struthiopteris

Pteridium aquilinum

Onoclea sensibilis

Osmunda cinnamomea

O. claytoniana

O. regalis

Pellaea species

Thelypteris kunthii

T. ovata

T. palustris

Woodsia ilvensis

W. polystichoides

Ferns for Wet Spots

(SWAMPS OR SMALL PONDS)

Azolla filiculoides

Dryopteris carthusiana

D. celsa

D. clintoniana

D. cristata

Equisetum fluviatile

Osmunda cinnamomea

O. regalis

Marsilea species

Matteuccia struthiopteris

Onoclea sensibilis

Salvinia species

Thelypteris palustris

Woodwardia areolata

W. virginica

Especially Good Evergreen Ferns

Asplenium trichomanes

Blechnum penna-marina

B. spicant

Cyrtomium species

Dryopteris championii

D. erythrosora

D. intermedia

D. marginalis

D. uniformis

continued

continued from previous page

Polypodium species
Polystichum acrostichoides
P. braunii

P. makinoi
P. munitum
P. neolobatum
P. tagawanum

Species Good for Beginners

Adiantum aleuticum
A. pedatum
A. venustum
Athyrium angustum
A. filix-femina and varieties
A. niponicum 'Pictum'
A. thelypteroides
Cyrtomium fortunei
Cystopteris bulbifera
C. protrusa
Dennstaedtia punctilobula
Diplazium pycnocarpon
Dryopteris affinis 'Cristata'
D. championii
D. crassirhizoma
D. erythrosora
D. filix-mas and varieties,
    esp. 'Barnesii'

D. goldiana
D. intermedia
D. marginalis
D. tokyoensis
D. uniformis 'Cristata'
Matteuccia struthiopteris
Onoclea sensibilis
Osmunda cinnamomea
O. claytoniana
O. regalis
Polystichum acrostichoides
P. makinoi
P. munitum
P. polyblepharum
Thelypteris noveboracensis
T. phegopteris
Woodsia polystichoides
Woodwardia areolata

Some Personal Favorites

Athyrium cyclosorum
A. filix-femina × niponicum
    'Pictum'
A. otophorum
Ceterach officinarum
Cystopteris tennesseensis
Dryopteris × australis
D. bissetiana

D. × boottii
D. campyloptera
D. celsa
D. clintoniana
D. complexa
D. cristata
D. dilatata
D. × mickelii

D. pseudo-filix-mas

D. remota

Equisetum hyemale

Lygodium japonicum

Phyllitis scolopendrium and
varieties

Polystichum aculeatum

P. andersonii

P. setiferum and varieties

P. tagawanum

P. tripteron

Selaginella braunii

S. moellendorffii

Thelypteris decursive-pinnata

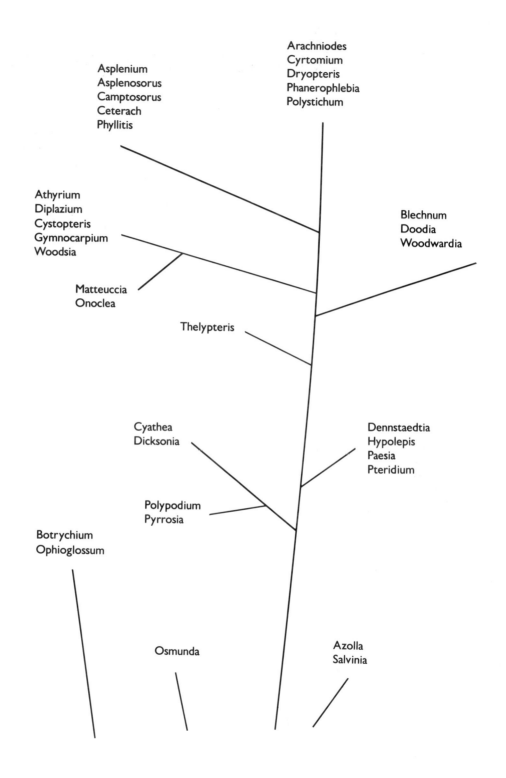

Arachniodes
Cyrtomium
Dryopteris
Phanerophlebia
Polystichum

Asplenium
Asplenosorus
Camptosorus
Ceterach
Phyllitis

Athyrium
Diplazium
Cystopteris
Gymnocarpium
Woodsia

Blechnum
Doodia
Woodwardia

Matteuccia
Onoclea

Thelypteris

Cyathea
Dicksonia

Dennstaedtia
Hypolepis
Paesia
Pteridium

Polypodium
Pyrrosia

Botrychium
Ophioglossum

Osmunda

Azolla
Salvinia

Relationships of Hardy Fern Genera

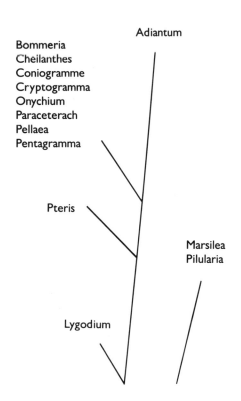

Adiantum

Bommeria
Cheilanthes
Coniogramme
Cryptogramma
Onychium
Paraceterach
Pellaea
Pentagramma

Pteris

Marsilea
Pilularia

Lygodium

Fern Societies

Although one can grow many ferns at home and learn a great deal about them from books, like many plants, gardeners seem to thrive in association with others. It is invigorating to share experiences and questions with others. Some cities or regions have a local fern group you can join, or you can organize your own.

AMERICAN FERN SOCIETY

The American Fern Society, organized in 1893, is an international organization composed of people interested in ferns and allied plants. The majority of its more than thirteen hundred members are amateurs interested in growing this group of plants or in studying them in the wild. Many professional fern scholars (pteridologists) and other botanists throughout the world also are members of the society.

The principal objective of the society is to foster scholarly and horticultural interest in ferns and fern allies. The society's spore exchange maintains a collection of fresh spores, which are available to members wishing to grow their own plants from spores. The bimonthly bulletin, *Fiddlehead Forum*, contains articles concerning native and cultivated ferns, field trip reports, and notices of society business. The spore list and questions from members are published regularly. The society's scientific publication, the *American Fern Journal*, is published quarterly and is of interest principally to professional and advanced amateur botanists.

For membership information, contact
American Fern Society
Dr. George A. Yatskievych
Missouri Botanical Garden
P.O. Box 299
St. Louis, MO 63166-0299

THE BRITISH PTERIDOLOGICAL SOCIETY

The British Pteridological Society has aims similar to those of the American Fern Society. It too has multiple publications: *The Bulletin* (reports of meetings, field trips, and other society business), *The Pteridologist* (articles and notes on fern cultivation and other items of general appeal), and *The Fern Gazette* (technical papers of interest primarily to professional pteridologists). For membership information, contact:

British Pteridological Society
Department of Botany
The Natural History Museum
Cromwell Road
London SW7 5BD, England

THE HARDY FERN FOUNDATION

The Hardy Fern Foundation, centered in the Seattle area, is an organization devoted to assembling a broad collection of the world's temperate ferns and testing their hardiness. Its primary planting site is with the Rhododendron Species Foundation at Federal Way, Washington, and associated satellite gardens in other parts of the country provide additional testing sites. The quarterly newsletter has notes on fern cultivation and news on the collection's progress. Membership, in addition to periodic news of the collection, gives associate membership in the Rhododendron Species Foundation. This includes reduced admission to the twenty-five acres of beautiful rhododendron and fern plantings. A spore exchange has been started for its members, and eventually plants will be available for sale at the garden site. Members have the satisfaction of being a part of a monumental international project that will greatly benefit fern horticulture and pteridology.

Hardy Fern Foundation
P.O. Box 166
Medina, WA 98039

OTHER NORTH AMERICAN FERN SOCIETIES INCLUDE:

Austin Fern Society
John Young
jdyoung@austin.cc.tx.us

Birmingham Fern Society
Birmingham Botanical Gardens
2612 Lane Park Road
Birmingham, AL 35223

Delaware Valley Fern and
    Wild Flower Society
Clara Bondinell
1512 Franklin Lane
Wayne, PA 19087

Los Angeles International Fern Society
P.O. Box 90943
Pasadena, CA 91109-0943

Louisiana Fern Society
Mary Elliott
41038 S. Range Road
Ponchatoula, LA 70454

Memphis Fern Society
Christine Spindel
3985 S. Galloway Drive
Memphis, TN 38111-6841

New York Fern Society
Dr. John T. Mickel
New York Botanical Garden
Bronx, NY 10458-5126

San Diego Fern Society
Amna Cornett
3905 Ibis Street
San Diego, CA 92103

Sarasota Fern Society
Marie Selby Botanical Gardens
811 S. Palm Avenue
Sarasota, FL 34136

Southwestern Fern Society
Ann Herrington
2121 Richwood Drive
Garland, TX 75044

Tampa Bay Fern Club
Carl Strohmenger
P.O. Box 15578
Tampa, FL 33684

Texas Gulf Coast Fern Society
Donna McGraw
8207 Colonial Oaks Lane
Spring, TX 77379-3908

Tropical Fern and
    Exotic Plant Society
6880 S.W. 75 Terrace
South Miami, FL 33143

Sources of Hardy Ferns

Of the numerous mail-order sources for hardy ferns in North America, some still obtain their material by collecting in the wild, a practice strongly to be discouraged. Listed below are a few nurseries that are known to sell only propagated materials. Additional sources may be found on the Web.

Andersen Horticultural Library's Source List of Plants and Seeds. University of Minnesota, St. Paul.

The Canadian Plant Sourcebook by Anne and Peter Ashley, Cheriton Graphics, Ottawa.

Gardening by Mail, by Barbara J. Barton. Houghton Mifflin Co., Boston

Hortus Source List, ed. Melissa Luckow. L. H. Bailey Hortorium, Cornell University, Ithaca, NY.

Nursery Sources, Native Plants and Wildflowers, ed Barbara F. Pryor. New England Wild Flower Society. 1987. (Garden in the Woods, Hemenway Rd, Framingham, MA 01701; phone [508] 877-7630.) Cites only companies that propagate 80 percent or more of their plants.

Collector's Nursery
16804 N.E. 102 Avenue
Battle Ground, WA 98604
(360) 574-3832
www.collectorsnursery.com

Eco-Gardens
P.O. Box 1227
Decatur, GA 30031
(404) 294-6468

Fancy Fronds
Judith Jones
P.O. Box 1090
Gold Bar, WA 98251
(360) 793-1472
www.fancyfronds.com

The Fernery
93 Magellan Way
Covington, KY 41015
fernery@aol.com

Foliage Gardens
2003 128 Avenue, S.E.
Bellevue, WA 98005
(425) 747-2998
www.foliagegardens.com

Forestfarm
990 Tetherow Road
Williams, OR 97544
(541) 846-6969
www.forestfarm.com

Heronswood Nursery
7530 N.E. 288 Street
Kingston, WA 98346
(360) 297-4172
www.heronswood.com

Plant Delights Nursery
9241 Sauls Road
Raleigh, NC 27603
(919) 772-4794
www.plantdelights.com

Roslyn Nursery
211 Burrs Lane
Dix Hills, NY 11746
(631) 643-9347
www.roslynnursery.com

Russell Graham
4030 Eagle Crest Road, N.W.
Salem, OR 97304
(503) 362-1135

Siskiyou Rare Plant Nursery
2825 Cummings Road
Medford, OR 97501
(541) 772-6846
www.srpn.net

Wild Earth Native Plant Nursery
P.O. Box 7258
Freehold, NJ 07728
(732) 308-9777

Bibliography

Many of the entries listed below are old books and articles which still provide a wealth of information on hardy fern cultivation. An asterisk designates the most broadly useful works.

Allen, David E. *The Victorian Fern Craze: A History of Pteridomania.* London: Hutchinson, 1969.

Boydston, Kathryn. "An Amateur Plants Fern Spores." *American Fern Journal* 48 (1958): 1–18.

"Brooklyn Botanic Garden Handbook on Ferns." *Plants and Gardens* 25 (1969): 1–77.

Clausen, Ruth R., and Nicolas H. Ekstrom. *Perennials for American Gardens.* New York: Random House, 1989.

Delendick, Tom, et al. "Hardy Ferns." *Fiddlehead Forum* 12 (1985): Part I: 9–12; Part II: 15–18; Part III: 21–24.

Druery, Charles T. *The Book of British Ferns.* London: Country Life, 1901.

*Druery, Charles T. *British Ferns and Their Varieties.* London: Routledge and Sons, 1910.

Druery, Charles T. *Choice British Ferns: Their Varieties and Culture.* London: Upcott Gill, 1888.

Duthie, Leslie. "Recreating Scott's Spleenwort." *Fiddlehead Forum* 17 (1990): 34–35.

Dyce, James W. "*Athyrium filix-femina* 'Plumosum superbum Drueryi'." *Pteridologist* 1 (1987): 148–153.

Dyce, James W. "British Fern Varieties— The Scolopendriums." *British Pteridological Society Newsletter* 10 (1972): 20–22.

*Dyce, James W. "Classification of Fern Variation in Britain." *Pteridologist* 1 (1987): 154–155.

Dyce, James W. "The Variation and Propagation of British Ferns." *British Pteridological Society, Special Publication* 3 (1991): 1–37.

Dyce, James W. "Variation in *Polystichum* in the British Isles." *British Fern Gazette* 9 (1963): 97–109.

Everett, Thomas H. *The New York Botanical Garden Illustrated Encyclopedia of Horticulture.* New York: Garland Publishing, 1981.

Finkbeiner, Frances. *Ferns under Fluorescents.* Light Gardening Cultural Guide No. 1. New York: Indoor Lighting Society of America, Inc., 1975.

*Foster, F. Gordon. *Ferns to Know and Grow.* New York: Hawthorn Books, Inc., 1976; 4th ed. Beaverton, OR: Timber Press, 1993.

Foster, F. Gordon. *The Gardener's Fern Book.* Princeton, NJ: Van Nostrand, 1964.

Harper, Pamela J. *Designing with Perennials.* New York: Macmillan Publishing Co., Inc., 1991.

Harper, Pamela J., and Fred McGourty. *Perennials: How to Select, Grow and Enjoy.* Tucson, Arizona: H. P. Books Inc., 1985.

Heim, Michael. "The Cultivation of our Native Clubmosses." *Minnesota Horticulturist* 116(1) (January 1988): 24–27.

Hemsley, Alfred. *The Book of Fern Culture.* London: J. Lane Co., 1908.

Hibberd, Shirley. *The Fern Garden.* 9th ed. London: Groombridge and Sons, 1881.

*Hoshizaki, Barbara. J. *Fern Growers Manual.* New York: Alfred A. Knopf, 1975.

Jones, David L. *Encyclopaedia of Ferns.* Portland, Oregon: Timber Press, 1987.

*Kaye, Reginald. *Hardy Ferns.* London: Faber & Faber, 1968.

Kaye, Reginald. "Variation in *Athyrium* in the British Isles." *British Fern Gazette* 9 (1965): 197–204.

Lovis, John D. "Fern Hybrids and Fern Hybridizing. 1: The work of Edward Joseph Lowe (1825–1900)." *British Fern Gazette* 9 (1967): 301–308.

Lowe, Edward J. *British Ferns and Where Found.* London: Swan Sonnenschein, 1890.

Lowe, Edward J. *Ferns: British and Exotic.* 8 vols. London: Groombridge and Sons, 1856–1860, 1867.

Lowe, Edward J. *Fern Growing.* London: Nimmo, 1895.

Lowe, Edward J. *Our Native Ferns.* 2 vols. London: Groombridge and Sons, 1865.

Macself, Albert James. *Ferns for Garden and Greenhouse.* New York: Transatlantic Arts, Inc., 1952.

Mickel, John T. "Ferns" in *Reader's Digest Illustrated Guide to Gardening.* Pleasantville, NY: Reader's Digest Association, Inc., 1978.

*Mickel, John T. *The Home Gardener's Book of Ferns.* New York: Ridge Press/Holt, Rinehart & Winston, 1979.

Mickel, John T., and Joseph M. Beitel. *Hardy Ferns: A Guide to the F. Gordon Foster Hardy Fern Collection at the New York Botanical Garden.* New York: New York Botanical Garden, 1987.

Mickel, John T., Warren H. Wagner, Jr., and Ernest M. Gifford. "Ferns and Other Lower Vascular Plants." *Encyclopaedia Britannica.* 19: 163–178. 1991.

Moore, Thomas. *British Ferns Nature Printed.* 2 vols. London: Bradbury & Sons, 1859–1860.

Moore, Thomas. *The Handbook of British Ferns.* 3rd ed. London: Groombridge and Sons, 1857.

Moore, Thomas. *Popular History of British Ferns.* London: Reeve & Bentham, 1851.

Perl, Philip, ed. *Ferns.* New York: Time-Life Books, 1977.

Phair, George. "Fern Allies for the Rock Garden." *Bulletin of the American Rock Garden Society* 47(3) (1989): 190–200.

Piggott, Anthony. "Cultivation of Horsetails." *Pteridologist* 1 (1988): 209–211.

Rickard, Martin. "Hardy Dwarf Ferns." *British Pteridological Society Bulletin* 2 (1992): 202–203.

Rickard, Martin. "Survey of Variation in British Polypodiums." *British Pteridological Society Bulletin* 2 (1981): 138–140.

Rush, Richard. "Choice Ferns: *Coniogramme.*" *Pteridologist* 1 (1984): 40–41.

*Rush, Richard. "A Guide to Hardy Ferns." *British Pteridological Society Special Publication.* 1984.

Rush, Richard. "A Hardy *Adiantum.*" *British Pteridological Society Bulletin* 2 (1983): 261–262.

Schneider, George. *The Book of Choice Ferns.* London: L. Upcott Gill, 1892.

Schneider, George. *Choice Ferns for Amateurs.* 3 vols. London: L. Upcott Gill, 1905.

Weatherby, Charles A. "A List of Varieties and Forms of the Ferns of Eastern North America." *American Fern Journal* 25 (1935): 45–51, 95–100; 26 (1936): 11–16, 60–69, 94–99, 131–136; 27 (1937): 51–56.

Woodward, Carol, ed. *Hardy Ferns and Their Culture.* New York Botanical Garden, 1940.

Woolson, Grace A. *Ferns and How to Grow Them.* New York: Doubleday, Page & Co., 1906.

REGIONAL IDENTIFICATION MANUALS OF NORTH AMERICA

Clute, Willard Nelson. *Our Ferns: Their Haunts, Habits and Folklore.* New York: Frederick A. Stokes Company, 1938.

Cobb, Boughton. *A Field Guide to the Ferns.* Boston: Houghton Mifflin Co., 1956.

Cronquist, Arthur, Arthur H. Holmgren, Noel H. Holmgren, and James L. Reveal. *Intermountain Flora: Vascular Plants of the Intermountain West, USA.* Vol. 1. New York: Hafner Publishing Co., 1972.

Dorn, Robert D., and Jane L. Dorn. *The Ferns and Other Pteridophytes of Montana, Wyoming, and the Black Hills of South Dakota.* Laramie, WY: by the authors, 1972.

Gleason, Henry A. *The New Britton and Brown Illustrated Flora.* 3 vols. New York: New York Botanical Garden, 1952.

Hallowell, Anne C., and Barbara G. Hallowell. *Fern Finder.* Berkeley, CA: Nature Study Guild, 1981.

Lellinger, David B. *A Field Manual of the Ferns and Fern Allies of the United States and Canada.* Washington, D.C.: Smithsonian Institution, 1985.

Mickel, John T. *How to Know the Ferns and Fern Allies*. Dubuque, IA: Wm. C. Brown Co., 1979.

Moran, Nancy, ed. *Flora of North America: Pteridophytes*. Oxford: Oxford University Press, 1993.

Ogden, Eugene C. "Field Guide to Northeastern Ferns." *New York State Museum Bulletin* 444: 1–122.

Small, John Kunkel. *Ferns of the Southeastern States*. Lancaster, PA: Science Press Printing Co., 1938.

Taylor, Thomas M. C. *Pacific Northwest Ferns and Their Allies*. Toronto: University of Toronto Press, 1970.

Wherry, Edgar T. *The Fern Guide*. New York: Doubleday & Co., 1961; reprinted, Philadelphia: Morris Arboretum, 1975.

Wherry, Edgar T. *The Southern Fern Guide*. New York: Doubleday & Co. 1964; reprinted, New York: New York Chapter, American Fern Society, 1977.

STATE FLORAS

ALABAMA

Dean, Blanche E. *Ferns of Alabama*. Rev. ed. Birmingham, AL: Southern University Press, 1969.

ALASKA

Hulten, Eric. *Flora of Alaska and Neighboring Territories*. Stanford, CA: Stanford University Press, 1968.

Welsh, Stanley L. *Anderson's Flora of Alaska and Adjacent Parts of Canada*. Provo, UT: Brigham Young University Press, 1974.

ARIZONA

Kearney, T. H., and R. H. Peebles. *Arizona Flora*. Berkeley: University of California Press, 1957.

CALIFORNIA

Grillos, Steve J. *Ferns and Fern Allies of California*. Berkeley: University of California Press, 1966.

Hickman, James, ed. *The Jepson Manual: Vascular Plants of California*. Berkeley: University of California Press, 1993.

Kiefer, Lawrence L., and Barbara Joe. "Checklist of California Pteridophytes." *Madrono* 19 (1967): 65–73.

Munz, P. A., and D. D. Keck. *A California Flora*. Berkeley: University of California Press, 1959.

CAROLINAS

Evans, A. Murray. "Pteridophytes" in: Radford, A., et al. *Manual of the Vascular Flora of the Carolinas*. Chapel Hill: University of North Carolina Press, 1964.

COLORADO

Harrington, H. D., and L. W. Durrell. *Colorado Ferns and Fern Allies*. Fort Collins: Colorado Agricultural Research Foundation, 1950.

FLORIDA

Lakela, Olga, and Robert W. Long. *Ferns of Florida*. Miami: Banyan Books, 1976.

Small, John Kunkel. *The Ferns of Florida*. New York: Science Press, 1932.

GEORGIA

McVaugh, Rogers, and Joseph H. Pyron. *Ferns of Georgia*. Athens: University of Georgia Press, 1951.

Snyder, Lloyd H., Jr., and James G. Bruce. *Field Guide to the Ferns and Other Pteridophytes of Georgia*. Athens: University of Georgia Press, 1986.

IDAHO

Flowers, Seville. "A List of the Ferns of Idaho." *American Fern Journal* 40 (1950): 121–131.

ILLINOIS

Mohlenbrock, Robert H. *The Illustrated Flora of Illinois: Ferns*. Carbondale: Southern Illinois University Press, 1967.

INDIANA

Clevenger, Sarah. "The Distribution of the Ferns and Fern Allies in Indiana." *Butler University Botanical Studies* 10 (1951): 1–11.

IOWA

Cooperrider, Thomas S. "The Ferns and Other Pteridophytes of Iowa." *State University of Iowa Studies in Natural History* 20(1) (1959): 1–66.

Peck, James. "Pteridophyte Flora of Iowa." *Proceedings of the Iowa Academy of Sciences* 83(1976): 143–163.

KANSAS

Brooks, Ralph. "Ferns in Kansas." *The Kansas School Naturalist* 13 (1967): 1–15.

McGregor, Ronald L. "Ferns and Fern Allies in Kansas." *American Fern Journal* 50 (1960): 62–66.

LOUISIANA

Brown, Clair A., and Donovan S. Correll. *Ferns and Fern Allies of Louisiana*. Baton Rouge: Louisiana State University Press, 1942.

MAINE

Ogden, Edith B. *The Ferns of Maine*. Reprinted from *The Maine Bulletin* 51, No. 3. Orono, ME: University Press, 1948.

MARYLAND

Reed, Clyde F. *Ferns and Fern Allies of Maryland, Delaware and District of Columbia*. Baltimore: Reed Herbarium, 1953.

MICHIGAN

Billington, Cecil. *Ferns of Michigan*. Bloomfield Hills, MI: Cranbrook Institute of Science, 1952.

MINNESOTA

Tryon, Rolla M., Jr. *The Ferns and Fern Allies of Minnesota*. 2nd ed. Minneapolis: University of Minnesota Press, 1977.

MISSISSIPPI

Jones, S. B., Jr. "The Pteridophytes of Mississippi." *Sida Contributions to Botany* 3 (1969): 359–364.

MISSOURI

Key, James S. *Field Guide to Missouri Ferns*. Jefferson City: Missouri Department of Conservation, 1982.

Steyermark, Julian A. *Flora of Missouri.* Ames: Iowa State University Press, 1963.

NEW HAMPSHIRE

Scamman, Edith. *Ferns and Fern Allies of New Hampshire. Bulletin of the New Hampshire Academy of Science* 2 (1947).

NEW JERSEY

Chrysler, M. A., and J. L. Edwards. *Ferns of New Jersey.* New Brunswick, NJ: Rutgers University Press, 1947.

Montgomery, James D., and David Fairbrothers. *New Jersey Ferns and Fern-Allies.* New Brunswick, NJ: Rutgers University Press, 1992.

NEW MEXICO

Dittmer, Howard J., Edward F. Castetter, and Ora M. Clark. *Ferns and Fern Allies of New Mexico.* University of New Mexico Publication in Biology No. 6. Albuquerque: University of New Mexico Press, 1954.

NEW YORK

Small, John Kunkel. *Ferns of the Vicinity of New York.* Lancaster, PA: Science Press Printing Co., 1935.

OHIO

Vannorsdall, Harry H. *Ferns of Ohio.* Wilmington, OH: by the author, 1956.

OKLAHOMA

Waterfall, U. T. *A Catalogue of the Flora of Oklahoma.* Stillwater, OK: Research Foundation, 1952.

PENNSYLVANIA

Canan, Elsie D. *A Key to the Ferns of Pennsylvania.* Lancaster, PA: Science Press, 1946.

RHODE ISLAND

Crandall, Dorothy L. "County Distribution of Ferns and Fern Allies in Rhode Island." *American Fern Journal* 55 (1965): 97–112.

SOUTH DAKOTA

Van Bruggen, T. "The Pteridophytes of South Dakota." *Proceedings of the South Dakota Academy of Sciences* 46 (1967): 126–144.

TENNESSEE

Shaver, Jesse M. *Ferns of Tennessee.* Nashville: George Peabody College for Teachers, 1954.

TEXAS

Correll, Donovan S. *Ferns and Fern Allies of Texas.* Renner: Texas Research Foundation, 1956.

VIRGINIA

Massey, A. B. *The Ferns and Fern Allies of Virginia.* 2nd ed. VPI Agricultural Extension Service Bulletin 256. Blacksburg, VA, 1958.

WEST VIRGINIA

Brooks, M. G., and A. S. Margolin. *The Pteridophytes of West Virginia.* West Virginia University Bulletin, Ser. 39, No. 2, 1938.

Strausbaugh, P. D., and Earl L. Core. *Flora of West Virginia, Part* 1. West Virginia University Bulletin., Ser. 52, No. 12–2, 1952.

WISCONSIN

Tryon, R. M., Jr., N. C. Fassett, D. W. Dunlop, and M. E. Diemer. *The Ferns and Fern Allies of Wisconsin.* 2nd ed. Madison: University of Wisconsin Press, 1953.

WYOMING

Porter, C. L. *A Flora of Wyoming, Part* 1. University of Wyoming Agricultural Experiment Station Bulletin 402, 1962.

COMMON NAMES
OF FERNS

Stewart, Ralph, David Johnson, and John T. Mickel. "Meanings of Generic Names." *Fiddlehead Forum* 10 (1983): 21–36.

Weatherby, Una F. "The English Names of North American Ferns." *American Fern Journal* 42 (1953): 134–151. Reprinted in *Fiddlehead Forum* 17 (1990): 11–14, 20–21.

OTHER USEFUL FERN
FLORAS OF TEMPERATE
REGIONS

Brownsey, Patrick J., and John C. Smith-Dodsworth. *New Zealand Ferns and Allied Plants.* Auckland: David Bateman, 1989.

Cody, William J., and Donald M. Britton. *Ferns and Fern Allies of Canada.* Research Branch Agriculture Canada Publication 1829/E. 1–430, 1989.

Flora of Taiwan, vol I. Taipei: Epoch Publishing Co. Ltd., 1975.

Iwatsuki, Kunio (ed.). *Ferns and Fern Allies of Japan.* Tokyo: Heibonsha Ltd., 1992.

Jermy, A. Clive, and Josephine M. Camus. *The Illustrated Field Guide to British Ferns and Allied Plants.* London: Natural History Museum, 1991.

Knobloch, Irving W., and Donovan S. Correll. *Ferns and Fern Allies of Chihuahua.* Renner: Texas Research Foundation, 1962.

Mickel, John T., and Joseph M. Beitel. "Pteridophyte Flora of Oaxaca, Mexico." *Memoirs of the New York Botanical Garden* 46 (1988): 1–568.

Ohwi, Jisaburo. *Flora of Japan.* Washington, DC: Smithsonian Institution, 1965.

Page, Christopher N. *The Ferns of Britain and Ireland.* Cambridge: Cambridge University Press, 1982.

Page, Christopher N. *Ferns: Their Habitats in the British and Irish Landscape* (New Naturalist). London: William Collins, 1988.

Tutin, T. G., et al., eds. *Flora Europaea.* vol. I. Cambridge: University Press, 1964.

GENERIC REVISIONS
AND MONOGRAPHS

ADIANTUM

Paris, Cathy A. "*Adiantum viridimontanum*, a New Maidenhair Fern in Eastern North America." *Rhodora* 93(1991): 105–121.

Arachniodes (as *Rumohra*)

Ching, Ren Chen. "A Revision of the Compound-leaved Polysticha and Other Related Species in the Continental Asia including Japan and Formosa." *Sinensia* 5 (1–2) (1934): 23–92.

ASPLENIUM

Wagner, Warren H., Jr. "Reticulate Evolution in the Appalachian Aspleniums." *Evolution* 8 (1954): 103–118.

ASTROLEPIS

Benham, Dale H., and Windham, Michael D. "Generic Affinities of the Star-scaled Cloak Ferns." *American Fern Journal* 82 (1992): 47–58.

AZOLLA

Svensen, H. K. "The New World Species of *Azolla*." *American Fern Journal* 34 (1944): 69–84.

BOTRYCHIUM

Clausen, Robert T. "A Monograph of the Ophioglossaceae." *Memoirs of the Torrey Botanical Club* 9 (2) (1938): 1–177.

Wagner, Florence S. "Moonworts Recently Discovered in the Great Lakes Area." *Fiddlehead Forum* 15 (1988): 2.

Wagner, Warren H. Jr., and Florence S. Wagner. "How to Find the Rare Grapeferns and Moonworts." *Fiddlehead Forum* 3 (1976): 2–3.

CYSTOPTERIS

Haufler, Christopher H., Michael D. Windham, and Thomas A. Ranker. "Biosystematic Analysis of the *Cystopteris tennesseensis* (Dryopteridaceae) Complex." *Annals of the Missouri Botanical Garden* 77 (1990): 314–329.

Blasdell, Robert F. "A Monographic Study of the Fern Genus *Cystopteris*." *Memoirs of the Torrey Botanical Club* 21 (4) (1963): 1–102.

DRYOPTERIS

Montgomery, James D. "*Dryopteris* in North America." I. *Fiddlehead Forum* 8 (1981): 25–31; II. *Fiddlehead Forum* 9 (1982): 23–30.

EQUISETUM

Hauke, Richard L. "Horsetails (*Equisetum*) in North America." *Fiddlehead Forum* 10 (1983): 39–42.

Hauke, Richard L. "A Taxonomic Monograph of the Genus *Equisetum* subgenus *Equisetum*." *Nova Hedwigia* 30 (1978): 385–455.

Hauke, Richard L. "A Taxonomic Monograph of the Genus *Equisetum* subgenus *Hippochaete*." *Beihefte zur Nova Hedwigia* 9 (1963): 1–123.

ISOETES

Taylor, W. Carl. "Lessons in Pteridology No. VIII. Quillworts." *Fiddlehead Forum* 6(3) (1979): 2.

LYCOPODIUM

Beitel, Joseph M. "Clubmosses (*Lycopodium*) in North America." *Fiddlehead Forum* 6(4/5) (1979): 1–8.

Wilce, Joan. "Section Complanata of the Genus *Lycopodium*." *Beihefte zur Nova Hedwigia* 19 (1965): 1–230 plus 40 plates.

MARSILEA

Johnson, David M. "An Introduction to the Water-clovers (*Marsilea*)." *Fiddlehead Forum* 14 (1987): 16–18.

Johnson, David M. "Systematics of the New World Species of *Marsilea* (Marsileaceae)." *Systematic Botany Monographs* 11 (1986): 1–87.

NOTHOLAENA

Tryon, Rolla M. "A Revision of the American Species of *Notholaena*." *Contributions of the Gray Herbarium* 179 (1956): 1–106.

ONOCLEOID FERNS

(*Onoclea* and *Matteuccia*)

Lloyd, Robert M. "Systematics of the Onocleoid Ferns." *University of California Publications in Botany* 61 (1971): 1–86.

OPHIOGLOSSUM

Clausen, Robert T. "A Monograph of the Ophioglossaceae." *Memoirs of the Torrey Botanical Club* 9 (2) (1938): 1–177.

OSMUNDA

Wagner, Warren H., Jr., Florence S. Wagner, C. N. Miller, Jr., and D. H. Wagner. "New Observations on the Royal Fern Hybrid *Osmunda* × *ruggii*." *Rhodora* 80 (1978): 92–106.

PELLAEA

Tryon, Alice. "A Revision of the Fern Genus *Pellaea* subgenus *Pellaea*." *Annals of the Missouri Botanical Garden* 44 (1957): 125–193.

PENTAGRAMMA

Yatskievych, George, Eckhard Wollenweber, and Michael Windham. "A Reconsideration of the Genus *Pityrogramma* (Adiantaceae) in Western North America." *American Fern Journal* 80 (1990): 9–17.

POLYPODIUM

Haufler, Christopher H., and Michael D. Windham. "New Species of North American *Cystopteris* and *Polypodium*, with Comments on Their Reticulate Relationships." *American Fern Journal* 81 (1991): 7–23.

POLYSTICHUM

Wagner, David. "Systematics of *Polystichum* in Western North America North of Mexico." *Pteridologia* 1 (1979): 1–64.

PTERIDIUM

Tryon, Rolla. "Revision of the Genus *Pteridium*." *Rhodora* 43 (1941): 1–31, 37–70.

SELAGINELLA

Tryon, Rolla. "*Selaginella rupestris* and Its Allies." *Annals of the Missouri Botanical Garden* 42 (1955): 1–99.

THELYPTERIS

Leonard, Steven W. "The Distribution of *Thelypteris torresiana* in the Southeastern United States." *American Fern Journal* 82(1972): 97–99.

Smith, Alan R. "Systematics of the Neotropical Species of *Thelypteris* section *Cyclosorus*." *University of California Publications in Botany* 59 (1971): 1–143.

WOODSIA

Brown, Donald F. M. "A monographic Study of the Fern Genus *Woodsia*." *Beihefte zur Nova Hedwigia* 16 (1964): 1–154.

Glossary

acroscopic: directed toward the apex of the organ on which it is borne; see *basiscopic*.

aerial stem: an erect stem arising from a horizontal rhizome.

annulus: the row of specialized cells of a fern sporangium that cause the sporangium to open and discharge its spores.

antheridium: the male sex organ, borne on the underside of the gametophyte, which produces sperms.

apical: pertaining to the tip, or apex.

apogamy: the process of forming a sporophyte directly from a gametophyte by budding rather than by sexual fusion.

appressed: lying flat against the surface.

archegonium: the female sex organ, borne on the underside of the gametophyte, which produces an egg.

articulate: jointed, having a line at the base where the frond, pinna, or segment falls off in old age.

auricle: an ear-shaped part, as the lobe at the base of a pinna.

axil: the acroscopic angle made by the meeting of two parts, as a leaf to a stem, or a pinna to a rachis.

axis: the central structure of a frond or pinna along which the pinnae or pinnules are arranged.

basiscopic: directed toward the base of the organ on which it is borne; see *acroscopic*.

bicolorous: having two colors, generally referring to rhizome scales with a dark central streak.

bipinnate: twice cut.

bipinnate-pinnatifid: twice cut with the pinnules partially cut.

bipinnatifid: twice cut but with the pinnae and pinnules broadly attached.

blade: the expanded part of the leaf, the part of the leaf other than the stipe.

bulblet or *bulbil:* a small, budlike structure that falls off a fern leaf to form a new plant.

calcareous: describing soils or rocks containing lime, consequently basic.

calciphilic: lime-loving; requiring, or at least preferring, to grow on limestone or in limy soil.

ciliate: bearing fine hairs, or cilia.

circinate vernation: the development of the frond from a tightly coiled condition, gradually maturing from the base to the tip.

circumneutral: about neutral in acidity, a little below to a little above neutral; pH 6.5 to 7.5.

concolorous: of one uniform color.

cone: a tight cluster of modified leaves or other structures bearing sporangia.

costa: the midvein of a pinna.

crested: the condition of having forking tips—for frond, pinnae, or segments.

crosier: the coiled developing leaf of a fern.

crown: the tip of a stem where a cluster of leaves arise.

deciduous: fronds not persisting the entire year; see *evergreen.*

depauperate: dwarfed, either through poor growing conditions or through genetic disfigurement (as in pinnae or segments of a particular cultivar or form).

dimorphic: describing the fertile and vegetative leaves or stems that are of distinctly different appearance.

disjunct: separated geographically.

dissection: referring to division, usually of a frond.

distal: away from the organ base or place of attachment; see *proximal.*

epiphytic: growing on other plants, generally on tree trunks or branches.

evergreen: bearing green leaves through the winter; see *deciduous.*

false indusium: a blade margin that is differentiated and rolled over a sorus, in function simulating an indusium.

fern ally: any pteridophyte other than a fern, including clubmosses (*Lycopodium*), spikemosses (*Selaginella*), quillworts (*Isoetes*), and horsetails (*Equisetum*).

fertile frond: a frond bearing sporangia.

fiddlehead: the coiled developing leaf of a fern.

fimbriate: fringed.

frond: the leaf of a fern.

gamete: a sex cell, sperm, or egg.

gametophyte: the small, independent generation that bears sex organs; the prothallus; see *sporophyte.*

gemma: a vegetative reproductive bud borne on the stem, as in *Lycopodium.*

glabrous: naked, lacking hairs or scales.

gland: secretory hair or other organ with specialized secretory cells.

habit: the general appearance of a plant or organ, whether erect, prostrate, spreading, etc.

hair: a form of leaf or stem covering, one or more cells long and only one cell wide; see *scale.*

hardy: enduring without protection, usually alluding to cold but may also refer to heat or drought; see *tender.*

heterophyllous: having more than one leaf size and shape, as in most species of *Selaginella.*

heterosporous: having two kinds of spores, generally differing in size.

homophyllous: having all leaves alike, as in some species of *Selaginella.*

homosporous: having spores of only one kind.

indument: the hairs and/or the scales of a plant, on the rhizome and fronds.

indusium: a specialized flap covering the sorus. A true indusium is a distinct organ arising in or beneath the sorus; see also *false indusium*, a differentiated portion of the leaf margin, in function simulating an indusium.

jointed: having stems that can be pulled apart easily at the joints (nodes), as in *Equisetum*.

medial: (especially of sori) located halfway between the midvein and the blade margin.

megaspore: in heterosporous plants a spore, commonly much larger than a microspore, that gives rise to a female gametophyte; see *microspore*.

microspore: in heterosporous plants a spore, usually minute, that gives rise to a male gametophyte; see *megaspore*.

midvein: the central vein of a leaf or any of its subdivisions.

monomorphic: having one shape, referring to spores, or sterile versus fertile blades.

noncalcareous: describing soils or rocks lacking lime, generally acidic.

papilla: a small, nipplelike projection.

paraphyses: hairs, or rarely scales, among the sporangia in a sorus.

pinna (plural, pinnae): one of the primary divisions of a fern leaf.

pinnate: having the leaflets (pinnae) arranged on both sides of the axis.

pinnate-pinnatifid: once-divided with deeply lobed pinnae.

pinnatifid: cut more than halfway to the midvein but the lobes are not separate segments.

pinnule: a secondary division of a fern leaf, e.g., a division of a pinna.

propagule: any structure that falls from the plant to form new plants, either vegetative (such as buds, bulblets) or sexual (such as spores).

prothallus (plural, prothalli): the small, independent generation that bears sex organs; the gametophyte.

proximal: toward the base or place of attachment of the frond or part in question; see *distal*.

pteridophyte: any member of the ferns and fern allies (clubmosses, spikemosses, quillworts, horsetails).

rachis: the central axis of a compound fern blade.

rhizoids: hairlike structures on the gametophyte that attach it to the soil and absorb water and minerals.

rhizome: a horizontal creeping stem, also applied to fern stems that are ascending at the tip or even upright.

scale: an epidermal outgrowth two or more cells wide and more or less flattened, on various parts of ferns, especially the rhizomes and stipes.

segment: an individual leaflet of a dissected fern leaf.

serpentine: a mineral, strong in magnesium and usually green, upon which relatively few plants can grow.

sinus: the space between two lobes, as on a pinna margin.

sorus (plural, sori): a discrete cluster of sporangia.

sporangium: (plural, sporangia): a small specialized case producing few to many spores.

spore: the one-celled reproductive unit of nonseed plants.

sporocarp: a hard, nutlike structure containing the sporangia of heterosporous ferns.

sporophyte: the generation that produces spores, the plant that you see in pteridophytes; see *gametophyte*.

stellate: starlike, bearing arms radiating from a central point, as in some hairs or scales.

sterile frond: a frond lacking sporangia.

stipe: the stalk of a fern leaf.

stipe bundles: the vascular bundles of the fern leaf stalk.

stolon: a slender, long-creeping branch from the primary stem, which produces new plants.

talus: a sloping mass of rocky fragments at the base of a cliff.

tender: unable to endure without protection from cold weather; see *hardy*.

tripinnate: three times divided.

vascular bundle: a tough strand of tissue running through the plant that conducts food, water, and minerals.

vegetative frond: a frond lacking sporangia.

whorled: leaves borne three or more around a stem at the same level.

xerophytic: growing in dry habitats.

Index of Common Names

Christmas fern: *Polystichum acrostichoides*
Cinnamon fern: *Osmunda cinnamomea*
Claw fern, Japanese: *Onychium japonicum*
Cliff brake: *Pellaea*
    Bridges': *Pellaea bridgesii*
    Flexuous: *Pellaea ovata*
    Intermediate: *Pellaea intermedia*
    Purple: *Pellaea atropurpurea*
    Sierra: *Pellaea brachyptera*
    Slender: *Cryptogramma stelleri*
    Smooth: *Pellaea glabella*
Climbing fern: *Lygodium*; *L. palmatum*
    Japanese: *Lygodium japonicum*
Cloak fern: *Cheilanthes*
    Beitel's: *Cheilanthes beitelii*
    Golden: *Cheilanthes bonariensis*
    Jones's: *Cheilanthes jonesii*
    Newberry's: *Cheilanthes newberryi*
    Powdery: *Cheilanthes dealbata*
    Small-leaved: *Cheilanthes parvifolia*
    Wavy: *Cheilanthes sinuata*
    Woolly: *Cheilanthes distans*
Clubmoss: *Lycopodium*
    Fir: *Lycopodium selago*
    Foxtail: *Lycopodium alopecuroides*
    Shining: *Lycopodium lucidulum*
    Tree: *Lycopodium dendroides*; *L. obscurum*
Coffee fern: *Pellaea andromedifolia*
Copper fern: *Bommeria hispida*
Cotton fern: *Cheilanthes newberryi*
Cup fern: *Dennstaedtia*
Deer fern: *Blechnum spicant*
    Japanese: *Blechnum niponicum*
Fairy swords: *Cheilanthes lindheimeri*
Fancy fern: *Dryopteris intermedia*
Felt fern: *Pyrrosia*; *P. lingua*

Firmoss: *Lycopodium*
    Northern: *Lycopodium selago*
    Shining: *Lycopodium lucidulum*
Five-finger fern: *Adiantum pedatum*
Floating fern: *Salvinia*
Flowering fern: *Osmunda*; *O. regalis*
Fragile fern: *Cystopteris*; *C. fragilis*
    Mountain: *Cystopteris montana*
    Slender: *Cystopteris tenuis*
    Southern: *Cystopteris protrusa*
    Southwestern: *Cystopteris reevesiana*
    Woodland: *Cystopteris protrusa*
Giant hypolepis: *Hypolepis tenuifolia*
Glade fern: *Diplazium pycnocarpon*
    Silvery: *Athyrium thelypteroides*
Goldback fern: *Pentagramma triangularis*
Grape fern: *Botrychium*
    Dissected: *Botrychium dissectum*
Green serpent: *Polypodium formosanum*
Ground fern, downy: *Hypolepis punctata*
Ground fern, lacy: *Dennstaedtia davallioides*
Ground fern, ruddy: *Hypolepis rugulosa*
Hard fern: *Blechnum*; *B. spicant*
    Little: *Blechnum penna-marina*
Hartford fern: *Lygodium palmatum*
Hart's-tongue fern: *Phyllitis*; *P. scolopendrium*
Hay-scented fern: *Dennstaedtia punctilobula*
Holly fern: *Arachniodes, Cyrtomium, Phanerophlebia, Polystichum*
    Alaska: *Polystichum setigerum* (mistakenly applied to *P. setiferum*)
    Anderson's: *Polystichum andersonii*
    Braun's: *Polystichum braunii*
    California: *Polystichum californicum*
    Dudley's: *Polystichum dudleyi*

Eared: *Phanerophlebia auriculata*
East Indian: *Arachniodes aristata*
Himalayan: *Polystichum lentum*
Japanese: *Cyrtomium falcatum*
Kruckeberg's: *Polystichum × kruckebergii*
Large-leaved: *Cyrtomium macrophyllum*
Long-eared: *Polystichum neolobatum*
Makino's: *Polystichum makinoi*
Nepal: *Polystichum nepalensis*
Northern: *Polystichum lonchitis*
Potter's: *Polystichum × potteri*
Prescott's: *Polystichum prescottianum*
Richard's: *Polystichum richardii*
Shasta: *Polystichum lemmonii*
Tagawa's: *Polystichum tagawanum*
Trifid: *Polystichum tripteron*
Tsus-sima: *Polystichum tsus-simense*
Variegated: *Arachniodes simplicior* var. *variegata*
Western: *Polystichum scopulinum*
Horsetail: *Equisetum*
Field: *Equisetum arvense*
Giant: *Equisetum telmateia*
Water: *Equisetum fluviatile*
Woodland: *Equisetum sylvaticum*
Indian's dream: *Cheilanthes siliquosa*
Interrupted fern: *Osmunda claytoniana*
Korean rock fern: *Polystichum tsus-simense*
Lace fern: *Cheilanthes gracillima*; *Paesia scaberula*
Lady fern: *Athyrium*
Alpine: *Athyrium distentifolium*
Black: *Athyrium japonicum*
Crenate: *Athyrium crenulato-serrulatum*
Eared: *Athyrium otophorum*
European: *Athyrium filix-femina*

Northern: *Athyrium angustum*
Southern: *Athyrium asplenioides*
Spinulose: *Athyrium spinulosum*
Western: *Athyrium cyclosorum*
Leather fern: *Rumohra adiantiformis*
Lemon-scented fern: *Thelypteris limbosperma*
Licorice fern: *Polypodium glycyrrhiza*
Lip fern: *Cheilanthes*
Alabama: *Cheilanthes alabamensis*
Beaded: *Cheilanthes myriophylla*
Coville's: *Cheilanthes covillei*
Eaton's: *Cheilanthes eatonii*
Fendler's: *Cheilanthes fendleri*
Glandular: *Cheilanthes kaulfussii*
Hairy: *Cheilanthes lanosa*
Lindheimer's: *Cheilanthes lindheimeri*
Slender: *Cheilanthes feei*
Woolly: *Cheilanthes tomentosa*
Wright's: *Cheilanthes wrightii*
Log fern: *Dryopteris celsa*
Maiden fern: *Thelypteris*
Marianna: *Thelypteris torresiana*
Oval: *Thelypteris ovata*
Southern: *Thelypteris kunthii*
Maidenhair fern: *Adiantum*
California: *Adiantum jordanii*
Dwarf: *Adiantum aleuticum* 'Subpumilum'
Himalayan: *Adiantum venustum*
Japanese: *Adiantum aleuticum* var. *japonicum*
Mexican: *Adiantum poiretii*
Northern: *Adiantum pedatum*
Rosy: *Adiantum hispidulum*

Rough: *Adiantum hispidulum*
Serpentine: *Adiantum aleuticum*
Southern: *Adiantum capillus-veneris*
Venus: *Adiantum capillus-veneris*
Western: *Adiantum aleuticum*
Male fern: *Dryopteris filix-mas*
  Dwarf: *Dryopteris oreades*
  Golden-scaled: *Dryopteris affinis*
  Mexican: *Dryopteris pseudo-filix-mas*
  Mountain: *Dryopteris oreades*
  Scaly: *Dryopteris affinis*
Mariannas fern: *Thelypteris torresiana*
Marsh fern: *Thelypteris palustris*
Massachusetts fern: *Thelypteris simulata*
Mosquito fern: *Azolla; A. filiculoides*
Mountain fern: *Thelypteris limbosperma*
  Sweet: *Thelypteris limbosperma*
Mouse-ear fern: *Paraceterach reynoldsii*
New York fern: *Thelypteris noveboracensis*
Oak fern: *Gymnocarpium; G. dryopteris*
  Limestone: *Gymnocarpium robertianum*
  Robert's: *Gymnocarpium robertianum*
Ostrich fern: *Matteuccia; M. struthiopteris*
  Oriental: *Matteuccia orientalis*
Painted fern, giant: *Athyrium filix-femina × niponicum* 'Pictum'
  Japanese: *Athyrium niponicum* 'Pictum'
Palmleaf fern: *Blechnum capense*
Parsley fern: *Cryptogramma acrostichoides, C. crispa*
Pepperwort: *Marsilea*
Pillwort: *Pilularia*

American: *Pilularia americana*
European: *Pilularia globulifera*
Pipes: *Equisetum fluviatile*
Polypody: *Polypodium*
  California polypody: *Polypodium californicum*
  Common: *Polypodium vulgare*
  Gray: *Polypodium polypodioides*
  Leathery: *Polypodium scouleri*
  Mountain: *Polypodium amorphum*
  Southern: *Polypodium cambricum*
  Virginia: *Polypodium virginianum*
  Western: *Polypodium hesperium*
Princess pine: *Lycopodium dendroideum, L. obscurum*
Rainbow moss: *Selaginella uncinata*
Rasp fern: *Doodia*
  Common: *Doodia media*
Rattlesnake fern: *Botrychium virginianum*
Resurrection fern: *Polypodium polypodioides*
Ribbon fern: *Pteris cretica*
River fern: *Thelypteris kunthii*
Rock brake: *Cryptogramma*
  American: *Cryptogramma acrostichoides*
  Asiatic: *Cryptogramma crispa*
Rock-cap fern: *Polypodium virginianum*
Rock fern
  Korean: *Polystichum tsus-simense*
Royal fern: *Osmunda regalis*
  Rugg's hybrid: *Osmunda × ruggii*
Rusty-back fern: *Ceterach officinarum*
Scouring rush: *Equisetum; E. hyemale*
  Dwarf: *Equisetum scirpoides*
  Evergreen: *Equisetum hyemale*
  Rough: *Equisetum hyemale*
  Smooth: *Equisetum laevigatum*

Variegated: *Equisetum*
variegatum
Sensitive fern. *Onoclea sensibilis*
Asian: *Onoclea sensibilis* var. *interrupta*
Shield fern: *Dryopteris, Polystichum*
Alpine: *Polystichum cystostegia*
Hard: *Polystichum aculeatum*
Mother: *Polystichum proliferum*
Prickly: *Polystichum vestitum*
Soft: *Polystichum setiferum*
Shuttlecock fern: *Matteuccia; M. struthiop-*
teris
Silver fern: *Cyathea dealbata*
Spikemoss: *Selaginella*
Braun's spikemoss: *Selaginella braunii*
Chinese lace-fern: *Selaginella braunii*
Desert: *Selaginella eremophila*
Douglas's: *Selaginella douglasii*
Gemmiferous: *Selaginella*
moellendorffii
Hansen's: *Selaginella hansenii*
Krauss's: *Selaginella kraussiana*
Meadow: *Selaginella apoda*
Oregon: *Selaginella oregana*
Peacock: *Selaginella uncinata*
Rock: *Selaginella rupestris*
Tree: *Selaginella involvens*
Wallace's: *Selaginella wallacei*
Watson's: *Selaginella watsonii*
Spleenwort: *Asplenium, Asplenosorus*
Acute-leaved: *Asplenium*
onopteris
Beijing: *Asplenium pekingense*
Black: *Asplenium adiantum-*
nigrum
Black-stemmed: *Asplenium*
resiliens
Bradley's: *Asplenium bradleyi*
Ebony: *Asplenium platyneuron*

Forked: *Asplenium septentrionale*
Fountain: *Asplenium fontanum*
Green: *Asplenium viride*
Hallberg's: *Asplenium hallbergii*
Lanceolate: *Asplenium billotii*
Lobed: *Asplenosorus pinnatifidus*
Maidenhair: *Asplenium trichomanes*
Mountain: *Asplenium montanum*
Narrow-leaved: *Diplazium*
pycnocarpon
Scaly: *Ceterach officinarum*
Scott's: *Asplenosorus ebenoides*
Silvery: *Athyrium thelypteroides*
Single-sorus: *Asplenium monanthes*
Smooth rock: *Asplenium*
fontanum
Wall rue: *Asplenium ruta-*
muraria
Swamp fern, narrow: *Dryopteris cristata*
Sweet mountain fern: *Thelypteris*
limbosperma
Sword fern: *Polystichum*
Dwarf western: *Polystichum*
imbricans
Western: *Polystichum munitum*
Tapering fern: *Thelypteris noveboracensis*
Tassel fern, Japanese: *Polystichum*
polyblepharum
Tatting fern: *Athyrium filix-femina*
'Frizelliae'
The King: *Dryopteris affinis* 'Cristata'
Thousand-leaved fern: *Hypolepis millefolium*
Tongue fern: *Pyrrosia lingua*
Tree fern: *Cyathea, Dicksonia*
Australian: *Cyathea cooperi*
Black: *Cyathea medullaris*
Soft: *Dicksonia antarctica*
Tasmanian: *Dicksonia antarctica*
Upside-down fern: *Arachniodes standishii*

Walking fern: *Camptosorus rhizophyllus*
    Asian: *Camptosorus sibiricus*
Wall rue: *Asplenium ruta-muraria*
Water clover: *Marsilea*
    European: *Marsilea quadrifolia*
    Golden: *Marsilea macropoda*
    Hairy: *Marsilea vestita*
Water fern, Sierra: *Thelypteris nevadensis*
Water spangles: *Salvinia*
Wood fern: *Dryopteris*
    Amur: *Dryopteris amurensis*
    Beaded: *Dryopteris bissetiana*
    Black: *Dryopteris cycadina*
    Boott's: *Dryopteris* × *boottii*
    Broad: *Dryopteris dilatata*
    California: *Dryopteris arguta*
    Champion's: *Dryopteris championii*
    Clinton's: *Dryopteris clintoniana*
    Coastal: *Dryopteris arguta*
    Crested: *Dryopteris cristata*
    Dixie: *Dryopteris* × *australis*
    Evergreen: *Dryopteris intermedia*
    Formosan: *Dryopteris formosana*
    Giant: *Dryopteris goldiana*
    Glandular: *Dryopteris intermedia*

    Goldie's: *Dryopteris goldiana*
    Hay-scented: *Dryopteris aemula*
    Leather: *Dryopteris marginalis*
    Limestone: *Dryopteris submontana*
    Marginal: *Dryopteris marginalis*
    Mexican: *Dryopteris pseudo-filix-mas*
    Mickel's: *Dryopteris* × *mickelii*
    Mountain: *Dryopteris campyloptera*
    Nevada: *Thelypteris nevadensis*
    Northern: *Dryopteris expansa*
    Scaly: *Dryopteris polylepis*
    Shaggy: *Dryopteris cycadina*
    Siebold's: *Dryopteris sieboldii*
    Southern: *Dryopteris ludoviciana*
    Spinulose: *Dryopteris carthusiana*
    Spreading: *Dryopteris campyloptera*, *D. expansa*
    Thick-stemmed: *Dryopteris crassirhizoma*
    Tokyo: *Dryopteris tokyoensis*
    Toothed: *Dryopteris carthusiana*
    Wallich's: *Dryopteris wallichiana*
    Western: *Dryopteris arguta*
Woodsia: *Woodsia*

Index

Numerals in *italics* indicate illustrations.

Wild blue phlox (*Phlox divaricata*), 44

Wood fern (*Dryopteris*), 7, 13, 14, *14*, 16, 17, 18, 21, 23, 29, 46, 54, 62, 68–69, 88, 106, 109, 170–203, *172–203*, 305, 330; Amur (*Dryopteris amurensis*), 174; Arching (*Dryopteris expansa*), 67, 186, *186*, 187; Beaded (*Dryopteris bissetiana*), 70, 176, *177*; Black (*Dryopteris cycadina*), 183, *183*; Boott's (*Dryopteris* × *boottii*), 176, *177*; Broad (*Dryopteris dilatata*), 16, 184, *184*, 185; California (*Dryopteris arguta*), 174, *174*, 175; Champion's (*Dryopteris championii*), 20, 179, *179*; Clinton's (*Dryopteris clintoniana*), 9, 180, *181*, 191; Coastal (*Dryopteris arguta*), 174, *174*, 175; Crested (*Dryopteris cristata*), 9, 32, 51, 178, 182–183, *183*, 191; Dixie (*Dryopteris* × *australis*), 9, 36, 46, 175, *175*; Evergreen (*Dryopteris intermedia*), 20, 32, 177, 178, 191–192, *192*; Formosan (*Dryopteris formosana*), 16, 91, 189–190, *190*; Giant (*Dryopteris goldiana*), 9, 38, 46, 51, 178, 190–191, *191*; Glandular (*Dryopteris intermedia*), 20, 32, 177, 178, 191–192, *192*; Goldie's (*Dryopteris goldiana*), 9, 38, 46, 51, 178, 190–191, *191*; Hay-scented (*Dryopteris aemula*), 171–172; Leather (*Dryopteris marginalis*),

Wood fern (*continued*) 18, 20, 46, 191, 192, 194–195, *195*; Marginal (*Dryopteris marginalis*), 18, 20, 46, 191, 192, 194–195, *195*; Mexican (*Dryopteris pseudo-filix-mas*), 196, 198, *199*; Mountain (*Dryopteris campyloptera*), 16, 176–177, *177*, 186, 187; Northern (*Dryopteris expansa*), 67, 186, *186*, 187; Scaly (*Dryopteris polylepis*), 197–198; Shaggy (*Dryopteris cycadina*), 183, *183*; Siebold's (*Dryopteris sieboldii*), 200, *200*; Southern (*Dryopteris ludoviciana*), 36, 175, 178, 191, 194; Spinulose (*Dryopteris carthusiana*), 16, 51, 177–178; Spreading (*Dryopteris campyloptera*), 16, 176–177, *177*, 186, 187; Thick-stemmed (*Dryopteris crassirhizoma*), 181–182, *182*; Tokyo (*Dryopteris tokyoensis*), 201, *201*; Toothed (*Dryopteris carthusiana*), 16, 51, 177–178; Wallich's (*Dryopteris wallichiana*), 202–203, *203*; Western (*Dryopteris arguta*), 174, *174*, 175

Wood fern, Nevada (*Thelypteris nevadensis*), 308

Woodland fragile fern (*Cystopteris protrusa*), 47, 51, 158, 159, 160, *160*, 161, 164

Woodland horsetail (*Equisetum sylvaticum*), 208

Woodsia, 21, 49, 313–317, *313–316*, 330; *gracilis*, 313, *313*; *ilvensis*,

Woodsia (*continued*) 314, *314*, 326, 327; *intermedia*, 314; *manchuriensis*, 315; *obtusa*, 315, *315*, 326; *plummerae*, 316; *polystichoides*, 49, 316, *316*, 317, 326, 327, 328; *scopulina*, *316*, 317

Woodsia (*Woodsia*), 21, 49, 313–317, *313–316*, 330; Blunt-lobed (*Woodsia obtusa*), 315, *315*; Holly-fern (*Woodsia polystichoides*), 49, 316, *316*, 317; Manchurian (*Woodsia manchuriensis*), 315; Plummer's (*Woodsia plummerae*), 316; Rocky Mountain (*Woodsia scopulina*), *316*, 317; Rusty (*Woodsia ilvensis*), 314, *314*

Woodwardia, 17, 18, 62, 170, 317–321, *319–321*, 330; *areolata*, 32, 51, 70, 225, 318, *319*, 327, 328; *fimbriata*, 47, 317, 3̲1̲8–319, *319*, 325; *orientalis*, 59, *59*, 319, *319*, 320; *radicans*, 52, 58, *58*, 317, 320, *321*; *unigemmata*, 320, *321*; *virginica*, 51, 62, 320–321, *321*, 327

Woolly cloak fern (*Cheilanthes distans*), 138

Woolly lip fern (*Cheilanthes tomentosa*), 146, *146*

Wright's lip fern (*Cheilanthes wrightii*), 146, *146*

Yarrow (*Achillea*), 44

Yellow flag iris, 52